T0319906

A Handbook on Multi-Attribute Decision-Making Methods

Wiley Series in Operations Research and Management Science

Operations Research and Management Science (ORMS) is a broad, interdisciplinary branch of applied mathematics concerned with improving the quality of decisions and processes and is a major component of the global modern movement toward the use of advanced analytics in industry and scientific research. The *Wiley Series in Operations Research and Management Science* features a broad collection of books that meet the varied needs of researchers, practitioners, policy makers, and students who use or need to improve their use of analytics. Reflecting the wide range of current research within the ORMS community, the Series encompasses application, methodology, and theory and provides coverage of both classical and cutting edge ORMS concepts and developments. Written by recognized international experts in the field, this collection is appropriate for students as well as professionals from private and public sectors including industry, government, and nonprofit organization who are interested in ORMS at a technical level. The Series is comprised of four sections: Analytics; Decision and Risk Analysis; Optimization Models; and Stochastic Models.

Analytics

Yang and Lee • *Healthcare Analytics: From Data to Knowledge to Healthcare Improvement*

Forthcoming Titles

Attoh-Okine • *Big Data and Differential Privacy: Analysis Strategies for Railway Track Engineering*
Kong and Zhang • *Decision Analytics and Optimization in Disease Prevention and Treatment*

Decision and Risk Analysis

Barron • *Game Theory: An Introduction,* Second Edition
Bozorg-Haddad, Zolghadr-Asli, and Loáiciga • *A Handbook on Multi-Attribute Decision-Making Methods*

Brailsford, Churilov, and Dangerfield • *Discrete-Event Simulation and System Dynamics for Management Decision Making*
Johnson, Keisler, Solak, Turcotte, Bayram, and Drew • *Decision Science for Housing and Community Development: Localized and Evidence-Based Responses to Distressed Housing and Blighted Communities*
Mislick and Nussbaum • *Cost Estimation: Methods and Tools*

Forthcoming Titles

Aleman and Carter • *Healthcare Engineering*

Optimization Models

Ghiani, Laporte, and Musmanno • *Introduction to Logistics Systems Management,* Second Edition

Forthcoming Titles

Smith • *Learning Operations Research Through Puzzles and Games*
Tone • *Advances in DEA Theory and Applications: With Examples in Forecasting Models*

Stochastic Models

Ibe • Random Walk and Diffusion Processes

Forthcoming Titles

Donohue, Katok, and Leider • *The Handbook of Behavioral Operations*
Matis • *Applied Markov Based Modelling of Random Processes*

A Handbook on Multi-Attribute Decision-Making Methods

Omid Bozorg-Haddad
University of Tehran
Alborz, Iran

Babak Zolghadr-Asli
University of Tehran
Alborz, Iran

Hugo A. Loáiciga
University of California
Santa Barbara, United States

This edition first published 2021

Registered Office
John Wiley & Sons, Inc., 111 River Street, Hoboken, NJ 07030, USA

Editorial Office
111 River Street, Hoboken, NJ 07030, USA

For details of our global editorial offices, customer services, and more information about Wiley products visit us at www.wiley.com.

Wiley also publishes its books in a variety of electronic formats and by print-on-demand. Some content that appears in standard print versions of this book may not be available in other formats.

Library of Congress Cataloging-in-Publication Data

Names: Bozorg-Haddad, Omid, 1974- author. | Zolghadr-Asli, Babak, author. | Loáiciga, Hugo A., author.
Title: A handbook on multi-attribute decision-making methods / Omid Bozorg-Haddad, Babak Zolghadr-Asli, Hugo A. Loáiciga.
Description: Hoboken, NJ : Wiley, 2021. | Series: Wiley series in operations research and management science | Includes bibliographical references and index.
Identifiers: LCCN 2020034049 (print) | LCCN 2020034050 (ebook) | ISBN 9781119563495 (cloth) | ISBN 9781119563471 (adobe pdf) | ISBN 9781119563389 (epub) | ISBN 9781119563501 (obook)
Subjects: LCSH: Multiple criteria decision making.
Classification: LCC T57.95 .B69 2021 (print) | LCC T57.95 (ebook) | DDC 658.4/03–dc23
LC record available at https://lccn.loc.gov/2020034049
LC ebook record available at https://lccn.loc.gov/2020034050

Cover Design: Wiley
Cover Image: © connel/Shutterstock

Set in 9.5/12.5pt STIXTwoText by SPi Global, Chennai, India

Contents

Preface

Multi-attribute decision-making (MADM) problems describe a situation in which the decision-makers evaluate a finite number of pre-defined alternatives that are explicitly known at the beginning of the solution process with regard to a set of often conflictive evaluating criteria. It would not be an exaggeration to state that almost everyone, whether in their personal or professional life, faces decision-making problems on a daily basis. Although there are numerous MADM methods at the decision-makers' disposal to cope with real-world decision-making problems there is still lacking a source that compiles and explains the various MADM methods in a clear and systematic manner that would make their understanding, comparison, and application straightforward for those who require implementing these techniques. Most existing sources that deal with MADM methods are generally focused on results of the applications of these methods, but overlook basic and unifying concepts. Therefore, those who are eager to gain an overview of these methods must endure hardships of searching through various sources which are written in specialized form and are difficult to understand.

The book at hand fills the cited knowledge and educational gap and describes the most important MADM methods, with an assessment of their performance in solving multiple problems encompassing many fields of inquiry and practice in a clear and systematic manner. The proposed book contains 12 chapters plus two appendices. Chapter 1 provides an overview of the decision-making and its fundamental concepts. Each of chapters 2 through 12 is devoted to a separate MADM method. In total, some 20 MADM methods are presented in the book. Appendix I describes a weight assignment method; Appendix II contains an application of MADM methods. The chapters are arranged based on pedagogical purposes so that the audience can easily engage with the presented materials in each given chapter. Nevertheless, the basic idea is to ensure that each chapter can stand alone by providing the audience with a brief description of the materials and methods required to cover every aspect and mathematical concepts used in each given method. In other words, while a highly engaged audience can go through the entire book to gain a deep understanding of MADM methods and their theoretical foundation, some can aim at a specific chapter without facing any difficulty in understanding the materials presented for the reviewed MADM methods. In essence, each chapter describing a specific MADM method, or in some case a family of methods, starts with a brief literature review of the methods' development followed by a description of its theoretical origins. The philosophical foundations of each method are discussed and mapped to the mathematical framework of the specified MADM method. Each chapter contains a stepwise description of its pertinent method that serves as the guideline for implementing the method with the purpose of coping with real-world MADM problems.

February 14, 2021
Iran and USA

Omid Bozorg-Haddad
Babak Zolghadr-Asli
Hugo A. Loáiciga

1 An Overview of the Art of Decision-making

1.1 Introduction

What motivates one to make a decision? Finding the precise reason behind these motivations might not be as easy as it might seem. Nevertheless, given that these choices are shaping the world around us, it would not be an exaggeration to claim that the answer to the aforementioned question may facilitate understanding the workings of many world phenomena. Just for a moment consider the possibility of knowing the motivations prompting person to make decisions. If that were achieved, predicting humans' behavior from the simple every-day activity to the most sophisticated social, economic, and political contexts would be possible.

Now let us change the scope of the question; *how can one make a good choice*? This time we may be more successful in finding a more proper answer. Let us take a moment to consider the description of the act of decision-making. The Oxford dictionary defines decision-making as "*the process of deciding about something important, especially in a group of people or in an organization.*" From a psychological point of view, however, decision-making is regarded as the cognitive process resulting in the selection of a belief or a course of action among several alternative possibilities. Each decision-making process produces a final choice, which may or may not prompt action (Tzeng and Huang 2011). In other words, the decision-making merely refers to the act choosing among a set of solutions, rather than the procedural requirements of executing the selected set of alternatives.

The decision-making process is founded on a four-stage analytical procedure (Vroom and Jago 1974; Bell et al. 1988; Weber and Coskunoglu 1990; Kleindorfer et al. 1993). The first stage of the decision-making process is better known as descriptive analytics or positive analytics, which is concerned with describing observed behaviors of the stakeholders who are involved in the decision-making process, mainly by looking at the their past performance and understanding such behavior either by mining historical data sets, and/or looking for the behavioral and social, psychological, and even neurology reasoning motivations that can best

A Handbook on Multi-Attribute Decision-Making Methods, First Edition.
Omid Bozorg-Haddad, Babak Zolghadr-Asli, and Hugo A. Loáiciga.

describe the course of actions made by the stockholders of the decision-making problem (Tzeng and Huang 2011; Santos and Rosati 2015). Descriptive analysis is outside the scope of this book in spite of its psychological nature being pertinent to decision-making process.

The predictive analytic stage concerns the prediction of what is likely to occur given a set of circumstances, which takes place after discerning the motivational patterns behind decision-making problems through descriptive analytical techniques. The application of predictive analysis is limited to the decision-making under uncertainty and, admittedly, not all decision-making problems require such approach. Nevertheless, if necessary, the historical data sets may be reviewed during this second stage to determine the probability of an event or the likelihood of a situation's occurrence (Bell et al. 1988; Kleindorfer et al. 1993). Exploring this phase of the decision-making process is left to readers given the scope and aims of this book.

The third stage of the decision-making process is the normative analysis. The term "normative" generally refers to relating an item to an evaluative standard through assessing and making judgments about the item's behavior or outcomes (Kahneman and Tversky 1984; Tversky and Kahneman 1986). Normative analysis, subsequently, is concerned with techniques through which the decision-makers would be able to evaluate the feasible alternatives in a mathematical sense (Bell et al. 1988; Kleindorfer et al. 1993). Note that traditional normative analysis is based on the assumption of rationalism through the evolved entities of the decision-making problem, which, loosely speaking, is a term that refers to decision-makers pursuing what was described through the previous stages, as their interests and goals. Naturally, making a decision irrationally is beyond the scope of this book, though methods are introduced throughout this book that would enable decision-makers to cope with different types of criteria, including intangible criteria.

The final stage of the decision-making process is called prescriptive analysis. In this stage, decision-makers go beyond predicting future outcomes to determine which alternatives would be the most advantageous or desirable solutions to the problem at hand (Saad 2001). In other words, prescriptive analytics combine the information gathered through studying the behavioral patterns of the stockholders (descriptive analysis), the likelihood of random events inherent to the decision-making problems (predictive analysis), which would be expressed in mathematical-oriented frameworks (normative analysis), to obtain the best course of actions for the decision-makers. Furthermore, through the realms of prescriptive analysis, decision-makers can explore the possible options on how to take advantage of future opportunities or coping with future risks, and, eventually, evaluate the implication of each feasible decision option based on the nature the decision-making problem at hand (Bell et al. 1988; Kleindorfer et al. 1993; Tzeng and Huang 2011).

Having defined decision-making, we consider what is a good choice or alternative in a decision-making problem. Indeed, the notion of a "good alternative" may differ among decision-makers' viewpoints due to their different personal desires, experiences, and backgrounds. In other words, one's idea of a "good choice" may not necessarily represent every decision-makers' ideal choice. Furthermore, the selection procedure of decision-makers may differ from one another, when facing the same decision-making problem. Nevertheless, the decision-makers' selection procedure is founded on a basic and similar principle, which is that decision-makers would have to choose a set of solutions that would outperform other feasible alternatives based on a set of evaluation criteria defined either explicitly or implicitly by the decision-makers for the specific problem at hand. In fact, this decision paradigm underlies multicriteria decision-making (MCDM) in general. In practice, almost everyone may face an MCDM problem on a daily bases, which most cope with by aggregating the criteria through an intuition-oriented weighting mechanism. Nevertheless implementing a systematic MCDM approach is essential to making informed and logical decision.

In technical terms, MCDM is a procedure by which the decision-maker explicitly evaluates a set of alternatives with regard to multiple, usually conflicting, criteria. Decision makers apply MCDMs to restructure and redefine the decision-making problem to make an informed decision. Although developing and implementing MCDM methods are not novel ideas, there have been undeniable advances in this field since the blooming era of computational intelligence (CI) during the early 1960 and 1970s, especially in the form of mathematically oriented methods that recapture and redefine MCDM. MCDM has been an active area of research that has played a crucial role in an array of disciplines, ranging from politics and business to the environment and energy (Zolghadr-Asli et al. 2018a).

Hwang and Yoon (1981) proposed clustering MCDM problems based on the nature of solutions that are available for the problem in hand into two main categories, namely, multiobjective decision-making (MODM), and multiattribute decision-making (MADM). Essentially, the aforementioned classification is based on whether the solutions are explicitly or implicitly defined (Mendoza and Martins 2006; Tzeng and Huang 2011; Velasquez and Hester 2013).

MODM problems describe a situation in which decision-makers are searching for a set of solutions that would satisfy the constraints imposed on the given problem and obtain results that constitute an optimal set of solutions based on the decision-makers objectives (Hwang and Yoon 1981). In essence, MODM is suitable for tackling design and planning problems, in which the decision-makers aim to achieve states objectives or goals by considering the various interactions within the given constraints. The decision space of MODM problems can be described as a multidimensional Cartesian space, with each (conflicting) objective acting as an axis, defined by a set of constraints that separate the feasible and infeasible solutions. MODM can solve problems with continuous or discrete decision spaces.

MODM solution methods are usually associated with mathematical programming methods (Tzeng and Huang 2011).

In general, MODM involve trade-off and scale problems (Tzeng and Huang 2011; Zolghadr-Asli et al. 2018a). MODM involves more than one objective, therefore, the optimal solutions to a MODM problem must be posed in terms of Pareto fronts or production possibility frontier (after the Italian economist Vilfredo Pareto 1848–1923), which are sets of points representing combinations of the values of the objective functions with the best tradeoffs among objectives that are achievable for the problem being solved. In classic MODM techniques, an optimal solution is commonly obtained with mathematical programming. This means multiple objectives are merged into a single-objective problem through a weighting of the various objectives. The process of obtaining a proper weighting scheme for the objectives is a trade-off problem. If such trade-off information is unavailable, Pareto solutions must be derived. Pareto solutions to MODM problems are expressed as a set of nondominated solutions. A nondominated solution has the property that it is not possible to improve the solution's utility or degree of preference without degrading at least one objective (Zolghadr-Asli et al. 2017, 2018a). The MODM's scaling problem, on the other hand, is a computational challenge surrounding most real-world, practical, decision-making problems, whereby the stakeholders must consider several conflicting objectives. As the number of objectives increases the decision makers face *the curse of dimensionality*, whereby the computational costs of solving a MODM problem become burdensome in the extreme, and sometimes computationally unassailable (Bozorg-Haddad et al. 2017; Zolghadr-Asli et al. 2017, 2018a). In an attempt to surmount this challenge, meta-heuristic algorithms have arisen to search within the decision-space and identify potential solutions to a MODM problem (Bozorg-Haddad et al. 2017, Zolghadr-Asli et al. 2018b,c,d).

MADM problems describe a situation in which the decision-makers evaluate a finite number of predefined alternatives. The alternatives are known at the beginning of the solution process. The decision-makers attempt to systematically assess each alternative via a discrete preference rating mechanism. The rating mechanism used by decision-makers to evaluate and compare the performance of each of the alternatives under consideration is defined either explicitly or implicitly (Hwang and Yoon 1981). Table 1.1 compares the main characteristic of MCDM approaches, namely, MODM and MADM (Malczewski 1999; Mendoza and Martins 2006; Tzeng and Huang 2011; Velasquez and Hester 2013).

Nowadays, decision-makers have numerous methods and techniques at their disposal to deal with MCDM problems, ranging from simple, easy-to-use approaches to complex techniques. Given the important role of MADM, it is vital for decision-makers to know the merits and drawbacks of MADM methods. This book introduces some of the fundamental MADM methods that have been

Table 1.1 Comparison of MODM and MADM approaches.

Criteria for comparison	MODM	MADM
Criteria defined	Objectives	Attributes
Objective defined	Explicitly	Implicitly
Attributes defined	Implicitly	Explicitly
Constraints defined	Explicitly	Implicitly
Alternatives defined	Implicitly	Explicitly
Number of alternatives	Infinite	Finite
Decision-makers' control	Significant	Limited
Decision modeling paradigm	Process-oriented	Outcome-oriented
Relevant to	Design/operation	Evaluation/choice

proven to be effective and practical solution-searching tools. Section 1.2 describes the foundations of MADM methods and their classification.

1.2 Classification of MADM Methods

There are numerous ways through which one can classify the MADM methods. A sound classification relies on the core principles and assumptions of MADM to categorize these methods. Familiarity with MADM methods is paramount to choose adequately among them to solve a decision problem at hand. Accordingly, based on the decision-makers' prioritizing system, the interactions among attributes, the mathematical nature of attributes' values, and the number of decision-makers, numerous classifications have been proposed for MADM methods.

1.2.1 Preference Evaluation Mechanism

Every MADM method requires a preference evaluation mechanism for the purpose of reflecting the stockholders' preferences in the decision-making process. These mechanisms act as a measure that enables decision-makers evaluating alternatives according to their attributes. The mechanism can be defined either explicitly (where the preference values are computable through a set of predefined boundaries or mathematical functions), or they can be defined implicitly so that the decision-makers' experiences, expertise, perception, and instincts are reflected in the alternatives' preference evaluation.

A classification based on the notion of preference evaluation mechanism divides MADM methods into multiattribute utility theory (MAUT) and outranking methods (Belton and Stewart 2002; Mendoza and Martins 2006). On the basis of Bernoulli's utility theory MAUT methods obtain the decision-makers' preferences, which can usually be represented as a hierarchical structure by using an appropriate utility function. By evaluating the utility function the alternative with the highest utility value can be identified as the solution to the MADM problem at hand. In spite of their reliance of solid axiomatic background of MAUT methods, they are criticized by their unrealistic assumption of preferential independencies (Tzeng and Huang 2011). Preferential independence describes situations in which the preferred outcome of one criterion over another is not influenced by the remaining criteria. However, it so happens that the criteria are usually interactive in real-world MADM problems. Alternatively, instead of building complex utility functions, outranking methods compare the preference relations among alternatives to determine on the best alternatives. The outranking methods were introduced to overcome the empirical difficulties experienced with the utility function in handling practical problems. Yet they lack axiomatic foundation, such as is the case with classical aggregate problems and structural problems (Tzeng and Huang 2011).

The previous classification categorizes classical MADM methods, yet it may face difficulties categorizing some of the modern MADM methods whose features do not fit either one of the previously cited categories. Belton and Stewart (2002) proposed a more sophisticated classification system for MADM methods that addresses the latter classification difficulties. The alternate classification categorizes the MADM methods within three classes, namely, value measurement, goal aspirations or reference level, and outranking methods. This classification is a reviewed next.

Value-measurement MADM methods implement numerical scales to represent the degree to which a feasible alternative may be preferable to another. The scores obtained for each alternative are developed initially for each individual evaluation criterion and are then synthesized to rate the overall performance of the alternatives. The scores assigned to each of the feasible alternatives reflect a preference order. These preferences must be consistent with a set of axioms, which are as follows (Belton and Stewart 2002; Mendoza and Martins 2006):

(I) Constant discipline and roles must be imposed by the decision-maker in the construction procedure of preference measurement scales;
(II) Provide a framework through which the decision-makers are able to systematically analyze the obtained preference values and gain a deeper understanding of the process that led to the final results; and
(III) Promoting explicit statements, rather than implicit judgments regarding the trade-offs between evaluation criteria.

Desirable or satisfactory levels of achievement must be defined by the decision-makers for each evaluation criterion. Through these reference level methods, those alternatives that are closest to achieving the goals or aspirations are identified. These types of MADM methods are recommended for those cases in which decision-makers may not be able to express trade-offs or identify importance weights of the evaluation criteria. Nevertheless, the most desirable outcome can be portrayed through arbitrary aspirations or goals for each criterion. As far as these branches of MADM is concerned, an alternative that represents the most similarities with the arbitrary defined ideal solution can best reflect the stakeholders' interests in the process of decision-making. Through the framework represented by this branch of MADM methods, the feasible alternatives, which are available courses of actions, are systematically eliminated until achieving a solution that best fits the stakeholders' ideal outcome for the MADM problem at hand (Belton and Stewart 2002; Mendoza and Martins 2006).

Lastly, outranking MADM methods evaluate alternatives' relative performances against one another using a comparison-oriented framework. Outranking MADM methods, the first evaluate feasible alternatives by the decision-makers in terms of evaluation criteria to establish their merits. This is followed by an aggregation stage whereby the gathered information is used as evidence to obtain an alternative that outrank others and emerges as the optimal solution. The aggregation stage establishes the relations between the alternatives in terms of preference, indifference, and incomparability. Consequently, a complete ranking of alternatives is produced.

1.2.2 Attributes' Interactions

In any MADM, the decision-maker is dealing with the presence of a number of evaluation criteria. In essence, each MADM method offers a different approach to aggregate each criterion's value to obtain an optimal solution. Based on that notion MADM methods are divided into two main categories, namely, compensatory and noncompensatory (Jeffreys 2004). In compensatory techniques, the poor performance of an alternative in some criteria can be compensated by high performance in some other criteria. Therefore, the aggregated performance of an alternative might not reveal its weakness area. In contrast, in noncompensatory techniques, the significant poor performance of an alternative in some criteria cannot be compensated with high performance in other criteria. The aggregated performance reflect this fact. In other words, each criterion can independently play a crucial rule in the aggregated performance of an alternative (Banihabib et al. 2017).

1.2.3 The Mathematical Nature of Attributes' Values

From a mathematical point of view, variables, and in this case evaluating criteria, can have different nature, such as, deterministic vs. nondeterministic, and fuzzy vs. crisp. MADM methods can be divided into the following categories.

1.2.3.1 Deterministic Vs. Nondeterministic

Deterministic MADM methods involve decision-makers who are certain about the occurrence of the set of outcomes in a decision-making problem. On the other hand, nondeterministic problems involve the occurrence of outcomes with stochastic components of a random-based nature (Pearl 1996; Tzeng and Huang 2011). In such case, the likelihood of an outcome would play a direct role in selecting the most suitable alternative (Coombs and Pruitt 1960). Nondeterministic methods are beyond the scope of this book.

1.2.3.2 Fuzzy Vs. Crisp

Crip MADM modeling expresses the decision-makers' preferences with numeric values. However, there are cases in which the subjective uncertainties that are surrounding decision-makers prevent the stockholders to express their preferences with a crisp number (Tzeng and Huang 2011). In such situations, decision-makers may rely on a fuzzy set that can best describe the stockholders' preferences. Fuzzy sets offer the benefit of implying linguistic evaluation, which in turn, would ease the evaluation process of the decision-makers (Bellman and Zadeh 1970).

It is vital for decision-makers to distinguish the fuzzy-uncertainty logic from the probability-uncertainty logic, and to use them in the proper context. In cases where the certainty of outcomes is in question, the probability-uncertainty logic is the recommended tool. In such situations, the decision-makers' decision-tree is founded on at least one uncertain event. Consequently, the probability of each outcome would play a role in determining the most suitable alternative. On the other hand, when the decision-makers are not certain on how to express the preference of an alternative, the fuzzy logic becomes the favored option. Fuzzy evaluation enables decision-makers to describe an alternative's preference through a fuzzy set employing membership functions. In essence, while the probability-uncertainty logic deals with the probability of outcomes in a decision-tree, the fuzzy logic offers the possibility of preference evaluation by the decision-makers. Exploring the realms of nondeterministic evaluation and fuzzy description of performances lays beyond the scope of this book.

1.2.4 Number of Involved Decision-makers

MADM methods can be classified as single or group decision-making methods depending on the number of decision-makers involved (Black 1948). In the case of single decision-maker methods, the opinion of that single individual forms the preference evaluation mechanism of the decision-making process. On the other hand, group decision-making enables a number of experts and stakeholders to contribute and influence the decision-making process (Kiesler and Sproull 1992). Group decision-making methods are founded on the basis of single decision-making methods; yet, they require an additional strategy through which, each decision-maker's opinion is aggregated and integrated with others' viewpoints to form the final result. Exploring such strategies falls outside the scope of this book.

1.3 Brief Chronicle of MADM Methods

The historical origins of MADM can be traced back to series of correspondence letter between Nicolas Bernoulli (1687–1759) and Pierre Rémond de Montmort (1678–1719), while discussing a mathematical brain teaser, known as the *St. Petersburg paradox* (Tzeng and Huang 2011). In brief, the St. Petersburg paradox can be portrayed as follows (Bernstein 1996):

> "This is a game of chance for a single player who tosses a fair coin at each stage of the game. The player keeps tossing the coin until it turns tails. If the first flip is tails the player wins \$2; if the first tails is on the second flip the player wins \$4; if the first tails is on the third flip the player wins \$8, etc. Concretely if first tails is on the nth flip the player wins \$$2^n$." The question here is: *how much would a prospective gambler be willing to pay to play this game?*

To grasp the magnitude of the described conundrum, consider for a moment, the answer of classical mathematics to the described question. The expected value of the prize resulting from playing this game is (Bernoulli 1738):

$$EV = \frac{1}{2} \times \text{US\$}2 + \frac{1}{4} \times \text{US\$}4 + \frac{1}{8} \times \text{US\$}8 + \ldots = \sum_{n=1}^{\infty} \frac{1}{2^n} \times \text{US\$}2^n = \infty \tag{1.1}$$

in which EV = the expected value turns out to be infinity. Accordingly, a player would be willing to pay any price to participate in the described game. However, this result defies human behavior since no one would be willing to pay a limitless amount of cash to engage in this game (Rieger and Wang 2006). The answer to the St. Petersburg paradox, which revolutionized the way in which decision-making problems were analyzed, did not surface itself until Daniel Bernoulli (1700–1782) published his influential research on utility theory in 1738. The concrete discussions describing the solution of the St. Petersburg paradox in detail are skipped here; yet, it is noteworthy that the remarkable solution that enabled *Daniel Bernoulli* to solve the aforementioned paradox relied on the fact that humans make decisions based not on the expected value, but rather, on the utility value. Specifically, assume that a prospective player has a wealth of w dollars, that the charge for entering the game equals c dollars, and that the player's utility function is $U(w) = \ln(w)$. It can be shown that under these circumstances, the expected incremental (or marginal) utility of playing this game $[E\Delta(U)]$ is finite:

$$E\Delta(U) = \sum_{n=1}^{\infty} \frac{1}{2^k} \left[\ln\left(w + 2^k - c\right) - \ln(w)\right] < \infty \tag{1.2}$$

Therefore, a prospective player whose wealth equals US\$$10^6$ should be willing to pay up to US\$20.88 to play the game; or US\$10.95 if the wealth is US\$$10^3$, and so on and so forth, because the amounts the player would be willing to pay maximize his expected incremental utility. The implication of the utility value is that humans choose the alternative with the highest expected utility value when confronting the MADM problems. A chronologic overview of the most fundamental and influential MADM methods, which would be discussed within this book, is presented in Table 1.2.

1.4 Conclusion

Almost everyone, on a daily bases, faces decision-making problems. It would not be exaggerated to state that these decisions constitute the nature of mankind and of the society that humans form. When it comes to real-world decision-making problems, the decision-makers often find judgment a challenging task. This is so because of the notion that the interest of the stakeholders can be only represented through the evaluation of a set of conflictive criteria. Whenever the decision-makers face a set of feasible, discrete, alternatives, the problem at hand involves MADM. Numerous methods have been presented by been reported to ensure a sound and reliable decision-making process. MADM is one of the main branches of operational research; it is an active field of study with multiple overlaps with many scientific disciplines, and has numerous practical applications. This chapter reviewed the principles of MADM. Furthermore, the best well-known MADMs were herein classified and reviewed.

Table 1.2 A chronologic overview of the most influential MADM methods.

MADM Methods	Utility function	Bernoulli (1738)
	Weighted sum method (WSM)	Churchman and Ackoff (1954)
	ELECTERE I	Benayoun et al. (1966)
	ELECTERE II	Roy and Bertier (1971)
	Analytic hierarchy process (AHP)	Saaty (1977)
	ELECTERE III	Roy (1978)
	TOPSIS	Hwang and Yoon (1981)
	ELECTERE IV	Roy and Hugonnard (1982)
	PROMETHEE I	Brans (1982)
	PROMETHEE II	Vincke and Brans (1985)
	PROMETHEE III	Brans et al. (1986)
	PROMETHEE IV	Mladineo et al. (1987)
	Grey relational analysis	Deng (1989)
	Analytic network process (ANP)	Saaty (1996)
	VIKOR	Opricovic (1998)
	Superiority and inferiority ranking (SIR)	Xu (2001)
	PAPRIKA	Hansen and Ombler (2008)
	Best-worst method (BWM)	Rezaei et al. (2015)
Weighting Methods	Entropy method	Shannon (1948)
	Delphi method	Dalkey and Helmer (1963)
	Eigenvector method	Saaty (1977)
	Weighted least square method	Chu et al. (1979)
	Multiple objective programming model	Choo and Wedley (1985)
	Principal element analysis	Fan (1996)
	Modified Delphi method	Custer et al. (1999)

References

Banihabib, M.E., Hashemi-Madani, F.S., and Forghani, A. (2017). Comparison of compensatory and non-compensatory multi criteria decision making models in water resources strategic management. *Water Resources Management* 31 (12): 3745–3759.

Bell, D.E., Raiffa, H., and Tversky, A. (1988). *Decision Making: Descriptive, Normative, and Prescriptive Interactions*. Cambridge, UK: Cambridge University Press.

Bellman, R.E. and Zadeh, L.A. (1970). Decision-making in a fuzzy environment. *Management Science* 17 (4): 141–164.

Belton, V. and Stewart, T. (2002). *Multiple Criteria Decision Analysis: An Integrated Approach*. Massachusetts, BST: Kluwer Academic Publishers.

Benayoun, R., Roy, B., and Sussman, B. (1966). ELECTRE: Une méthode pour guider le choix en présence de points de vue multiples. Note de travail 49, SEMA-METRA International, Direction Scientifique, Paris, France.

Bernstein, P. (1996). *Against the Gods: The Remarkable Story of Risk*. New York, NY: Wiley.

Bernoulli, D. (1738). Specimen theoriae novae de mensura sortis. *Comentarii Academiae Scientiarum Imperiales Petropolitanae* 1738 (5): 175–192.

Black, D. (1948). On the rationale of group decision-making. *Journal of Political Economy* 56 (1): 23–34.

Bozorg-Haddad, O., Solgi, M., and Loáiciga, H.A. (2017). *Meta-heuristic and Evolutionary Algorithms for Engineering Optimization*. Hoboken, NJ: Wiley.

Brans, J.P. (1982). L'ingénierie de la decision. Elaboration d'instruments d'aide a la decision: Methode PROMETHEE. In: *L'aide a la Decision: Nature, Instruments et Perspectives D'avenir* (eds. R. Nadeau and M. Landry), 183–214. Québec, Canada: Presses de Universite Laval.

Brans, J.P., Vincke, P., and Mareschal, B. (1986). How to select and how to rank projects: the PROMETHEE method. *European Journal of Operational Research* 24 (2): 228–238.

Choo, E.U. and Wedley, W.C. (1985). Optimal criterion weights in repetitive multicriteria decision-making. *Journal of the Operational Research Society* 36 (11): 983–992.

Chu, A.T.W., Kalaba, R.E., and Spingarn, K. (1979). A comparison of two methods for determining the weights of belonging to fuzzy sets. *Journal of Optimization Theory and Applications* 27 (4): 531–538.

Churchman, C.W. and Ackoff, R.L. (1954). An approximate measure of value. *Journal of the Operations Research Society of America* 2 (2): 172–187.

Coombs, C.H. and Pruitt, D.G. (1960). Components of risk in decision making: probability and variance preferences. *Journal of Experimental Psychology* 60 (5): 265.

Custer, R.L., Scarcella, J.A., and Stewart, B.R. (1999). The modified Delphi technique: a rotational modification. *Journal of Career and Technical Education* 15 (2): 50–58.

Dalkey, N. and Helmer, O. (1963). An experimental application of the Delphi method to the use of experts. *Management Science* 9 (3): 458–467.

Deng, J. (1989). Introduction to grey system theory. *The Journal of Grey System* 1 (1): 1–24.

Fan, Z.P. (1996). Complicated multiple attribute decision making: theory and applications. Ph.D. Dissertation. Northeastern University. Shenyang, China.

Hansen, P. and Ombler, F. (2008). A new method for scoring additive multi-attribute value models using pairwise rankings of alternatives. *Journal of Multi-Criteria Decision Analysis* 15 (3–4): 87–107.

Hwang, C.L. and Yoon, K. (1981). Methods for multiple attribute decision making. In: *Multiple Attribute Decision Making: Lecture Notes in Economics and Mathematical Systems* (eds. C.L. Hwang and K. Yoon), 58–191. Heidelberg, Germany: Springer Publication Company.

Jeffreys, I. (2004). The use of compensatory and non-compensatory multi-criteria analysis for small-scale forestry. *Small-Scale Forest Economics, Management and Policy* 3 (1): 99–117.

Kahneman, D. and Tversky, A. (1984). Choices, values, and frames. *American Psychologist* 39 (4): 341.

Kiesler, S. and Sproull, L. (1992). Group decision making and communication technology. *Organizational Behavior and Human Decision Processes* 52 (1): 96–123.

Kleindorfer, P.R., Kunreuther, H., and Schoemaker, P.J. (1993). *Decision Sciences: An Integrative Perspective*. Cambridge, UK: Cambridge University Press.

Malczewski, J. (1999). *GIS and Multicriteria Decision Analysis*. New York, NY: Wiley.

Mendoza, G.A. and Martins, H. (2006). Multi-criteria decision analysis in natural resource management: a critical review of methods and new modelling paradigms. *Forest Ecology and Management* 230 (1–3): 1–22.

Mladineo, N., Margeta, J., Brans, J.P., and Mareschal, B. (1987). Multicriteria ranking of alternative locations for small scale hydro plants. *European Journal of Operational Research* 31 (2): 215–222.

Opricovic, S. (1998). Multicriteria optimization of civil engineering systems. Ph.D. Thesis. Faculty of Civil Engineering. Belgrade, Serbia.

Pearl, J. (1996). Decision making under uncertainty. *ACM Computing Surveys* 28 (1): 89–92.

Rezaei, J., Wang, J., and Tavasszy, L. (2015). Linking supplier development to supplier segmentation using best-worst method. *Expert Systems with Applications* 42 (23): 9152–9164.

Rieger, M.O. and Wang, M. (2006). Cumulative prospect theory and the St. Petersburg paradox. *Economic Theory* 28 (3): 665–679.

Roy, B. (1978). ELECTRE III: Un algorithme de classement fondé sur une représentation floue des préférences en présence de critères multiples. *Cahiers du Centre d'Etudes de Recherche Opérationnelle* 20 (1): 3–24.

Roy, B. and Bertier, P. (1971). La méthode ELECTRE II: Note de travail 142. SEMA-METRA. Metra International.

Roy, B. and Hugonnard, J.C. (1982). Ranking of suburban line extension projects on the Paris metro system by a multicriteria method. *Transportation Research Part A: General* 16 (4): 301–312.

Saad, G.H. (2001). Strategic performance evaluation: descriptive and prescriptive analysis. *Industrial Management and Data Systems* 101 (8): 390–399.

Saaty, T.L. (1977). A scaling method for priorities in hierarchical structures. *Journal of Mathematical Psychology* 15 (3): 234–281.

Saaty, T.L. (1996). *Decision Making with Dependence and Feedback: The Analytic Network Process*. Pittsburgh, PA: RWS Publications.

Santos, L.R. and Rosati, A.G. (2015). The evolutionary roots of human decision making. *Annual Review of Psychology* 66: 321–347.

Shannon, C.E. (1948). A mathematical theory of communication. *Bell System Technical Journal* 27 (3): 379–423.

Tversky, A. and Kahneman, D. (1986). Rational choice and the framing of decisions. *Journal of Business*: S251–S278.

Tzeng, G.H. and Huang, J.J. (2011). *Multiple Attribute Decision Making: Methods and Applications*. Boca Raton, FL: CRC Press.

Velasquez, M. and Hester, P.T. (2013). An analysis of multi-criteria decision making methods. *International Journal of Operations Research* 10 (2): 56–66.

Vincke, J.P. and Brans, P. (1985). A preference ranking organization method: the PROMETHEE method for MCDM. *Management Science* 31 (6): 647–656.

Vroom, V.H. and Jago, A.G. (1974). Decision making as a social process: normative and descriptive models of leader behavior. *Decision Sciences* 5 (4): 743–769.

Weber, E.U. and Coskunoglu, O. (1990). Descriptive and prescriptive models of decision-making: implications for the development of decision aids. *IEEE Transactions on Systems, Man, and Cybernetics* 20 (2): 310–317.

Xu, X. (2001). The SIR method: a superiority and inferiority ranking method for multiple criteria decision making. *European Journal of Operational Research* 131 (3): 587–602.

Zolghadr-Asli, B., Bozorg-Haddad, O., and Chu, X. (2018a). Chapter 1: Introduction. In: *Advanced Optimization by Nature-Inspired Algorithms*. Singapore: Springer International Publishing AG.

Zolghadr-Asli, B., Bozorg-Haddad, O., and Chu, X. (2018b). Crow search algorithm (CSA). In: *Advanced Optimization by Nature-Inspired Algorithms*. Singapore: Springer.

Zolghadr-Asli, B., Bozorg-Haddad, O., and Chu, X. (2018c). Dragonfly algorithm (DA). In: *Advanced Optimization by Nature-Inspired Algorithms*. Singapore: Springer.

Zolghadr-Asli, B., Bozorg-Haddad, O., and Chu, X. (2018d). Krill herd algorithm (KHA). In: *Advanced Optimization by Nature-Inspired Algorithms*. Singapore: Springer.

Zolghadr-Asli, B., Bozorg-Haddad, O., and Loáiciga, H.A. (2017). Discussion of 'Optimization of Phenol Removal Using Ti/PbO 2 Anode with Response Surface Methodology' by C. García-Gómez, JA Vidales-Contreras, J. Nápoles-Armenta, and P. Gortáres-Moroyoqui. *Journal of Environmental Engineering* 143 (9): 07017001.

2

Simple Weighting Methods: Weighted Sum and Weighted Product Methods

2.1 Introduction

To reach a better understanding of any decision-making problem, one must employ information-gathering methods, including but not limited to surveys, questionnaires, examination, and sampling, to collect as much practical information as possible. Eventually, such attempts increase the chance of choosing the most suitable alternative, that would better reflect the needs and interests of the stakeholders of the MADM problem at hand (Tzeng and Huang 2011).

From the MADM point of view, the gathered information regarding the problem in question is generally represented in a matrix form, commonly referred to as the decision-matrix. Based on the decision-matrix, the decision-maker can anticipate the stakeholders' desires and preferences, which eventually lead to choosing the most suitable available option through a mathematically supported framework. The choosing process proceeds and their assumptions are what distinguishes between the MADM methods.

A MADM problem is composed of a set of alternatives, which are the feasible discrete solutions available to the decision-maker, and a set of evaluation criteria, which are the instruments through which the stakeholders describe their objective. Subsequently, a decision-matrix in extended form is constructed based on the four following information sets (Yu 1990):

(1) The set of feasible alternatives, denoted by $\{a_i \mid i = 1, 2, \ldots, m\}$. Notice that each alternative represents a row in the decision-matrix (D);
(2) The set of predefined evaluation criteria denoted by $\{c_j \mid j = 1, 2, \ldots, n\}$. Each criterion represents a column in the decision-matrix (D);
(3) The anticipated value or performance of the alternatives with regard to each given criterion. Let $v_{(i,j)}$ represent the value of the ith alternative with respect to the jth criterion, then a $m \times n$ matrix is constructed with $v_{(i,j)}$ as the elements; and

A Handbook on Multi-Attribute Decision-Making Methods, First Edition.
Omid Bozorg-Haddad, Babak Zolghadr-Asli, and Hugo A. Loáiciga.

(4) The decision-maker prioritizes based on the weights, denoted by $\{w_j \mid j = 1, 2, \ldots, n\}$. Each w_j reflects the importance of the ith criterion. This step involves a weighting procedure.

Consequently, the decision-matrix (D) is represented as follows (Yu 1990):

$$D = \begin{array}{c} \\ a_1 \\ \vdots \\ a_m \end{array} \begin{array}{c} \begin{array}{ccc} c_1 & \cdots & c_n \end{array} \\ \begin{bmatrix} v_{(1,1)} & \cdots & v_{(1,n)} \\ \vdots & \ddots & \vdots \\ v_{(m,1)} & \cdots & v_{(m,n)} \end{bmatrix} \end{array} \tag{2.1}$$

In addition to the decision-matrix on occasion, the decision-makers define extreme alternatives, namely, ideal (a^+) and inferior (a^-) alternatives. The ideal alternative is an arbitrarily defined vector of choices describing the aspired solution to the given problem, which, in practice, may or may not be achievable. The inferior alternative is a solution that represents the most undesirable option for the given MADM problem. There are two main methods to compose the ideal and inferior alternatives. One can use the best and worst values in the jth column of the decision-matrix to compose the jth component of the ideal and inferior alternatives, respectively. On the other hand, one could also use the upper and lower boundaries of the feasible range of the jth criterion to compose these arbitrarily defined alternatives. In such cases, if the criterion is considered to be positive, where the larger the value the better the situation, the upper and lower boundaries represent the ideal and inferior alternatives, respectively. Conversely, a negative criterion, where the smaller the value, the better the situation, the lower and upper boundaries represent the ideal and inferior alternatives, respectively. These arbitrarily defined alternatives can then be represented as follows (Tzeng and Huang 2011):

$$a^+ = (v_1^+, v_2^+, \ldots, v_j^+, \ldots, v_n^+) \tag{2.2}$$

$$a^- = (v_1^-, v_2^-, \ldots, v_j^-, \ldots, v_n^-) \tag{2.3}$$

in which v_j^+ and v_j^- = the components of the ideal and inferior alternatives with regard to the jth criterion, respectively.

The admissibility of each alternative in a MADM problem hinges on their performances with regards to the predefined evaluation criteria, which may be of different mathematical nature. In fact, an MADM problem commonly involves multiple criteria with different dimensions and measure of scales. One of the main challenges of the MADM is for the decision-maker to aggregate the performance of alternatives with regard to each given criterion so that the overall preference of alternatives can be achieved. However, the former cannot be achieved while the evaluation criteria are not of the same dimension, measuring unit, and scale. Consequently, through a mathematical procedure, better known as normalization, the decision-matrix is transformed into a dimensionless matrix. There are various normalization procedures, such as the Z-score transformation; yet, the following two forms are the most recommended for MADM problems, mainly, because they are easy to interpret (Ebert and Welsch 2004; Zhou et al. 2006; Tzeng and Huang 2011):

Form I: This normalization process, linearly, transforms all the performance values, so that the relative order of magnitude of the ratings remains equal. The procedure can be set up as follows (Chang and Yeh 2001):

- *For positive criteria*:

$$r_{(i,j)} = \frac{v_{(i,j)}}{v_j^+} \tag{2.4}$$

- *For negative criteria*:

$$r_{(i,j)} = \frac{1/v_{(i,j)}}{1/v_j^+} = \frac{v_j^+}{v_{(i,j)}} \tag{2.5}$$

in which $r_{(i,j)}$ = the normalized performance value for the ith alternatives with respect to the jth criterion.

Form II: In this normalizing procedure, which is slightly more advanced than the former technique, both ideal and inferior alternatives are used to normalize the performance values, as follows (Ma et al. 1999):

- *For positive criteria*:

$$r_{(i,j)} = \frac{v_{(i,j)} - v_j^-}{v_j^+ - v_j^-} \tag{2.6}$$

- *For negative criteria*:

$$r_{(i,j)} = \frac{v_j^- - v_{(i,j)}}{v_j^- - v_j^+} \tag{2.7}$$

The cited normalization procedure yields dimensionless performance values of the decision-matrix in which the $[r_{(i,j)}]$ range between 0 and 1.

Through the normalization procedure, the decision-maker transforms the elements of a decision-matrix into commensurable values. The next step is for the decision-maker to combine these values in a way that the alternatives' overall preferences can be evaluated. Herein, assume that the decision-maker evaluated the importance of each criterion and derive the set of weights that best reflect the stakeholder's priorities. Let w_j denote the assigned weight to the jth criterion; the following holds for the assigned weight set:

$$\sum_{j=1}^{n} w_j = 1 \tag{2.8}$$

Assigning the proper weight to each criterion is a challenging procedure that is discussed later in the appendix section. The challenge remains, however, on how these values can be combined to form an overall preference for each given alternative. Sections 2.2 and 2.3 describe, in detail, two basic methods to aggregate the alternatives' performances and obtain the alternatives' overall preference.

2.2 The Weighted Sum Method

The weighted sum method (WSM), also referred to as the simple additive weighting (SAW) method, is the best known and simplest MADM method for evaluating a number of alternatives in terms of a number of decision criteria. The basic logic of WSM, which was perhaps the first logical solution that enabled the decision-makers to cope with the MADM problems, is to obtain a weighted sum of the performance values of each alternative's overall attributes. Churchman and Ackoff (1954) were among the first to employ the WSM method to cope with a portfolio selection problem (Tzeng and Huang 2011). Ever since, due to the simplistic nature of the method, it quickly became a popular tool to cope with a MADM problem (Zanakis et al. 1995, 1998). Notable examples of applying WSM in different fields would be in agroecosystem management (Andrews and Carroll 2001), airlines' strategic planning and management (Chang and Yeh 2001), energy planning and management (San Cristóbal 2011), construction management (Jato-Espino et al. 2014), environmental assessments (Kang 2002; Zhou et al. 2006), forestry management (Howard 1991), industrial management (Ma et al. 1999), industrial robot selection (Athawale and Chakraborty 2011), landfill site selection (Şener et al. 2006), mobile network selection (Savitha and Chandrasekar 2011), software evaluation (Olson et al. 1995), wastewater management (Zarghami 2011), and water supply planning (Goicoechea et al. 1992; Hobbs et al. 1992), to name a few.

The following is a detailed stepwise instruction to implement WSM as an MADM solving method:

2.2.1 Step 1: Defining the Decision-making Problem

The initial step of the WSM would be for the decision-maker to determine the elements of the decision-matrix. It goes without saying that the integrity of the final result would rely heavily on this step. A well-defined decision-matrix is the basic requirement of any MADM method.

2.2.2 Step 2: Normalizing the Elements of the Decision-matrix

At this junction, the decision-maker creates a commensurable decision-matrix by normalizing the elements of the matrix, using Eqs. (2.4–2.7). This step is vital to compose a logical and viable decision-making process, for otherwise, combining the nonnormalized values to obtain the overall scores of the alternatives would yield meaningless elements.

2.2.3 Step 3: Aggregating the Preference of Alternatives

The following equation is employed to aggregate the normalized preference values of alternatives (Churchman and Ackoff 1954):

$$V_i = \sum_{j=1}^{n} w_j \times r_{(i,j)} \quad \forall i \tag{2.9}$$

in which V_i = the overall preference of the ith alternative. Equation (2.9) is found on most compensatory methods and implies that poor performance of an alternative with respect to some criteria can be compensated for by high performance by other criteria.

Despite its simplicity, the WSM remains a top choice of decision-makers for evaluating an MADM problem. A conceptually similar method to WSM is the weighted product method (WPM), which is discussed in Section 2.3.

2.3 The Weighted Product Method

The WPM employs multiplication for synthesizing the attributes' performance values, each of which is raised to the power of the corresponding attributes' weights. In essence, compared to the WSM, the WPM penalizes alternatives with poor attribute preference values more heavily (Triantaphyllou and Mann 1989; Chang and Yeh 2001; San Cristóbal 2012). WPM has been successfully implemented in bidding strategies (Wang et al. 2010), business strategic planning (Chang and Yeh 2001), energy resources management (Pohekar and Ramachandran 2004), environmental evaluations (Zhou et al. 2006), technological instrument selection (Savitha and Chandrasekar 2011), supply chain management (Chou et al. 2008), and waste management (Cheng et al. 2003).

The WPM follows the same basic steps applied in the WSM. The following is a stepwise procedure to implement the WPM in an MADM problem:

Step 1: *Defining the decision-making problem*
Step 2: *Normalizing the elements of the decision-matrix*
Step 3: *Aggregating the preference of alternatives*

Equation (2.10) synthesizes the alternatives' performance values (Chang and Yeh 2001):

$$V_i = \prod_{j=1}^{n} [r_{(i,j)}]^{w_j} \quad \forall i \tag{2.10}$$

This method is also considered as a compensatory MADM method where the assumption of criteria independency is made (Saaty and Ergu 2015).

2.4 Conclusion

MADM problems have extensive theoretical and practical foundations. Concerning MADM it has been demonstrated how to mathematically express decision-making problem through an instrument called the decision-matrix. A decision-matrix is, generally, composed of four features, namely, alternatives, criteria, the weights of criteria, and the performance value of alternatives. Additionally, the importance of normalizing the element of the decision-matrix, which is a mathematical procedure through which the preference values of the decision-matrix are rendered dimensionless, was also reviewed in this chapter. Lastly, two of the majorly implemented, basic MADM methods, namely, WSM and WPM, were presented, and stepwise instructions for each method were listed. The WSM and WPM are compensatory methods founded on the assumption of criteria independence. Tough and more advanced methods are available, the WSM and WPM remain relevant. They constitute the foundation on which most state-of-the-arts MADM methods are founded upon.

References

Andrews, S.S. and Carroll, C.R. (2001). Designing a soil quality assessment tool for sustainable agroecosystem management. *Ecological Applications* 11 (6): 1573–1585.

Athawale, V.M. and Chakraborty, S. (2011). A comparative study on the ranking performance of some multi-criteria decision-making methods for industrial robot selection. *International Journal of Industrial Engineering Computations* 2 (4): 831–850.

Chang, Y.H. and Yeh, C.H. (2001). Evaluating airline competitiveness using multiattribute decision making. *Omega* 29 (5): 405–415.

Cheng, S., Chan, C.W., and Huang, G.H. (2003). An integrated multi-criteria decision analysis and inexact mixed integer linear programming approach for solid waste management. *Engineering Applications of Artificial Intelligence* 16 (5-6): 543–554.

Chou, S.Y., Chang, Y.H., and Shen, C.Y. (2008). A fuzzy simple additive weighting system under group decision-making for facility location selection with objective/subjective attributes. *European Journal of Operational Research* 189 (1): 132–145.

Churchman, C.W. and Ackoff, R.L. (1954). An approximate measure of value. *Journal of the Operations Research Society of America* 2 (2): 172–187.

Ebert, U. and Welsch, H. (2004). Meaningful environmental indices: A social choice approach. *Journal of Environmental Economics and Management* 47 (2): 270–283.

Goicoechea, A., Stakhiv, E.Z., and Li, F. (1992). Experimental evaluation of multiple criteria decision models for application to water resources planning. *Journal of the American Water Resources Association* 28 (1): 89–102.

Hobbs, B.F., Chankong, V., Hamadeh, W., and Stakhiv, E.Z. (1992). Does choice of multicriteria method matter? An experiment in water resources planning. *Water Resources Research* 28 (7): 1767–1779.

Howard, A.F. (1991). A critical look at multiple criteria decision making techniques with reference to forestry applications. *Canadian Journal of Forest Research* 21 (11): 1649–1659.

Jato-Espino, D., Castillo-Lopez, E., Rodriguez-Hernandez, J., and Canteras-Jordana, J.C. (2014). A review of application of multi-criteria decision making methods in construction. *Automation in Construction* 45: 151–162.

Kang, S.M. (2002). A sensitivity analysis of the Korean composite environmental index. *Ecological Economics* 43 (2): 159–174.

Ma, J., Fan, Z.P., and Huang, L.H. (1999). A subjective and objective integrated approach to determine attribute weights. *European Journal of Operational Research* 112 (2): 397–404.

Olson, D.L., Moshkovich, H.M., Schellenberger, R., and Mechitov, A.I. (1995). Consistency and accuracy in decision aids: experiments with four multiattribute systems. *Decision Sciences* 26 (6): 723–747.

Pohekar, S.D. and Ramachandran, M. (2004). Application of multi-criteria decision making to sustainable energy planning: a review. *Renewable and Sustainable Energy Reviews* 8 (4): 365–381.

Saaty, T.L. and Ergu, D. (2015). When is a decision-making method trustworthy? Criteria for evaluating multi-criteria decision-making methods. *International Journal of Information Technology and Decision Making* 14 (06): 1171–1187.

San Cristóbal, J.R. (2011). Multi-criteria decision-making in the selection of a renewable energy project in Spain: the VIKOR method. *Renewable Energy* 36 (2): 498–502.

San Cristóbal, J.R. (2012). Weighted sum method and weighted product method. In: *Multi Criteria Analysis in the Renewable Energy Industry* (ed. J.R. San Cristobal), 19–22. London, UK: Springer.

Savitha, K. and Chandrasekar, C. (2011). Vertical Handover decision schemes using SAW and WPM for network selection in heterogeneous wireless networks. *Global Journal of Computer Science and Technology* 11 (9): 19–24.

Şener, B., Süzen, M.L., and Doyuran, V. (2006). Landfill site selection by using geographic information systems. *Environmental Geology* 49 (3): 376–388.

Triantaphyllou, E. and Mann, S.H. (1989). An examination of the effectiveness of multi-dimensional decision-making methods: a decision-making paradox. *Decision Support Systems* 5 (3): 303–312.

Tzeng, G.H. and Huang, J.J. (2011). *Multiple Attribute Decision Making: Methods and Applications*. Boca Raton, FL: CRC Press.

Wang, M., Liu, S., Wang, S., and Lai, K.K. (2010). A weighted product method for bidding strategies in multi-attribute auctions. *Journal of Systems Science and Complexity* 23 (1): 194–208.

Yu, P.L. (1990). *Forming Winning Strategies: An Integrated Theory of Habitual Domains*. Heidelberg, Germany: Springer Science and Business Media Publication.

Zanakis, S.H., Mandakovic, T., Gupta, S.K. et al. (1995). A review of program evaluation and fund allocation methods within the service and government sectors. *Socio-Economic Planning Sciences* 29 (1): 59–79.

Zanakis, S.H., Solomon, A., Wishart, N., and Dublish, S. (1998). Multi-attribute decision making: a simulation comparison of select methods. *European Journal of Operational Research* 107 (3): 507–529.

Zarghami, M. (2011). Effective watershed management; case study of Urmia Lake, Iran. *Lake and Reservoir Management* 27 (1): 87–94.

Zhou, P., Ang, B.W., and Poh, K.L. (2006). Comparing aggregating methods for constructing the composite environmental index: an objective measure. *Ecological Economics* 59 (3): 305–311.

3

Analytic Hierarchy Process (AHP)

3.1 Introduction

A skeptical mind might argue that the philosophical foundation of multicriteria, in general, and multiattribute decision-making (MADM) process, is similar to any other decision-making process seeking to achieve participant satisfaction and ensure the interest of the stakeholders. There may be some truth in this unifying view of decision-making because a multi attribute decision-making process can be transformed into a single criterion problem with the objective of optimizing the stakeholders' utility. This viewpoint, however, is flawed because stakeholders' interests may differ from one another and representing their goals with a single mathematical objective function is a moot attempt. Furthermore, even in cases with a solitary stakeholder, guaranteeing the satisfaction of the beneficiary may, in turn, relay on underlying objectives or evaluating criteria. These criteria may be of conflicting natures and are, in all likelihood, of different importance to the stakeholders. Consequently, such reasoning would lead the decision-maker back were the argument started, where the interest of stakeholders would be represented by evaluation criteria, and the objective is to forage these criteria to find the ideal set of solution(s) that would best represent the interest of the participants in the decision-making process.

The process of decision-making is a subjective procedure, which relies in part on the cognitive understanding of the experts. It can be described as assigning a set of arbitrarily selected weights to each given criteria, thus transforming the problem into a single objective function (Dyer 1990; Saaty 1990a). Though most, if not all, MADM methods are founded upon a similar procedure, different experts may derive different sets of arbitrary weights thus arriving at a different sets of solution(s) for the same MADM problem. The above reasoning does not undermine the important role of subjective reasoning in the MADM process. Yet, a decision support theory is unique in the representation of the experts' judgments, and in the synthesis obtained from these judgments (Saaty 1985, 1990b). The above

A Handbook on Multi-Attribute Decision-Making Methods, First Edition.
Omid Bozorg-Haddad, Babak Zolghadr-Asli, and Hugo A. Loáiciga.

comments do not mean that a sound decision-making method arrives at a unique set of solutions regardless of the decision-making cognitive assessment of the problem in hand, but rather, that such method should partly neutralize and mitigate the magnitude of such influence through a set of mathematically and logically supported procedures.

Basically, a sound MADM method provides the tools with which the decision-makers would be able to find the most suited alternative for any given problem. To do so, the decision-maker must first represent the stakeholders' interest in terms of a set of evaluating criteria. The sole purpose of this mathematically and/or linguistically expressed set is to represent different perspectives of the stakeholders' interests, and such derived set would serve as a benchmark to compare the acceptability of a set of feasible alternatives for the given problem. The first challenge of any sound MADM method is to propose a framework through which the decision-makers would be empowered to cope with the complex, multidimensional real-world problems, without inducing any notable simplification errors to ease computations. In other words, a sound decision-making method ought to balance the role of accurate estimation of the final solution and the ease of computation. Furthermore, a sound MADM method must provide a means with which the decision-makers can realistically and accurately reflect the interests of the stakeholders. This entails evaluating and ranking the feasible solutions to any given decision-making problem using a set of predefined evaluation criteria. Such mechanism must be able to cope with both tangible and intangible criteria. In the case of intangible criteria, the decision-makers would have to employ an ambiguous, and, often, linguistically expressed metrics, which would further complicate an already complex process.

The analytic hierarchy process (AHP), which can be identified as a compensatory MADM method, was first theorized by Saaty (1977), and further developed in the late 1970s (Saaty 1980). In light of the AHP, an MADM problem is expressed in terms of smaller, independent, yet connected units, each of which has the structure of a single objective decision-making problem. The decision-maker is then encouraged to make cognitive comparisons of the units. Through the framework of the AHP, the aforementioned comparisons are combined allowing the decision-maker to choose the most suitable solution for the given MADM problem. Given that this framework is pairwise comparison-oriented, it can be employed to cope with MADM problems that feature tangible and intangible evaluation criteria. The AHP method is rigorously concerned with the scaling of measurement, or metrics, used in the process of decision-making. Therefore, the AHP method employs implicitly defined scales of measurement to evaluate and map the elements of the decision-making process, whether they are criteria, subcriteria, or alternatives (Saaty 1990b).

The AHP method and has been numerously employed in various fields of study, including but not limited to: ecological evaluation (Anselin et al. 1989), energy resources planning and management (Kumar et al. 2017), engineering (Triantaphyllou and Mann 1995), environmental management (Ramanathan 2001; Handfield et al. 2002), financial management (Yalcin et al. 2011), firm management (Hafeez et al. 2002), healthcare agendas (Brent et al. 2007; Liberatore and Nydick 2008), maintenance strategy management (Bevilacqua and Braglia 2000), marketing application (Wind and Saaty 1980), military products manufacturing (Cheng and Mon 1994), operation management (Partovi et al. 1990; Subramanian and Ramanathan 2012), project risk management (Mustafa and Al-Bahar 1991), public transportation site selection (Mohajeri and Amin 2010), social network analysis (Liebowitz 2005), supplier selection (Barbarosoglu and Yazgac 1997), supply chain selection (Nydick and Hill 1992), and watershed management (Pourghasemi et al. 2012). This chapter reviews the foundation of the AHP method, followed by a stepwise procedure to implement this method.

3.2 The Hierarchical Structure

The initial and a noticeable challenge of real-life MADM problems is their complex nature. The decision-maker in such situation is confronted by numerous vital elements, each of which plays a crucial role in the final result of the decision-making. These elements include (Yu 1990):

(1) The main purpose of the decision-making or the goal of the decision-maker;
(2) A set of evaluation factors, better known as criteria, that shall express different aspects of interest to the stakeholders; and, lastly,
(3) A set of feasible solutions, better known as the alternatives, that ought to represent the most viable options under consideration.

Let a_i denote the ith alternative and c_j represent the jth criterion, and the sets of alternatives and criteria are composed of m and n members, respectively. The first task of any sound decision-making is to understand the structure through which the decision-making takes place. In real-life MADM problems, the relationship between the elements of the decision-making, including the evaluation criteria and feasible alternatives, are so interwoven that finding the most suitable solution to the problem at hand becomes a difficult and, even, an impossible task.

For this reason, it is logical to divide the complex problem into a number of smaller unit decision-making problems, and tackle these individual, less-complicated problems separately. Subsequently, the final solution can be sought by combining the result of these individual evaluations. The adoption of this simplifying procedure following a hierarchical structure is the main tool at the disposal of decision-makers. The hierarchical structure is similar to the commonly known decision tree, yet, it is not quite a traditional decision tree. Through the hierarchical structure, the MADM problem is expressed in terms of several layers, where the top layer is reserved for the main goal of the decision-maker, and the bottom layer is where the feasible alternatives of the problems are located, and in between these two is where the evaluation criteria are housed. The hierarchical structure enables the decision-makers to cluster a set of evaluation criteria, and, if need be, create a subcriteria branch. This feature allows the decision-maker to categorize the evaluation criteria, which, in turn, can facilitate the task of setting the priorities or to sharpen the focus on one or more parts of the system by inserting or eliminating levels and elements as needed. Specifically, elements that have a global character can be represented at the higher levels of the hierarchy, and others that characterize the problem at hand can be developed in greater depth (Harker and Vargas 1987; Forman and Gass 2001; Ishizaka and Nemery 2013). Figure 3.1 demonstrates the scheme of a hierarchical structure.

It is seen in Figure 3.1 the hierarchical structure maps the connections from the main objective of the decision-making to the feasible alternatives at the root level. Note that these connections, which are demonstrated by a straight line that links the parent element in the upper level to the child element in the lower level, guide the decision-maker to synthesize the evaluation of the alternatives with respect to the set of predefined criteria (Saaty 1994). At the bottom level, these connections are linked between the set of alternatives and the covering criteria, which is a technical term used to refer to any criteria/sub-criteria that are directly connected to the alternatives at the root level. In technical terms, a hierarchical structure in which every element at any given level has a direct link to the elements in the level below is called a complete hierarchy. Conversely, in an incomplete hierarchy, there exists an element at a given level that does not have an immediate link to at least one of the elements in the level below (Saaty 1980). Elements with the similar level that are connected to the same parent element are referred to as siblings (Saaty 1980).

The hierarchical structure, which is one of the key features of the AHP method, provides a framework through which the decision-maker evaluates each element with respect to the elements located in the higher level. This layered structure facilitates coping with complex MADM problems by focusing the evaluation on a solitary criterion and helps the decision-maker gain a better understanding of the basic foundation of the decision-making problem at hand (Saaty 1977). Before embarking upon how the AHP synthesizes the decision-makers' to choose the most suitable alternative, Section 3.3 sheds light on another key feature of the AHP method called the pairwise comparison.

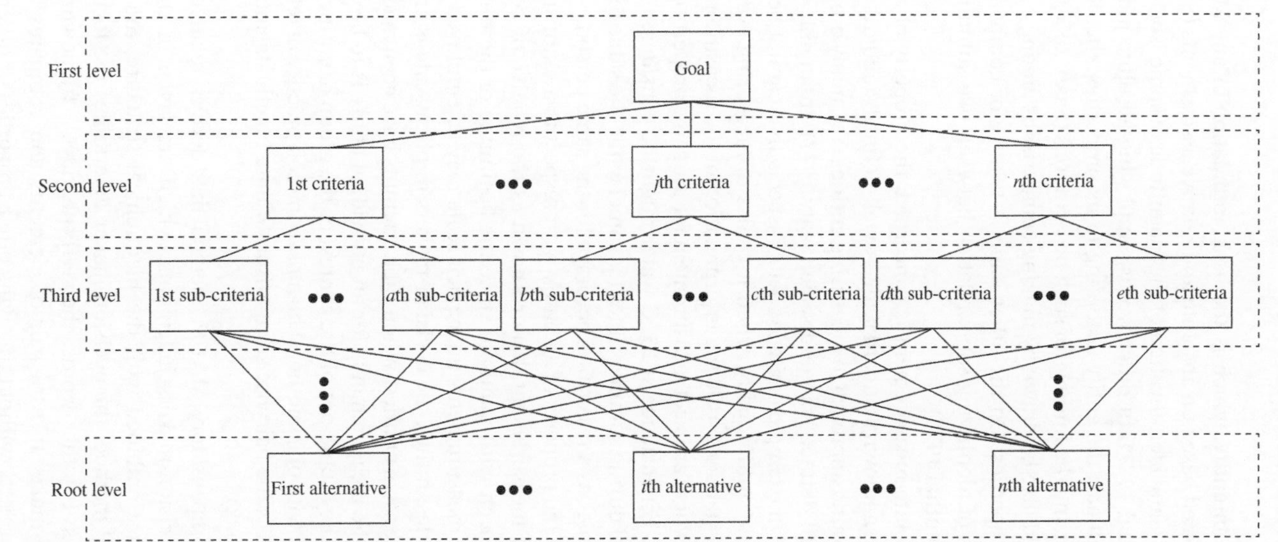

Figure 3.1 A scheme of hierarchical structure of an MADM problem.

3.3 The Pairwise Comparison

A judgment about an entity, which is the basic foundation of any MADM process, can be established based on absolute and relative assessments (Saaty 1977). Absolute judgment is the identification of the magnitude of some isolated entity's property (Blumenthal 1977). In other words, employing absolute judgment the decision-maker evaluates the entity according to its properties, then draws conclusions by synthesizing the findings of such observations (Saaty 2008). However, the conclusion could also be drawn by making comparisons among a set of entities with similar properties. On the other hand, a relative or comparative judgment is the process of identifying some relation between two stimuli sensed by the observer (Blumenthal 1977).

As far as the absolute measurement is concerned, the property of an entity is sized with respect to a known standard scale. A well-defined standard scale could be considered as a sound approach to measuring entities. Yet, many properties and attributes lack a well-defined standard scale (Saaty 1977). Intangible properties, for one, are merely an example of a wide set of aspects that cannot be measured with a standard scale. Additionally, when it comes to measuring even with the presence of a sound standard scale the interpretation of the measurements could be case dependent, where an exact measurement for the same property could carry different meanings. For instance, a 25 °C water might be considered "pleasant" for a swimming pool during summer times for some, while the same temperature might be "undesirable" as a refreshing beverage for the same person.

One can measure the property of an entity with respect to a set of similar entities. This branch of measurement, better known as the relative or comparative measurement, has been with mankind since the beginning of the time. In relative or comparative measurements no explicit scale may be employed to size the property of the entities; rather, the decision-makers implicit scale is employed to size and measure the set of entities. When such attempts have been made to assess a certain property, the measurements for an individual entity is to be considered meaningless when they stand out of the context of the group of entities to which they were compared with one another. The most common practice of relative measurement in MADM is the pairwise comparison-oriented methods, including the AHP (Saaty 1977, 1988).

The AHP is a compensatory MADM method that derives relative, implicit, scales using the decision-makers judgments, which are given in the form of paired comparisons. Combined with the hierarchical structure, the other key element of the AHP method, the decision-maker determines the focus on each of several properties. In other words, the AHP provides a framework through which the decision-maker takes a pair of elements and compares them with regard to a single property without involving other properties or other elements.

With respect to the unique hierarchical structure of any given MADM problem, the AHP's methodology provides a path to synthesize these individual pairwise comparisons so that the most suitable alternative can emerge as the final result.

At this junction, let $A = \{a_1, a_2, \ldots, a_m\}$ denote the set of feasible alternatives (a), and $O = \{c_1, c_2, \ldots, c_n\}$ represent the set of predefined evaluation criteria (c). The pairwise comparison matrix is the instrument through which the AHP method derives the preference value of each given set of elements with respect to the parent element. For instance, let P denote a pairwise comparison matrix, which compares the alternatives housed in the root level of the hierarchical structure with respect their parent element, say, the kth criterion (c_k). The matrix in this instance is expressed as follows (Saaty 1977):

$$P = \begin{array}{c} \\ a_1 \\ \vdots \\ a_m \end{array} \begin{array}{c} \begin{array}{ccc} a_1 & \cdots & a_m \end{array} \\ \begin{bmatrix} p_{(1,1)} & \cdots & p_{(1,m)} \\ \vdots & \ddots & \vdots \\ p_{(m,1)} & \cdots & p_{(m,m)} \end{bmatrix} \end{array} \quad p_{(i,i)} = 1 \tag{3.1}$$

in which $p_{(i,j)}$ = the pairwise comparison of the ith and jth alternatives. Pairwise comparison matrices are constructed for the n criteria. A complete hierarchy structured with m alternatives, n criteria/sub-criteria has $m+n+1$ (number of alternatives plus criteria/sub-criteria, and the main objective) elements, and such hierarchical structure requires $n+1$ pairwise comparison matrices.

The matrix P is the pairwise comparison matrix of the feasible alternatives formed by the implicit scales of the decision-maker. Therefore, the elements of the matrix can be employed to derive the preference value of each alternative. In other words, given the relative nature of the elements of such matrix they are expressed as follows (Saaty 1977):

$$p_{(i,j)} = v_i / v_j \tag{3.2}$$

in which v_i and v_j = the absolute preference value of the ith and jth alternatives, respectively. Logic dictates that any pairwise comparison matrix must satisfy the following property, better known as the reciprocal property (Saaty 1986):

$$p_{(i,j)} = 1/p_{(j,i)} \tag{3.3}$$

Each element in the pairwise comparison matrix P is selected based on an implicit scale used by the expert or decision-maker to demonstrate the relative preference values of each given alternative. Consequently, given the comparative nature of such measurement, the decision-maker can easily evaluate both tangible and intangible properties in light of such framework. The decision-maker or experts could employ any numerical scale to make the pairwise comparison. Table 3.1 contains a 1–9 scale that can be employed for such pairwise comparison required in the procedure of the AHP assessments (Saaty 1980).

Table 3.1 A typical pairwise comparison scale for the AHP method.

Intensity of decision-maker's preference	Definition
1	Equally important
3	Moderate preference of the ith criteria over the jth one
5	Strong preference of the ith criteria over the jth one
7	Very strong preference of the ith criteria over the jth one
9	Extreme preference of the ith criteria over the jth one
2, 4, 6, 8	Intermediate values between the two adjacent judgments

Source: Modified from Saaty (1980).

Based on Eq. (3.2) the pairwise comparison matrix introduced in Eq. (3.1) is revised as follows (Saaty 1977):

$$P = \begin{array}{c} \\ a_1 \\ \vdots \\ a_m \end{array} \begin{array}{c} \begin{array}{ccc} a_1 & \cdots & a_m \end{array} \\ \begin{bmatrix} {}^{v_1}/_{v_1} & \cdots & {}^{v_1}/_{v_m} \\ \vdots & \ddots & \vdots \\ {}^{v_m}/_{v_1} & \cdots & {}^{v_m}/_{v_m} \end{bmatrix} \end{array} \tag{3.4}$$

The decision-maker derives a preference weight vector, denoted by $W = (v_1, v_2, \ldots, v_i, \ldots, v_m)$, where v_i represents the normalized preference value of the ith alternative. Mathematically, we have that (Saaty 1977):

$$\begin{bmatrix} v_1/v_1 & \cdots & v_1/v_m \\ \vdots & \ddots & \vdots \\ v_m/v_1 & \cdots & v_m/v_m \end{bmatrix} \times \begin{bmatrix} v_1 \\ \vdots \\ v_m \end{bmatrix} = m \times \begin{bmatrix} v_1 \\ \vdots \\ v_m \end{bmatrix} \tag{3.5}$$

Equation (3.5) implies the result of multiplying the pairwise comparison matrix P by the weights vector $W = (v_1, v_2, \ldots, v_i, \ldots, v_m)^T$, is equal to m, which is the number of alternatives time the weights vector (Saaty 1980). m is expressed as an eigenvalue of the pairwise comparison matrix P, and W is the eigenvector associated with it. The sum of the eigenvalues of a matrix is equal to its trace, the sum of the diagonal elements, and in this case the trace of the pairwise comparison matrix P is equal to m. Therefore, m is the largest, or principal eigenvalue of P. The solution of $P \times W = n \times W$ is called the principal right eigenvector of P. It consists of positive entries and is unique to within a multiplicative constant (Saaty 1990b).

The aforementioned calculation is based on the judgments that formed the pairwise comparison matrix P, and is accurate, rational, and consistent. However, as the complexity of real-life MADM increases, the decision-makers in all likelihood would induce perturbation in their assessment of the relative scales measurements, and in turn, the elements of the pairwise comparison matrix are merely an estimation of their true values. In other words, the error in judgments induced by the subjective and inexact assessments made by the decision-makers and experts in forming the pairwise comparison matrix most likely introduces inconsistency in the MADM results. Section 3.4 discusses how to derive the preference value of elements with respect to such inconsistency and how to quantify such inconsistency, also.

3.4 Inconsistency

The most significant challenge for MADM methods founded on the basis of the pairwise comparison is to maintain the consistency of the pairwise comparison matrices, which is challenging in practical problems (Herman and Koczkodaj 1996). Maintaining consistency in a pairwise comparison matrix would not necessarily validate the authenticity and accuracy of the results, but rather reflects the existence of the rationality in the decision-maker judgments. Consider, for instance, a case where the decision-maker evaluates that the preference of item A is a time more significant than item B, while item B's preference is b times more significant when it is compered to item C. Rationality, consequently, would dictate for the preference of item A to be $a \times b$ more significant than item C. If the decision-maker's judgment is in line with the aforementioned rational statement, the pairwise comparison is considered to be consistent. Regardless, error in judgments by the decision-makers' evaluation of either a or b could induce inaccuracy to the pairwise comparison. While using experts' opinions would dramatically decrease the inaccuracy of the decision-making process maintaining a certain acceptable level of consistency remains an challenge for MADM methods that are based on pairwise comparisons.

Recall the pairwise comparison matrix, where each element $p_{(i,j)}$ represented an estimation of the preference value of the ith alternative (v_i) with respect to the preference value of the jth one (v_j). If full consistency hold throughout the entire pairwise comparison matrix P, the following is obtained (Saaty 1980):

$$p_{(i,j)} = p_{(i,k)} \times p_{(k,j)} \quad \forall i, j, k \tag{3.6}$$

As stated earlier, the judgments made by experts and decision-makers may induce errors to the elements of the pairwise comparison matrix, which are expressed as follows (Saaty 1980):

$$p_{(i,j)} \cong {}^{v_i}\!/_{v_j} \quad \forall i, j \tag{3.7}$$

According to the eigenvalue theory, a small perturbation about a simple eigenvalue (as is the case of m when P is not fully consistent) leads to an eigenvalue problem of the form (Saaty 1980):

$$P \times W = \lambda_{max} \times W \tag{3.8}$$

in which λ_{max} = the principal (largest) eigenvalue of the pairwise comparison matrix P, where P may no longer be fully consistent but is still reciprocal (Parlett and Reinsch 1971; Tzeng and Huang 2011). The following theorem applies to the principal eigenvalue of the pairwise comparison matrix P (Saaty 1990b):

$$\lambda_{max} \geq m \tag{3.9}$$

where $\lambda_{max} = m$, if and only if, the pairwise comparison matrix P is fully consistent.

At this junction, following a simple mathematical procedure, the decision-maker could derive an estimation of the preference weight vector. However, the integrity of the estimated results in terms of the presence of consistency in the estimated values remains under question. To quantify the inconsistency in the pairwise comparison matrix P, one must first compute the consistency index (IC), which can be expressed as follows (Saaty 1977, 1980):

$$IC = \frac{\lambda_{max} - m}{m - 1} \tag{3.10}$$

The value computed for the consistency index is then compared with the same index obtained as an average over a large number of reciprocal matrices of the same order whose entries are of random nature, namely the random index (RI) (Vargas 1982; Saaty 1990b). The random index for matrices of different order can be found in Table 3.2 (Tzeng and Huang 2011).

The order of the pairwise comparison matrix in Table 3.2 is limited to 9 from studies revealing that experts can only process information involving simultaneously only a few facts. Specifically, 7 ± 2, otherwise possible confusions may jeopardize the decision-makers ability to analyze the results (Miller 1956).

As for the final stage of quantifying the inconsistency of the pairwise comparison matrix, the inconsistency ratio (IR) is calculated as follows (Saaty 1990b):

$$IR = \frac{IC}{RI} \tag{3.11}$$

Table 3.2 The random index value for matrices of different orders.

The order of the pairwise comparison matrix	**1**	**2**	**3**	**4**	**5**	**6**	**7**	**8**	**9**
Random index (RI)	0.00	0.00	0.52	0.89	1.11	1.25	1.35	1.40	1.49

Source: Modified from Tzeng and Huang (2011).

If the aforementioned ratio (IR) is under 0.1 or less, the estimate of the preference weight vector W is accepted. Otherwise, the decision-maker is encouraged to improve the consistency of the estimated preference weight vector (Saaty 1990b; Tzeng and Huang 2011).

Before embarking upon the pragmatic framework to employ the AHP method, it is beneficial to go through the basic principles and axioms of the AHP method. Section 3.5 is dedicated to the theoretical foundation on which the AHP rests.

3.5 Quadruple Axioms of the AHP

Like any sound decision-making method, the AHP is based upon a rational, mathematically supported foundation. This foundation can be expressed as a set of quadruple axioms, as follows (Saaty 1986):

Axiom 3.1 ***The reciprocal property***
Considering that the elements of the pairwise comparison matrix are relative preference value of one entity logic dictates that if the decision-maker evaluates item A to be a times more valuable than item B, then item B must be have $1/a$ value compared to item A. This axiom is expressed by Eq. (3.3).

Axiom 3.2 ***The homogeneity property***
In order to achieve sound decision-making, one must ensure that the sibling elements or alternatives are of the same magnitude of importance so that the comparisons can be made among homogenous elements. Additionally, the homogeneity axiom prescribes the inconsistencies that may be injected to the result due to perturbations introduced by the decision-maker (Saaty 1990b).

Axiom 3.3 ***The dependency property***
The third axiom states the dependence of a lower level on the adjacent higher level. This property that ensures the presence of the continuity in the hierarchical structure enables the decision-maker to aggregate the results of the pairwise comparison matrices and choose the most suitable alternative.

Axiom 3.4 ***The property of expectation***
The fourth axiom states the idea that an outcome can only reflect expectations when the latter are well represented in the hierarchical structure. In other words, only an accurately, well-defined hierarchical structure can lead to the selection of the most desirable alternative for an MADM problem.

3.6 Stepwise Description of the AHP Method

3.6.1 Step 1: Defining the Decision-making Problem

The first task for the decision-maker is to lay the framework through which the decision-making process takes place. The integrity of the final result relies heavily on the accuracy of this vital step. The main idea of this step is for the decision-maker to mathematically express the decision-making problem through a set of criteria, for example $\{c_1, c_2, \ldots, c_n\}$, and alternatives, for example $\{a_1, a_2, \ldots, a_m\}$. In addition, the decision-maker must provide a hierarchy for the MADM problem. At this stage, the elements of the MADM problem are formed in a hierarchical structure, and if need be, clustered in specific groups. The decision-maker can ensure homogeneity throughout the hierarchical structure via the proper clustering of the elements.

There are three types of clustering of elements in a hierarchical structure (Saaty 1990b):

(1) *The elementary approach*: Given n elements in a level of the hierarchical structure one may first make a quick pass through them by comparing one element with another, dropping elements with seemingly lower priority and picking another and continuing the comparison process. Hence, through these eliminations, the largest element is selected in the $n - 1$th attempt. A similar process is repeated for the remaining $n - 1$ elements to identify the second largest element, and so on. At the end of the process, the decision-maker is left with a set of arranged elements in a descending order of magnitude or intensity according to an evaluation criterion which is clustered into groupings of a few elements based on the desires of the decision-maker and the unique characteristics of the hierarchical structure. This procedure involve $(n - 1)!$ comparisons, such renders the computational effort burdensome even for relatively small n;

(2) *Trial and error clustering*: The elements of the same level are first classified into groups of large, medium, and small sizes. Then the decision-maker attempts to cluster the elements of each category into several smaller groups. At this stage, a quick pass through the clustered elements identifies the misplaced elements, which are then removed and reclustered with the appropriate categories. The aforementioned trial and error oriented process is repeated until for each evaluation criterion until the decision-maker determines the clustered elements are of the similar and comparable importance; and, finally:

(3) *Clustering by absolute measurements*: Each alternative is evaluated by absolute measurement of an attribute, and thus is rearranged in descending order on the basis of an evaluation criterion. These rearranged elements are clustered into small groups. It should be noted that though this procedure is considered to be highly efficient it cannot be performed for intangible criteria.

3.6.2 Step 2: Performing the Pairwise Comparison Through the Hierarchical Structure

At this stage, the decision-maker prioritizes the feasible alternatives and the evaluation criteria through constructing a series of pairwise comparison matrices (Eq. (3.4)). Based on the unique hierarchical structure of the problem at hand each of these constructed pairwise comparison matrices performs a comparison between sibling elements. The decision-maker employs a scale similar to what has been introduced in Table 3.1 to conduct such comparison, though other scales could also be adopted for such task. The key assumption embedded in conducting such comparisons is that the elements of the hierarchical structure must be independent of one another (Saaty 1980). In other words, one can only consider adopting the AHP method if there are no feedbacks in the hierarchical structure of the problem at hand.

3.6.3 Step 3: Estimating the Preference Value Vectors

The decision-maker must derive the preference values of the alternatives and the weights of the criteria/sub-criteria. As stated earlier, each element of the pairwise comparison matrices carries valuable information regarding the preference value of alternatives and the importance of criteria/subcriteria. To extract the proper weights from these elements, the following procedure must be conducted for each given pairwise comparison matrix located in the hierarchical structure. First, the decision-maker must normalize the elements of the pairwise comparison matrix P. Though several types of normalization, procedures have been introduced the following formulations are recommended for the AHP method (Saaty and Vargas 2006):

$$k_{(i,j)} = \frac{p_{(i,j)}}{\sum_{i=1}^{m} p_{(i,j)}} \tag{3.12}$$

and

$$k_{(i,j)} = \frac{p_{(i,j)}}{\max_{i} [p_{(i,j)}]} \tag{3.13}$$

in which $k_{(i,j)}$ = the normalized pairwise comparison of the ith alternative/criterion with the jth one. An AHP method that employs Eq. (3.12) as its normalizing technique is called the distributive mode of AHP. Conversely, an AHP method that uses Eq. (3.13) is called the ideal mode of AHP (Saaty 1980). The distributive mode assumes the existence of dependency between one criterion and the number and quality of other criteria housed in the hierarchical structure of the problem at hand (Saaty and Vargas 2006).

The preference value of the ith alternative (v_i) equals the average of the normalized pairwise comparisons of the ith alternative/criterion of each row of the matrix P:

$$v_i = \frac{\sum_{j=1}^{m} k_{(i,j)}}{m} \tag{3.14}$$

Through a similar procedure the weights of each element (e.g. alternatives, criteria, and subcriteria) located in the hierarchical structure of the MADM problem are computed.

3.6.4 Step 4: Synthesizing and Computing the Overall Preference Value of Alternatives

Up to this point all the elements of the hierarchical structure is evaluated and normalized, which enables the decision-maker to express the MADM problem through the following format (Saaty 1977):

$$D = \begin{matrix} & c_1 & \cdots & c_n \\ a_1 & k_{(1,1)} & \cdots & k_{(1,n)} \\ \vdots & \vdots & \ddots & \vdots \\ a_m & k_{(m,1)} & \cdots & k_{(m,n)} \end{matrix} \tag{3.15}$$

in which D = the decision-matrix. Each evaluation criterion, say c_j, is correlated with a weight, denoted by w_j, which is computed and normalized as covered in the previous step.

At this junction, the decision-maker must aggregate the computed values with the following equation (Saaty 1977):

$$V_i = \sum_{j=1}^{n} w_j \times k_{(i,j)} \quad \forall i \tag{3.16}$$

in which V_i = the overall preference value of the ith feasible alternative.

3.6.5 Step 5: Evaluating the Results' Rationality and Selecting the Best Alternative

At this point, the decision-maker has already synthesized the individual implicit/explicit judgments with the aggregation function written in Eq. (3.16). Yet, the integrity of the chosen solution on the base of rationality is something that still needs to be evaluated. In other words, the decision-maker must look for any sign of inconsistency in the process of the decision-making. In light of the eigenvalue theory, the decision-maker must obtain the principal eigenvalue of every pairwise comparison matrices (λ_{max}) in the hierarchical structure of the problem at hand. As stated in Section 3.4, Eq. (3.8) is the key feature of this process. Next, the decision-maker computes the consistency index, and hence, the inconsistency ratio for each pairwise comparison matrix housed in the hierarchical structure, and evaluates the rationality applied in conducting these comparison matrices. If the rationality holds the decision-maker can trust the chosen solution; otherwise, appropriate adjustments must be made to the pairwise matrices with anomalous comparisons.

3.7 Conclusion

The decision-maker attempts to pursue a solution that best reflects the interest of the stakeholders of a MADM problem. Within the process of the decision-making, one evaluates the preferences of the predetermined set of alternatives with regard to the set of predefined evaluation criteria. The decision-maker employs implicit and explicitly defined measuring scales through the procedure of choosing the most desirable solution. The pairwise comparison-oriented methods are a branch of MADM which constitutes a framework whereby the decision-makers employ implicit and explicit measuring scales without inducing any notable error to the final emerging solution set. The AHP is an MADM method that is based on the aforementioned notion. Additionally, through the elaborate framework of the AHP method the decision-maker breaks the structure of the main problem into smaller, single, attribute decision-making problems, and presents them in as a hierarchical structure. This restructured problem facilitates the process of decision-making. The decision-maker constructs pairwise comparison matrices and derives the preference value of each element on these matrices. The final solution is chosen by synthesizing these derived weights and preference values. However, it should be noted that in pairwise comparison-oriented methods it is likely that the subjective assessments of the experts may induce irrationality to the emerging results. Consequently, the AHP provides the decision-makers with a mathematical procedure, that is the inconsistency ratio, to quantify the amount of irrationality induced in the decision-making process. Therefore, the final solution of the AHP method shall be tested and validated for the existence of rationality through the decision-making process. Thanks to the pairwise comparisons and the hierarchical structure the AHP method has become a popular method to solve real-world, complex MADM problems.

References

Anselin, A., Meire, P.M., and Anselin, L. (1989). Multicriteria techniques in ecological evaluation: an example using the analytical hierarchy process. *Biological Conservation* 49 (3): 215–229.

Barbarosoglu, G. and Yazgac, T. (1997). An application of the analytic hierarchy process to the supplier selection problem. *Production and Inventory Management Journal* 38 (1): 14.

Bevilacqua, M. and Braglia, M. (2000). The analytic hierarchy process applied to maintenance strategy selection. *Reliability Engineering and System Safety* 70 (1): 71–83.

Blumenthal, A.L. (1977). *The Process of Cognition.*" Englewood Cliffs, NJ. New Jersey, NJ: Prentice-Hall.

Brent, A.C., Rogers, D.E., Ramabitsa-Siimane, T.S., and Rohwer, M.B. (2007). Application of the analytical hierarchy process to establish health care waste management systems that minimise infection risks in developing countries. *European Journal of Operational Research* 181 (1): 403–424.

Cheng, C.H. and Mon, D.L. (1994). Evaluating weapon system by analytical hierarchy process based on fuzzy scales. *Fuzzy Sets and Systems* 63 (1): 1–10.

Dyer, J.S. (1990). Remarks on the analytic hierarchy process. *Management Science* 36 (3): 249–258.

Forman, E.H. and Gass, S.I. (2001). The analytic hierarchy process: an exposition. *Operations Research* 49 (4): 469–486.

Hafeez, K., Zhang, Y., and Malak, N. (2002). Determining key capabilities of a firm using analytic hierarchy process. *International Journal of Production Economics* 76 (1): 39–51.

Handfield, R., Walton, S.V., Sroufe, R., and Melnyk, S.A. (2002). Applying environmental criteria to supplier assessment: a study in the application of the analytical hierarchy process. *European Journal of Operational Research* 141 (1): 70–87.

Harker, P.T. and Vargas, L.G. (1987). The theory of ratio scale estimation: Saaty's analytic hierarchy process. *Management Science* 33 (11): 1383–1403.

Herman, M.W. and Koczkodaj, W.W. (1996). A Monte Carlo study of pairwise comparison. *Information Processing Letters* 57 (1): 25–29.

Ishizaka, A. and Nemery, P. (2013). *Multi-Criteria Decision Analysis: Methods and Software*, 13–54. Wiley ISBN: 978-1-118-64489-8.

Kumar, A., Sah, B., Singh, A.R. et al. (2017). A review of multi criteria decision making (MCDM) towards sustainable renewable energy development. *Renewable and Sustainable Energy Reviews* 69: 596–609.

Liberatore, M.J. and Nydick, R.L. (2008). The analytic hierarchy process in medical and health care decision making: a literature review. *European Journal of Operational Research* 189 (1): 194–207.

Liebowitz, J. (2005). Linking social network analysis with the analytic hierarchy process for knowledge mapping in organizations. *Journal of Knowledge Management* 9 (1): 76–86.

Miller, G.A. (1956). The magical number seven, plus or minus two: some limits on our capacity for processing information. *Psychological Review* 63 (2): 81.

Mohajeri, N. and Amin, G.R. (2010). Railway station site selection using analytical hierarchy process and data envelopment analysis. *Computers and Industrial Engineering* 59 (1): 107–114.

Mustafa, M.A. and Al-Bahar, J.F. (1991). Project risk assessment using the analytic hierarchy process. *IEEE Transactions on Engineering Management* 38 (1): 46–52.

Nydick, R.L. and Hill, R.P. (1992). Using the analytic hierarchy process to structure the supplier selection procedure. *Journal of Supply Chain Management* 28 (2): 31–36.

Partovi, F.Y., Burton, J., and Banerjee, A. (1990). Application of analytical hierarchy process in operations management. *International Journal of Operations & Production Management* 10 (3): 5–19.

Parlett, B.N. and Reinsch, C. (1971). Balancing a matrix for calculation of eigenvalues and eigenvectors. In: *Handbook for Automatic Computation* (eds. J.H. Wilkinson and C. Reinsch), 315–326. Berlin, Heidelberg: Springer.

Pourghasemi, H.R., Pradhan, B., and Gokceoglu, C. (2012). Application of fuzzy logic and analytical hierarchy process (AHP) to landslide susceptibility mapping at Haraz watershed, Iran. *Natural Hazards* 63 (2): 965–996.

Ramanathan, R. (2001). A note on the use of the analytic hierarchy process for environmental impact assessment. *Journal of Environmental Management* 63 (1): 27–35.

Saaty, T.L. (1977). A scaling method for priorities in hierarchical structures. *Journal of Mathematical Psychology* 15 (3): 234–281.

Saaty, T.L. (1980). *The Analytic Hierarchy Process*. New York, NY: McGraw-Hill Education.

Saaty, T.L. (1985). Decision making for leaders. *IEEE Transactions on Systems, Man, and Cybernetics* 3: 450–452.

Saaty, T.L. (1986). Axiomatic foundation of the analytic hierarchy process. *Management Science* 32 (7): 841–855.

Saaty, T.L. (1988). What is the analytic hierarchy process? In: *Mathematical Models for Decision Support* (eds. G. Mitra, H.J. Greenberg, F.A. Lootsma, et al.), 109–121. Berlin, Heidelberg: Springer.

Saaty, T.L. (1990a). An exposition of the AHP in reply to the paper remarks on the analytic hierarchy process. *Management Science* 36 (3): 259–268.

Saaty, T.L. (1990b). How to make a decision: the analytic hierarchy process. *European Journal of Operational Research* 48 (1): 9–26.

Saaty, T.L. (1994). Highlights and critical points in the theory and application of the analytic hierarchy process. *European Journal of Operational Research* 74 (3): 426–447.

Saaty, T.L. (2008). Decision making with the analytic hierarchy process. *International Journal of Services Sciences* 1 (1): 83–98.

Saaty, T.L. and Vargas, L. (2006). *Decision Making with the Analytic Network Process: Economics, Political, Social and Technological Applications with Benefits, Opportunities, Costs, and Risks*. NY: Springer.

Subramanian, N. and Ramanathan, R. (2012). A review of applications of analytic hierarchy process in operations management. *International Journal of Production Economics* 138 (2): 215–241.

Triantaphyllou, E. and Mann, S.H. (1995). Using the analytic hierarchy process for decision making in engineering applications: some challenges. *International Journal of Industrial Engineering: Applications and Practice* 2 (1): 35–44.

Tzeng, G.H. and Huang, J.J. (2011). *Multiple Attribute Decision Making: Methods and Applications*. Boca Raton, FL: CRC Press.

Vargas, L.G. (1982). Reciprocal matrices with random coefficients. *Mathematical Modelling* 3 (1): 69–81.

Wind, Y. and Saaty, T.L. (1980). Marketing applications of the analytic hierarchy process. *Management Science* 26 (7): 641–658.

Yalcin, A., Reis, S., Aydinoglu, A.C., and Yomralioglu, T. (2011). A GIS-based comparative study of frequency ratio, analytical hierarchy process, bivariate statistics and logistics regression methods for landslide susceptibility mapping in Trabzon, NE Turkey. *Catena* 85 (3): 274–287.

Yu, P.L. (1990). *Forming Winning Strategies: An Integrated Theory of Habitual Domains*. Heidelberg, Germany: Springer Science and Business Media Publication.

4

Analytic Network Process (ANP)

4.1 Introduction

Quite often real-world decision-making problems can be described as situations in which the stakeholders' interests can only be portrayed through a set of evaluation criteria, while the decision-maker is faced with a set of viable, feasible, alternatives, which cannot fully outperform and dominate one another. Multiattribute decision-making (MADM) can provide the decision-makers with elaborate frameworks composed of logically supported instruments and mathematically expressed procedures to deal with the aforementioned circumstances. In light of MADM, one should first attempt to assess the feasible alternatives with regard to the predefined evaluation criteria using measuring scales. Note that these measuring scales could be defined both explicitly, where exists a standard and generally approved scale (i.e. direct measurements) or implicitly, where the decision-makers' subjective judgments would form an arbitrarily defined measuring scale (i.e. relative measurements; Saaty 1977). Thus, this would be where the decision-makers' expertise and experience on the matter at hand can help the whole decision-making process to arrive at a reliable conclusion (Saaty 1980). The challenge behind such a procedure, as it happens in most practical, real-world cases of decision-making, is where the stakeholders' interest is represented by some intangible criteria. This is where employing relative measurements have proven to be beneficial for the decision-making process (Saaty 1985, 1986, 1988). The aforementioned notion describes the core ideology behind a branch of MADM techniques better known as the pairwise-oriented methods. The analytic hierarchy process (AHP) is a fairly recognized representative for such methods (Saaty 1977, 1980).

The other challenge that usually accompanies the real-world cases of MADM is the complex, multilevel nature of these problems. A sound MADM method should provide a framework through which the decision-maker could cope with such complexities that surround these problems. For the sake of argument, if one would

A Handbook on Multi-Attribute Decision-Making Methods, First Edition.
Omid Bozorg-Haddad, Babak Zolghadr-Asli, and Hugo A. Loáiciga.

be able to decompose the large MADM problem into smaller units that would immensely help the decision-making process. Representing a problem in the form of a hierarchy is one way to tackle the described challenge (Saaty 1980). A hierarchy structure represents the MADM problem in the form of linearly positioned elements, where each element could represent the feasible alternatives, criteria, subcriteria, or even the main goal. Essentially, in a hierarchical representation of the decision-making problem, the main objective or goal would be housed on the top level and the alternatives would be located on the bottom or root level, while a series of linked criteria and sub/criteria are the bridges that compose the final structure of the problem in hand. Note that in a hierarchical structure that could be described as a muted version of a decision tree, the lines of connections are designed to be of a top-down nature. Hence, given the nature of these lines, one can conclude that each element in such a structure can be only influenced by a directly linked element housed in one layer above (Saaty 1986). Note that this indicates that in a hierarchical structure, the elements ought to be independent of those located at the same level. While the described formation is a legitimate approach to model many MADM problems, there may be cases where the assumption of independence between iso-level elements and/or lack of bottom-up connections would not be realistic. Thus, a more advanced and sophisticated form of structure is required to accurately represent such MADM problems. A network structure might be one of the plausible keys to overcoming this challenge (Saaty 1996).

Theorized by Saaty in 1996 the analytic network process (ANP) can be seen as the advanced, expanded, and generalized version of the AHP method (Saaty 2004, 2006). Note that the term “analytic” represents the core philosophy behind AHP and ANP methods, which means breaking down the MADM problems into their constituent components to study their isolated individual behavior and then aggregating the results to obtain a glance at the bigger picture and finding the most desirable solution for the MADM problem at hand. In contrast to the AHP method, which uses a hierarchy structure for such task, the ANP method benefits from a network structure (Saaty 1996). While the hierarchy can represent the elements connected in a lineal form, a network can be seen as a web of connections that enables the decision-maker to map the dependency of elements in multiple directions (Saaty 2008; Ishizaka and Nemery 2013).

The ANP method has been successfully applied in many fields, including but not limited to: construction management (Cakmak and Cakmak 2014), economic assessments (Niemira and Saaty 2004), educational issues (Momeni et al. 2011), energy markets (Köne and Büke 2007), environmental assessment (Tran et al. 2004), financial management (Amiri et al. 2012), forest management (Wolfslehner et al. 2005), logistics management (Çelebi et al. 2010), research and development (R&D) planning (Meade and Presley 2002), risk evaluation (Ghorbanzadeh et al. 2018), transportation (Mohajeri and Amin 2010), software marketing

(Mulebeke and Zheng 2006), selection of logistics service provider (Jharkharia and Shankar 2007), supplier selection (Gencer and Gürpinar 2007), and supply chain management (Zhu et al. 2010). Note that this method has been linked with other mathematical theories to make it more compatible with real-world MADM problems. For instance, Fuzzy-ANP (Li and Sun 2001; Mikhailov and Singh 2003; Cheng and Li 2005; Wu et al. 2009), a hybrid decision-making trial and evaluation laboratory (DEMATEL) with ANP (Yang et al. 2008; Tsai and Chou 2009); grey-ANP (Tseng and Chiu 2012; Dou et al. 2014), a combination of preference ranking organization method for enrichment evaluations (PROMETHEE) and ANP (Peng and Xiao 2013) are merely few examples of hybrid ANP methods. This chapter presents the basic structure of the ANP method, a stepwise description of the standard ANP method, and ends with conclusions.

4.2 Network Vs. Hierarchy Structure

The AHP and ANP methods are founded on a basic principle, which is breaking a complex MADM problem into smaller, yet connected units (Saaty 1977, 1996). Thus, the decision-maker would then be able to tackle each of these isolated decision-making problems individually and synthesize these separate assessments using the network of connections between the elements of the problem at hand to arrive at the final conclusion, which would be the set of most desirable alternatives. The AHP method, for instance, employs a hierarchical structure to map the connections between the elements of the decision-making (Saaty 1977). The hierarchical structure of the AHP method arranges its elements, which are the main objective, feasible alternatives, evaluation criteria, and subcriteria, in a top-down, linearly designed structure, with the main objective located at the top level, and the least desirable alternative placed at the root of the hierarchy structure. Note that the hierarchical structure would enable the decision-makers to form clusters, which is a combination of elements that share a common property and thus can be categorized with each other. This key feature of the hierarchical structure would dramatically decrease the chance of introducing errors in the decision-making process, especially for cases in which implicit measuring scales and subjective judgments are employed by the decision-makers to evaluate the elements of the decision-making problem. Note that the aforementioned notion applies to the key features of the network structure of the ANP method (Saaty 1996). However, unlike the ANP method, the critical assumption of the hierarchy structure of the AHP method is that for each element located in the hierarchy structure is only dependent on the upper-level elements, hence, each element's preference value is evaluated with regard to the linked elements located in the upper level. Conversely, this limitation in constructing an MADM problem is

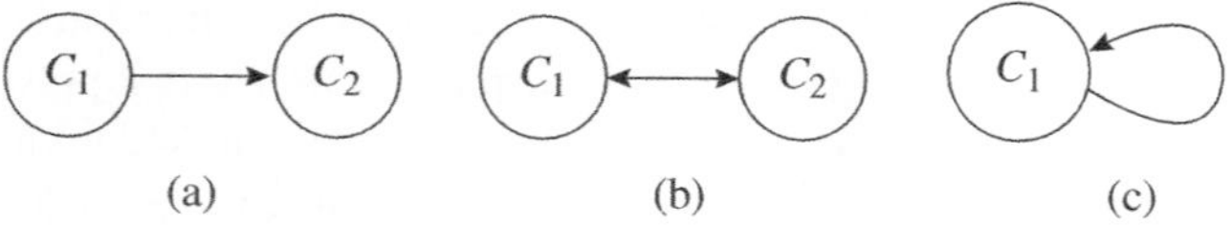

Figure 4.1 The forms of connection in the structure of a network, (a) linear connection, (b) cyclic connection, and (c) loop connection.

resolved through the network structure of the ANP method. In contrast to the AHP method, which is bounded due to its linear, leveled formation, the ANP's nonlinear, web-like formation of the network structure enables the decision-maker to express the presence of dependency between the elements in any desired direction (Saaty 1996).

A network is composed of two basic entities, namely, the components and the connections (Saaty 1996, 2004). The basic function of a network is to represent the decision-maker with a map that links the components of the decision-making through a series of web-shaped connections. Basically, these connections, which represent the presence of dependency among the components of the decision-making, can be of three forms: (i) linear connections; (ii) cyclic connections; and (iii) loop connections (Figure 4.1).

A linear connection describes the dependency of one component to another one (Figure 4.1a). For instance, in Figure 4.1a, the component C_2 is dependent on the component C_1. Note that all connections in a hierarchy structure, which would link the elements in the upper level to the elements in the lower level, are of this nature. A cycle connection, however, describes the connection of two codependent components, where exist a line of feedback among the components (Figure 4.1b). For instance, in Figure 4.1b, not only component C_1 is dependent on component C_2, but, at the same time, component C_2 is dependent on component C_1. In other words, component C_1 can influence and be influenced by component C_2. Note that interoperating and in turn evaluating, the feedback structure which is of a nonlinear nature, are challenging tasks for the decision-makers, for this type of connection involves cycling, and technically speaking, cycling can be seen as an infinite process (Saaty 2004, 2006). However, the ANP method provides a framework that would enable the decision-makers to evaluate and, eventually, quantify the influence of such components over one another. Lastly, the loop connection describes a situation where the elements of a component are interdependent and thus can influence the preference of one another (Figure 4.1c). While interoperating the loop connections, which are of nonlinear nature and, thus, can also be seen as an infinite process, is a difficult task for any MADM technique, the ANP method provides the decision-makers with a procedure to handle such situations.

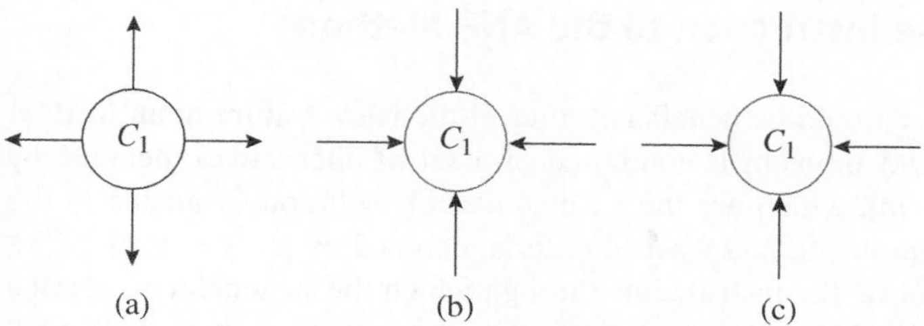

Figure 4.2 The forms of components in the structure of a network, (a) source component, (b) sink component, and (c) intermediate component. Source: Modified from Saaty (1996).

It is worth citing that the linear and cyclic connections are referred to as outer dependent connections, while the loop connections are known as the inner dependent connections (Saaty 2004, 2006).

Components, as the second piece of the puzzle that helps form a network structure, are made of elements that share a common feature or property. In essence, there are three types of components, namely (i) source components; (ii) sink components; and, lastly, (iii) intermediate components (Figure 4.2; Saaty 1996).

A sink component is the origin of series of paths of influence or connections and never the destination of such sorts of paths (Figure 4.2a). In other words, while there is at least one component that is influenced or its preference value depends on the source component, there could be no component that influences the source component. The main objective component is, usually but not necessarily, of this nature. Conversely, a sink component is the destination of a series of paths of influence or connections and never the origin of such paths (Figure 4.2b). In other words, while there is at least one component that influences the sink component, there could be no component that is influenced or its preference value depends on the sink component. The criteria and subcriteria components are of this nature. Finally, there exist components that are the origins of some lines of influential paths and the destination of others (Figure 4.2c). These components are referred to as the intermediate components. The alternative component is, commonly but not necessarily, of this nature. A full network is composed of the combination of source, sink, and intermediate components.

The key point that one should consider while forming a network is that the final structure that represents an MADM problem must perform as a single, fully, linked web of components (Saaty 1996). Note that the final network cannot be divided into a number of individual and separated parts, for in such cases, the lack of connection between the components makes their comparison infeasible. Section 4.3 would provide a detailed stepwise instruction to the ANP method.

4.3 Stepwise Instruction to the ANP Method

At this junction, it would be beneficial to recall the basic feature of an MADM problem. A MADM problem is composed of a set of alternatives, denoted by $\{a_i \mid i = 1, 2, \ldots, m\}$, which are the feasible discrete solutions available to the decision-making problem, and a set of criteria, denoted by $\{c_j \mid j = 1, 2, \ldots, n\}$, which are, in essence, the instruments through which the stakeholders describe their main objective. The following is a stepwise description to employ the ANP method to cope with the schematic MADM problem described above.

4.3.1 Step 1: Defining the Decision-making Problem

The basic idea is that MADM methods are as good as the decision-makers' ability to describe and mathematically express the decision-making problem at hand. Hence, a well-defined problem is the crucial beginning step of the whole process that is the decision-making. Defining an MADM problem, in most cases, requires the decision-maker to mathematically describe the stakeholders' main objective, a set of feasible alternatives, and a set of criteria to evaluate and measure the properties of the latter. In light of the ANP method, however, the decision-maker must take the whole process one step further that is portraying the problem at hand in a network structure.

As stated earlier on, the network structured is formed out of two main entities, that is the components and the connections. The components are the clusters of elements, that is alternatives, criteria, and the main objective, that share a common property. The process of forming a component is quite similar to the clustering procedure in the AHP method. Basically, the decision-makers' expertise and experience would aid them to thoroughly search the elements of the decision-making problem, and through a trial and error process, group those elements that are of similar nature. The decision-maker then attempts to map the connections that would link these newly formed components to one another. Chiefly, the components that have influence over each other would be linked together via an arrow. In light of the ANP method, three types of connections could be formed namely a linear, cyclic, and loop connection. In a linear connection, the influential component would be the origin of an arrow, while the destination of such link would be the influenced component. The relation between those components that both have influence over one another is illustrated by the cycle connection. Lastly, a loop connection is used to demonstrate those components that are composed of elements with interdependency. Note that these verities of options that enable the decision-makers to express the inner and outer dependency of components would make the ANP method an ideal option to deal with complex, real-world, MADM problems.

4.3.2 Step 2: Conducting a Pairwise Comparison of the Elements of the Decision-making Problem

The ANP method was founded on the idea of employing explicit and implicit measuring scales, through a mathematical framework better known as the pairwise comparisons. In light of this framework, the decision-maker would form pairwise comparison matrices that are the instruments through which one would derive the preference value of each given elements of the influenced component with respect to the elements of the influential component. For instance, let C_j be the component with influence over the component C_j. That is indicated by an arrow with C_j component as the origin would descend to the C_j component. Let the ith and the jth components be composed of g and h individual elements, respectively. Resultantly, $C_i = \{e_1^i, e_2^i, \ldots, e_g^i\}$ and $C_j = \{e_1^j, e_2^j, \ldots, e_z^j, \ldots, e_h^j\}$ are the sets that mathematically express these components. Note that e_z^j denotes the zth element of the jth component. Consequently, let $P_{(i,e_z^j)}$ denote the pairwise comparison matrix of the elements of the ith component, with respect to the zth element of the influential component C_j, which can be mathematically expressed as follows (Saaty 1996):

$$P_{(i,e_z^j)} = \begin{array}{c} \\ e_1^i \\ \vdots \\ e_g^i \end{array} \begin{array}{c} \begin{array}{ccc} e_1^i & \cdots & e_g^i \end{array} \\ \begin{bmatrix} p_{(e_1^i,e_1^i)}^{e_z^j} & \cdots & p_{(e_1^i,e_g^i)}^{e_z^j} \\ \vdots & \ddots & \vdots \\ p_{(e_g^i,e_1^i)}^{e_z^j} & \cdots & p_{(e_g^i,e_g^i)}^{e_z^j} \end{bmatrix} \end{array} \tag{4.1}$$

in which $p_{(e_s^i,e_d^i)}^{e_z^j}$ = the pairwise comparison of the sth element of C_i component with the dth element of the C_i component, with respect to the zth element of C_j component. Note that the aforementioned matrix must have the quadruple axioms of the standard pairwise comparison matrix namely (i) the reciprocal property; (ii) the homogeneity property; (iii) the dependency property; and (iv) the property of expectation (Saaty 1986). That, in turn, dictates that the following equation must hold for every pairwise comparison matrix (Saaty 1977):

$$p_{(e_s^i,e_d^i)}^{e_z^j} = 1/p_{(e_d^i,e_s^i)}^{e_z^j} \tag{4.2}$$

The next step for the decision-maker would obtain the preference values for each given element on the influenced component (C_i). Given the relative nature of the elements of the pairwise comparison matrix $P_{(i,e_z^j)}$, they can be expressed as follows (Saaty 1996):

$$p_{(e_s^i,e_d^i)}^{e_z^j} = v_{e_s^i}^{e_z^j} / v_{e_d^i}^{e_z^j} \tag{4.3}$$

Table 4.1 The fundamental scale for pairwise comparisons.

Intensity of decision-maker's preference	Definition
1	Equally important
3	Moderate preference of the *i*th criteria over the *j*th one
5	Strong preference of the *i*th criteria over the *j*th one
7	Very strong preference of the *i*th criteria over the *j*th one
9	Extreme preference of the *i*th criteria over the *j*th one
2, 4, 6, 8	Intermediate values between the two adjacent judgment

in which $v_{e_s^i}^{e_z^j}$ and $v_{e_d^i}^{e_z^j}$ = the absolute preference values of the *s*th and *d*th elements for the *i*th component with respect to the *z*th element of the *j*th component, respectively.

Note that each element in the pairwise comparison matrix $P_{(i,e_z^j)}$ is obtained based on an implicit measuring scale used by the decision-maker to quantify the relative preference values of each given element. Consequently, given the comparative nature of such relative measurements, the decision-maker can easily evaluate both tangible and intangible properties. The decision-maker is permitted to employ any numerical measuring scale to make these pairwise comparisons; yet, Table 4.1 contains a 1–9 scale that is recommended for the implicit measurements of both AHP and ANP methods. This scale has been derived through stimulus–response theory and validated for effectiveness not only in many real-world, practical, MADM cases but also through the theoretical justification of what scale one ought to employ in the comparison of homogeneous elements (Saaty 2004, 2006).

To assign the proper weights to each of these elements, the decision-maker must attempt to normalize the preference value of the pairwise comparison matrix $P_{(i,e_z^j)}$. The following formulations have been recommended for the ANP method (Saaty and Vargas 2006):

$$k_{(e_s^i,e_d^i)}^{e_z^j} = \frac{p_{(e_s^i,e_d^i)}^{e_z^j}}{\sum_{s=1}^{g} p_{(e_s^i,e_d^i)}^{e_z^j}} \tag{4.4}$$

and

$$k_{(e_s^i,e_d^i)}^{e_z^j} = \frac{p_{(e_s^i,e_d^i)}^{e_z^j}}{\max_s [p_{(e_s^i,e_d^i)}^{e_z^j}]} \tag{4.5}$$

in which $k^{e^j_z}_{(e^i_s,e^i_d)}$ = the normalized pairwise comparison of the e^i_s element with the e^i_d one with respect to e^j_z. In technical terms, the ANP method that employs Eq. (3.4) as its normalizing technique is called the distributive mode of ANP. Conversely, the ANP method that uses Eq. (4.5) is called the ideal mode of ANP (Saaty and Vargas 2006).

The preference value of the *s*th element of the *i*th component with respect to the *z*th element of the *j*th component ($v^{e^j_z}_{e^i_s}$) can be computed as follows, which, mathematically speaking, is the average of the normalized pairwise comparison of the *s*th element of each row of the matrix $P_{(i,e^j_z)}$ (Saaty 1996):

$$v^{e^j_z}_{e^i_s} = \frac{\sum_{d=1}^{g} k^{e^j_z}_{(e^i_s,e^i_d)}}{g} \tag{4.6}$$

Note that through a similar procedure, the weights of each element located in the network structure of the MADM problem can be computed. As the last stage to conduct the pairwise comparison measurements one must evaluate the results' rationality. If rationality were held, the decision-maker can trust the implicit measurements and subjective judgments, otherwise, the appropriate adjustments must be made for the pairwise matrices with irrational comparisons. In light of the eigenvalue theory, the decision-maker must obtain the principal eigenvalue of every pairwise comparison matrices (λ_{max}) in the network structure of the problem at hand. The following equation is the center of such computation (Saaty 1996):

$$P_{(i,e^j_z)} \times W_{(i,e^j_z)} = \lambda_{max} \times W_{(i,e^j_z)} \tag{4.7}$$

in which $W_{(i,e^j_z)}$ = the weights vector of the *i*th component with respect to *z*th element of the *j*th component, denoted by $(v^{e^j_z}_{e^i_1}, v^{e^j_z}_{e^i_2}, \ldots v^{e^j_z}_{e^i_s}, \ldots v^{e^j_z}_{e^i_g})^T$.

Next, the decision-maker computes the consistency index (*CI*), and hence, the inconsistency ratio (*IR*) for each give pairwise comparison matrix in the network structure via Eqs. (4.8, 4.9), respectively (Vargas 1982; Saaty 1990).

$$IC = \frac{\lambda_{max} - g}{g - 1} \tag{4.8}$$

$$IR = \frac{IC}{RI} \tag{4.9}$$

in which *RI* = the random index, and can be assigned based on the contents of Table 4.2 (Tzeng and Huang 2011).

Table 4.2 refers to random index (RI), while the mentioned sentence refers to inconsistency ration (IR), the estimate of the preference weight vector $W_{(i,e^j_z)}$ can be considered rational; otherwise, the decision-maker is encouraged to improve

Table 4.2 The random index value for pairwise comparison matrices of different orders.

The order of the pairwise comparison matrix	1	2	3	4	5	6	7	8	9
RI	0.00	0.00	0.52	0.89	1.11	1.25	1.35	1.40	1.49

Source: Modified from Tzeng and Huang (2011).

the consistency of the estimated preference weight vector (Saaty 1990; Tzeng and Huang 2011).

4.3.3 Step 3: Forming the Supermatrix

The supermatrix is formed to summarize the MADM problem in a matrix-based, mathematical framework. Through the supermatrix, the decision-maker intends to quantify the value of each given element located in the network structure with respect to the influence of other components. The supermatrix of an MADM problem with N component is composed as follows (Saaty 1996):

$$SM = \begin{array}{c} \\ C_1 \\ \vdots \\ C_N \end{array} \begin{array}{c} \begin{array}{ccc} C_1 & \cdots & C_N \end{array} \\ \begin{bmatrix} Z_{(1,1)} & \cdots & Z_{(1,N)} \\ \vdots & \ddots & \vdots \\ Z_{(N,1)} & \cdots & Z_{(N,N)} \end{bmatrix} \end{array} \tag{4.10}$$

in which SM = the supermatrix; $Z_{(i,j)}$ = the matrix of values of the ith component with respect to the elements of the jth component. Unsurprisingly, each $Z_{(i,j)}$, which in technical term is referred to as a block for the supermatrix (SM), is of matrix nature. Each block summaries the results of the preference values resulted from the pairwise comparisons made in the previous step. For instance, recall the case where the component C_j with h element, had an influence over the component C_i with g elements, which was illustrated using an arrow connecting the jth component to the ith one. The matrix of values for such situation can be described as follows (Saaty 1996):

$$Z_{(i,j)} = \begin{array}{c} \\ e_1^i \\ \vdots \\ e_g^i \end{array} \begin{array}{c} \begin{array}{ccc} e_1^j & \cdots & e_h^j \end{array} \\ \begin{bmatrix} v_{e_1^i}^{e_1^j} & \cdots & v_{e_1^i}^{e_h^j} \\ \vdots & \ddots & \vdots \\ v_{e_g^i}^{e_1^j} & \cdots & v_{e_g^i}^{e_g^i} \end{bmatrix} \end{array} \tag{4.11}$$

Note that in compiling the supermatrix zero matrices are assigned to those components that do not have influence over one another. For instance, in the supermatrix of the network structure illustrated in Figure 4.1a the $Z_{(1,2)}$ is a zero matrix. Additionally, there are two major approaches to reflect the self-feedback effects, which are demonstrated by a loop connection in the network structure of the MADM problem. An approach would be for one to simply place a 1 in diagonal elements, while the second approach requires the decision-maker to conduct a pairwise comparisons matrix for such cases (Tzeng and Huang 2011).

4.3.4 Step 4: Computing the Weighted Supermatrix

The main objective of this step is to derive limit priorities of influence form the supermatrix, that is, the relative weights that can be assigned to each element. To obtain such relative weights, the supermatrix must first be transformed to a matrix each of its column sums to unity. In technical terms, the transformed matrix would be referred to as a column stochastic or a stochastic supermatrix (*SSM*) (Saaty 2005; Tzeng and Huang 2011). The aforementioned notion is expressed as follows (Saaty 1996):

$$\sum_{s=1}^{g} v_{e_s^i}^{e_z^j} = 1 \tag{4.12}$$

It should be noted that using the normalized pairwise comparison, as recommended in the earlier stage of this stepwise instruction, leads to automatic obtainment of the properties required for this step.

4.3.5 Step 5: Computing the Global Priority Vectors and Choosing the Most Suitable Alternative

As the final step, the *SSM* is raised to limiting powers so that the global priority vector (*GPV*), that is the final value of each element, is computed as follows (Saaty 1996):

$$GPV = \lim_{b \to \infty} \frac{1}{M} \sum_{b=1}^{M} SSM^b \tag{4.13}$$

Note that purpose behind Eq. (4.13), which takes the limit of the average of a sequence of M of these powers of the *SSM*, that is, Cesaro's sum, is that, in compliance with the ANP method, the decision-maker is able to capture the transmission of influence along all possible paths of the *SSM*.

In computing the global property vectors (Eq. (4.13)), one must bear in mind that if the sequence converges to a limit, then it can be mathematically proven that the Cesaro sum also converges to the same limit (Saaty 1996). The sequence is defined by the powers of the matrix; therefore, it is sufficient to determine the limit of these powers. If, however, the sequence does not converge to a unique limit, the Cesaro sum averages out over the different limits of the sequences obtaining a unique limit (Saaty 1996). It goes without saying that the alternative with the largest value in the global property vector is the most desirable solution for the given MADM problem at hand under maximization.

4.4 Conclusion

Pairwise comparisons are the tools which would empower the decision-maker to make the subjective judgments and implicit measuring scales to the precise procedure of the decision-making. Based on the aforementioned notion the ANP method is able to cope with both tangible and intangible evaluation criteria.

On the other hand, relying solely on implicit measuring scales and subjective judgments of the decision-makers, experts, and elites in the real-world, practical MADM problems with the complex interaction of the elements, may induce errors to the solution finding the procedure. In light of the ANP method, the decision-maker is enabled to reconstruct the problem in a network structure, which in turn, can help facilitate the decision-making, immensely. A network structure is composed of sets of components, which are in essence, clustered elements that share a common property, and a series of connections. The connections, which demonstrate the influences and dependencies between the components, are of three major type, namely, linear, cyclic, and loop connections. After expressing the MADM problem in the form of a network structure, the ANP method provides the decision-maker with a path, that is a well-established mathematical procedure that starts with forming the supermatrix and ends with the global property vectors, which enables the experts to deal with a wide range of MADM real-world problems.

References

Amiri, M.P., Amiri, A.P., and Amiri, M.P. (2012). An analytical network process approach for evaluating banking performance based on balanced scorecard. *Trends in Applied Sciences Research* 7 (6): 456.

Cakmak, E. and Cakmak, P.I. (2014). An analysis of causes of disputes in the construction industry using analytical network process. *Procedia-Social and Behavioral Sciences* 109: 183–187.

Cheng, E.W. and Li, H. (2005). Analytic network process applied to project selection. *Journal of Construction Engineering and Management* 131 (4): 459–466.

Çelebi, D., Bayraktar, D., and Bingöl, L. (2010). Analytical network process for logistics management: a case study in a small electronic appliances manufacturer. *Computers and Industrial Engineering* 58 (3): 432–441.

Dou, Y., Zhu, Q., and Sarkis, J. (2014). Evaluating green supplier development programs with a grey-analytical network process-based methodology. *European Journal of Operational Research* 233 (2): 420–431.

Ishizaka, A. and Nemery, P. (2013). *Multi-criteria Decision Analysis: Methods and Software*, 13–54. Wiley ISBN: 978-1-118-64489-8.

Gencer, C. and Gürpinar, D. (2007). Analytic network process in supplier selection: a case study in an electronic firm. *Applied Mathematical Modelling* 31 (11): 2475–2486.

Ghorbanzadeh, O., Feizizadeh, B., and Blaschke, T. (2018). Multi-criteria risk evaluation by integrating an analytical network process approach into GIS-based sensitivity and uncertainty analyses. *Geomatics, Natural Hazards and Risk* 9 (1): 127–151.

Jharkharia, S. and Shankar, R. (2007). Selection of logistics service provider: an analytic network process (ANP) approach. *Omega* 35 (3): 274–289.

Köne, A.Ç. and Büke, T. (2007). An analytical network process (ANP) evaluation of alternative fuels for electricity generation in Turkey. *Energy Policy* 35 (10): 5220–5228.

Li, J. and Sun, Y. (2001). Application of F-ANP in risk evaluation of offshore wind power projects. *Journal of Liaoning Technical University (Natural Science)* 30: 96–99.

Meade, L.M. and Presley, A. (2002). R&D project selection using the analytic network process. *IEEE Transactions on Engineering Management* 49 (1): 59–66.

Mikhailov, L. and Singh, M.G. (2003). Fuzzy analytic network process and its application to the development of decision support systems. *IEEE Transactions on Systems, Man, and Cybernetics, Part C (Applications and Reviews)* 33 (1): 33–41.

Mohajeri, N. and Amin, G.R. (2010). Railway station site selection using analytical hierarchy process and data envelopment analysis. *Computers and Industrial Engineering* 59 (1): 107–114.

Momeni, M., Samimi, B., Afshari, M.A. et al. (2011). Selection process of supervisor for doctoral dissertation using analytical network process (ANP): an Iranian study. *Journal of Management and Strategy* 2 (2): 63.

Mulebeke, J.A. and Zheng, L. (2006). Analytical network process for software selection in product development: a case study. *Journal of Engineering and Technology Management* 23 (4): 337–352.

Niemira, M.P. and Saaty, T.L. (2004). An analytic network process model for financial-crisis forecasting. *International Journal of Forecasting* 20 (4): 573–587.

Peng, A.H. and Xiao, X.M. (2013). Material selection using PROMETHEE combined with analytic network process under hybrid environment. *Materials and Design* 47: 643–652.

Saaty, T.L. (1977). A scaling method for priorities in hierarchical structures. *Journal of Mathematical Psychology* 15 (3): 234–281.

Saaty, T.L. (1980). *The Analytic Hierarchy Process*. New York, NY: McGraw-Hill Education.

Saaty, T.L. (1985). Decision making for leaders. *IEEE Transactions on Systems, Man, and Cybernetics* 3: 450–452.

Saaty, T.L. (1986). Axiomatic foundation of the analytic hierarchy process. *Management Science* 32 (7): 841–855.

Saaty, T.L. (1988). What is the analytic hierarchy process? In: *Mathematical Models for Decision Support* (eds. G. Mitra, H.J. Greenberg, F.A. Lootsma, et al.), 109–121. Berlin, Heidelberg: Springer.

Saaty, T.L. (1990). How to make a decision: the analytic hierarchy process. *European Journal of Operational Research* 48 (1): 9–26.

Saaty, T.L. (1996). *Decision Making with Dependence and Feedback: The Analytic Network Process*. Pittsburgh, PA: RWS Publications.

Saaty, T.L. (2004). Fundamentals of the analytic network process: dependence and feedback in decision-making with a single network. *Journal of Systems Science and Systems Engineering* 13 (2): 129–157.

Saaty, T.L. (2005). *Theory and Applications of the Analytic Network Process: Decision Making with Benefits, Opportunities, Costs, and Risks*. Pittsburgh, PA: RWS Publications.

Saaty, T.L. (2006). The analytic network process. In: *Decision Making with the Analytic Network Process* (eds. T.L. Saaty and L.G. Vargas), 1–26. Boston, MA: Springer.

Saaty, T.L. (2008). The analytic network process. *Iranian Journal of Operations Research* 1 (1): 1–27.

Saaty, T.L. and Vargas, L. (2006). *Decision Making with the Analytic Network Process: Economics, Political, Social and Technological Applications with Benefits, Opportunities, Costs, and Risks*. NY: Springer.

Tran, L.T., Knight, C.G., O'neill, R.V., and Smith, E.R. (2004). Integrated environmental assessment of the mid-Atlantic region with analytical network process. *Environmental Monitoring and Assessment* 94 (1–3): 263–277.

Tsai, W.H. and Chou, W.C. (2009). Selecting management systems for sustainable development in SMEs: a novel hybrid model based on DEMATEL, ANP, and ZOGP. *Expert Systems with Applications* 36 (2): 1444–1458.

Tseng, M.L. and Chiu, A.S. (2012). Grey-entropy analytical network process for green innovation practices. *Procedia-Social and Behavioral Sciences* 57: 10–21.

Tzeng, G.H. and Huang, J.J. (2011). *Multiple Attribute Decision Making: Methods and Applications*. Boca Raton, FL: CRC Press.

Vargas, L.G. (1982). Reciprocal matrices with random coefficients. *Mathematical Modelling* 3 (1): 69–81.

Wolfslehner, B., Vacik, H., and Lexer, M.J. (2005). Application of the analytic network process in multi-criteria analysis of sustainable forest management. *Forest Ecology and Management* 207 (1–2): 157–170.

Wu, C.R., Lin, C.T., and Chen, H.C. (2009). Integrated environmental assessment of the location selection with fuzzy analytical network process. *Quality and Quantity* 43 (3): 351–380.

Yang, Y.P.O., Shieh, H.M., Leu, J.D., and Tzeng, G.H. (2008). A novel hybrid MCDM model combined with DEMATEL and ANP with applications. *International Journal of Operations Research* 5 (3): 160–168.

Zhu, Q., Dou, Y., and Sarkis, J. (2010). A portfolio-based analysis for green supplier management using the analytical network process. *Supply Chain Management: An International Journal* 15 (4): 306–319.

5

The Best-Worst Method (BWM)

5.1 Introduction

As established thus far a decision matrix plays a crucial rule in the multiattribute decision-making (MADM) process. A decision matrix (D) is described as follows (Yu 1990):

$$D = \begin{matrix} & \begin{matrix} c_1 & \cdots & c_n \end{matrix} \\ \begin{matrix} a_1 \\ \vdots \\ a_m \end{matrix} & \begin{bmatrix} r_{(1,1)} & \cdots & r_{(1,n)} \\ \vdots & \ddots & \vdots \\ r_{(m,1)} & \cdots & r_{(m,n)} \end{bmatrix} \end{matrix} \tag{5.1}$$

in which a_i = the predetermined, feasible alternative; c_j = the predefined evaluation criterion determined by the decision-maker; $r_{(i,j)}$ = the normalized value of the ith alternative with regard to the jth criterion; m = the number of feasible alternatives; and n = the number of criteria. The decision-maker attempts to choose the set of alternatives that would achieve the decision-makers main objective or goal that can be portrayed via a set of predetermined criteria. The MADM philosophy prescribes that if the poor performance of an alternative with regard to one of the predefined criterion is compensated by the alternative's good performance with regard to other criteria, such tradeoff can be accounted for by a compensatory method (Jeffreys 2004; Banihabib et al. 2017). Most compensatory MADM methods would attempt the aggregate the overall performance of each alternative through a weighting mechanism that assigns the proper weight to each of the predefined criteria. Such weighting mechanism is calculated mathematically as follows (Churchman and Ackoff 1954):

$$V_i = \sum_{j=1}^{n} w_j \times r_{(i,j)} \quad \forall i \tag{5.2}$$

in which V_i = the overall performance of the ith alternative; and w_j = the weight assigned to the jth criterion. As stated earlier not all MADM methods imply

A Handbook on Multi-Attribute Decision-Making Methods, First Edition.
Omid Bozorg-Haddad, Babak Zolghadr-Asli, and Hugo A. Loáiciga.

weighting functions to aggregate to the overall performance of the feasible alternative vector; nevertheless, most compensatory methods use the aforementioned notion as the core idea of computing the alternatives' overall performance. In such cases, the principles, techniques, and assumption employed to derive these weights are what distinguishes these compensatory MADM methods.

Using a scale of a sort is the most common practice in MADM methods; however, designing a well-defined scale is a challenge, especially, in cases where the decision-maker is faced with intangible, nonquantitative variables (Saaty 1985, 1986, 1994). Implementing pairwise comparisons constitutes an alternate approach to overcome such difficulties (Saaty 1980, 1990; Saaty and Vargas 2006).

The pairwise comparison method was introduced by Thurstone (1927). Pairwise comparison main implication is to structure the decision matrix, but many borrowed the core idea behind these comparisons to extract the weighting functions required to deal with MADM problems (Saaty 1977, 1988, 1996). Pairwise comparisons are a strategy for determining the decision-makers' relative preferences of either alternatives or criteria with respect to the decision-makers' predetermined criteria and the main goal, respectively (Saaty 2004). The pairwise comparison has proven to be an effective tactic to tackle MADM problems where it is unfeasible or meaningless to provide a conventional scale system to estimate the scores of alternatives or criteria (Saaty 2005, 2006). One can claim that although in such cases the decision-maker is not using an explicitly defined scaling measure, yet, comparisons, which are the core element in such methods, are made based on the decision-makers' expertise, experience, and cognitive abilities, which constitute an implicit scale of judgment made by the decision-makers. A common criticism to employ such implicit, cognitive-oriented, scales of measurement, which is the basic foundation for pairwise comparison MADM methods, is that it can introduce error in the decision-making process. This is so because subjective criteria depend on the decision-makers' knowledge, experience, expertise, and cognitive reasoning, rather than a consistent, mathematically defined, and logically supported scale (Dyer 1990). Note that every decision-making method relies heavily on the expert's judgments when it comes to assessing intangible, quantitative attributes. The fact stands that any measurement, of any sort, would be based on an arbitrarily defined scale (Saaty 2008). While implying standard scales are advantageous in practice not all attributes can be assessed through such instruments. Therefore, it is inevitable to depend on the decision-makers' judgments on a subject matter at hand. Thus, personal-oriented assessments of an informed, rational, and unbiased decision-maker could not jeopardize the integrity of the pairwise comparison-based MADM method. In technical terms, the aforementioned notion is known as consistent decision-making (Rezaei 2015).

The most significant challenge for MADM methods that are founded on the basis of the pairwise comparison, is to maintain the consistency of the pairwise comparison matrices, which usually becomes challenging in practical problems (Herman and Koczkodaj 1996). Note that maintaining consistency in a pairwise comparison matrix would not necessarily guarantee the authenticity and accuracy of the results, but rather ensures the existence of rationality in the decision-making process. Consider, for instance, a case where the decision-maker evaluates that the preference of item A is a time more significant than the item B, while the item B's preference is of b times more significant when it is compared to the item C. Rationality, consequently, would dictate for the preference of the item A to be of $a \times b$ more significant than the item C. If the decision-makers judgment would be in line with the aforementioned rational statement, the pairwise comparison is considered to be consistent. Yet, error in judgments regarding the decision-makers evaluation of either a or b could induce inaccuracy to the pairwise comparison. Using an expert's opinion would dramatically decrease the inaccuracy of the decision-making process, but maintaining a certain acceptable level of consistency remains an ongoing challenge for MADM methods that are pairwise comparison-oriented. Allegedly, limiting the number of pairwise comparisons seems to be a logical attempt to control and mitigate the inconsistency induced in such sorts of the decision-making process (Rezaei 2015).

The best–worst method (BWM), theorized by Rezaei (2015), is a compensatory MADM technique, which is based on a pairwise comparison of the best and the worst criteria or alternatives with regard the other criteria or alternatives, respectively. The preliminary studies illustrated its potential in solving practical, real-life MADM problems (Rezaei 2015, 2016). Since then, the BWM has been applied in numerous research fields including: Business planning (Torabi et al. 2016), educational and scientific agendas (Salimi and Rezaei 2016; Hafezalkotob and Hafezalkotob 2017), energy resources management (Ahmad et al. 2017), environmental and natural resources agendas (Chitsaz and Azarnivand 2017; Ren et al. 2017), human resources management (Yang et al. 2016), marketing (Rezaei et al. 2015, 2016), nation's strategic development planning (Gupta and Barua 2016), supplier section (Gupta and Barua 2017), transport policy appraisal (Annema et al. 2015), and transportation selection (Rezaei et al. 2017). Even though, some alternated, hyperlinked alteration has been suggested for the standard BWM (e.g. the fuzzy BWM (Mou et al. 2016; Guo and Zhao 2017), linked with a linear programming model (Rezaei 2016), and the BWM for an uncertain environment (Pamučar et al. 2017)), the reliable results and relative ease of computations made the BWM a promising method to handle real-world MADM problems. The following sections would contain a detailed description of the standard BWM methodology.

5.2 Basic Principles of the BWM

The decision matrix introduced in Eq. (5.1) is the key in the decision-making process of compensatory methods such as the BWM. The basic idea is to derive and assign the proper weights to each criterion so that the overall performance of each alternative could be estimated. Assume a problem in which the decision-maker identified n evaluating criteria for the MADM problem at hand. To do a pairwise comparison, the preference of all identified criteria are to be compared to one another and then rated in relative terms. In that regard, a pairwise comparison matrix is formed as follows (Saaty 1977):

$$P = \begin{matrix} & \begin{matrix} c_1 & \cdots & c_n \end{matrix} \\ \begin{matrix} c_1 \\ \vdots \\ c_n \end{matrix} & \begin{bmatrix} p_{(1,1)} & \cdots & p_{(1,n)} \\ \vdots & \ddots & \vdots \\ p_{(n,1)} & \cdots & p_{(n,n)} \end{bmatrix} \end{matrix} \quad \forall i \; p_{(i,i)} = 1 \tag{5.3}$$

in which P = the pairwise comparison matrix of the identified criteria, and $p_{(i,j)}$ = the pairwise comparison of the ith alternative/criterion with the jth one. The decision-maker can use any numerical scale to make the pairwise comparison, but it is advisable to use a 1–9 scale for the BWM. A typical scale that can be employed for such pairwise comparisons is demonstrated in Table 5.1 (Saaty 1977, 1980; Rezaei 2015).

The reciprocal property is one the major conditions for the pairwise comparison matrix. Consequently, in Eq. (5.3) each element of the matrix ought to satisfy the following condition (Saaty 1986):

$$p_{(i,j)} = {}^{1}/_{p_{(j,i)}} \quad \forall i, j \tag{5.4}$$

Every element of the pairwise comparison matrix reflects the decision-makers preference, yet some elements are more significant than others. With that regard Rezaei (2015) proposed to classify the elements of the pairwise comparison matrix

Table 5.1 A typical pairwise comparison scale for the BWM.

Intensity of decision-maker's preference	Definition
1	Equally important
3	Moderate preference of the ith criteria over the jth one
5	Strong preference of the ith criteria over the jth one
7	Very strong preference of the ith criteria over the jth one
9	Extreme preference of the ith criteria over the jth one
2, 4, 6, 8	Intermediate values between the two adjacent judgments

Source: Saaty (1977, 1980) and Rezaei et al. (2015).

into two main categories, namely, reference and secondary comparisons. Basically, a comparison $a_{(i,j)}$ is considered a reference comparison if i is the best element and/or j is the worst element, in any other case the $a_{(i,j)}$ belongs to the secondary comparison category. It can be shown that the number of reference comparisons would be equal to $2n - 3$ (Rezaei 2015, 2016).

The significance of limiting the decision-makers assessment to the set of reference comparisons is that one provides an environment through which the decision-maker is more likely to make more consistent comparisons due to the presence of a reference alternative/criteria (whether the best or worst alternative/criteria). In addition, the set of reference comparisons can be seen as an external information source that helps extract the set of secondary comparison, and thus the relative importance of every alternative/criteria in the pairwise comparison matrix without making any additional assessments. In mathematical terms, the aforementioned statement is based on the following characteristic of a consistent comparison (Saaty 1977):

$$p_{(i,j)} = p_{(i,k)} \times p_{(k,j)} \tag{5.5}$$

Equation (5.5) states reference comparisons are the external source of information, and each secondary comparison $p_{(i,j)}$ appears in two relational chains, whose two reference comparisons are as follows (Rezaei 2015):

$$p_{(B,i)} \times p_{(i,j)} = p_{(B,j)} \tag{5.6}$$

$$p_{(i,j)} \times p_{(j,W)} = p_{(i,W)} \tag{5.7}$$

in which $p_{(B,i)}$ and $p_{(B,j)}$ = the preference of the best alternative/criterion over the ith and jth alternative/criterion, respectively; and $p_{(i,W)}$ and $p_{(j,W)}$ = the preference of the ith and jth alternative/criterion over the worst alternative/criterion, respectively. Note that any deviation from the decision-makers estimation of $p_{(i,j)}$ and the $p_{(i,j)}$ calculated through Eqs. (5.6, 5.7) can be interoperated to evaluate the decision-makers' consistency of judgment, which will be discussed in the following sections.

The BWM is a pairwise comparison-oriented method, but unlike most practiced pairwise comparison MADM methods, it limits the decision-makers evaluation to the reference comparisons. Evidently, decreasing the number of comparisons made by the decision-maker would increase the accuracy and reliability of the decision-making process (Rezaei 2015). The following section presents a stepwise description of the BWM.

5.3 Stepwise Description of the BWM

The standard BWM is a five-step process involving pairwise comparisons matrix is employed to derive the weights of the criteria. These weights are used to obtain the alternatives' overall performance (see Eq. (5.2)).

5.3.1 Step 1: Defining the Decision-Making Problem

The first step of the BWM, as is the case with every other MADM method, is to lay the framework through which the decision-making process takes place. The integrity of the final result would rely heavily on the accuracy of this initial, yet, vital step. The main idea of this step is for the decision-maker to mathematically express the decision-making problem, through a set of criteria, e.g. $\{c_1, c_2, \ldots, c_n\}$, and alternatives, e.g. $\{a_1, a_2, \ldots, a_m\}$. The decision matrix is the ideal instrument to do so. To that end, the decision-maker evaluates the alternatives with regard to each criterion and then normalizes the results with respect to each column $[r_{(i,j)}]$. Subsequently, the final decision matrix has the following property (Ma et al. 1999; Chang and Yeh 2001):

$$\sum_{i=1}^{m} r_{(i,j)} = 1 \quad \forall j \tag{5.8}$$

5.3.2 Step 2: Determining the Reference Criteria

Recall each element of the pairwise comparison matrix is either a reference or secondary comparison. Reference comparisons, which are the keys to the BWM, are those comparisons the decision-maker makes to evaluate each given criterion to determine what is the most and/or least important criterion. To that end, the decision-maker makes an implicit and general evaluation of all the predetermined criteria to identify the best (most important) and the worst (least important) criteria. The decision-maker identifies more than one reference criteria (either best or worst criterion) based on the decision-makers cognitive reasoning (Rezaei 2015).

5.3.3 Step 3: Pairwise Comparisons

The BWM is based on using reference comparisons, which refers to the comparisons that are made between the best criterion and the rest of the remaining criteria and/or those that are made between the predetermined criteria and the worst criterion. It is recommended to use a 1–9 numerical scale (Table 5.1) to made such comparisons. The results would eventually lead to forming two vectors, namely, best-to-others (A_B) and others-to-worst (A_W) vectors, respectively. The best-to-others (A_B) and others-to-worst (A_W) vectors are expressed by Eqs. (5.9, 5.10), respectively (Rezaei 2015).

$$A_B = [p_{(B,1)}, p_{(B,2)}, \ldots, p_{(B,j)}, \ldots, p_{(B,n)}] \tag{5.9}$$

$$A_W = [p_{(1,W)}, p_{(2,W)}, \ldots, p_{(j,W)}, \ldots, p_{(n,W)}] \tag{5.10}$$

5.3.4 Step 4: Computing the Optimal Weights

This step combines the previously gathered information to assign proper weights to each give criteria. The following equations can be used to compute the weight of the jth criterion assuming that each pairwise comparison is the result of dividing the comparing criteria's weights (Rezaei 2015):

$$p_{(B,j)} = {}^{w_B}/_{w_j} \quad \forall j \tag{5.11}$$

$$p_{(j,W)} = {}^{w_j}/_{w_W} \quad \forall j \tag{5.12}$$

in which w_i, w_j, w_B, and w_W = the weights that are assigned to the ith, jth, the best, and the worst criteria, respectively. Notice the summation of assigned weights is equal to 1 (Rezaei 2015).

Ideally, if the decision-makers judgments are fully consistent, a single, elegant solution (set of weights) could be found that satisfy all the aforementioned conditions implied by Eqs. (5.11, 5.12). The BWM searches for a set of arrays of weights, say $(w_1^*, w_2^*, \dots, w_j^*, \dots, w_n^*)$, where w_j^* is the optimized assigned weight for the jth criterion that would cause the least amount of inconsistency. The aforementioned notion can be mathematically expressed as a *minimax* problem, as follows (Rezaei 2015):

$$\underset{j}{Min\,Max} \left\{ \left| \frac{w_B}{w_j} - p_{(B,j)} \right|, \left| \frac{w_j}{w_W} - p_{(j,W)} \right| \right\}$$

Subject to

$$\sum_{j=1}^{n} w_j = 1$$

$$w_j \geq 0 \quad \forall j \tag{5.13}$$

The above *minimax* problem can be described as the following linear programming problem (Rezaei 2015):

$$Min\ \xi$$

Subject to

$$\left| \frac{w_B}{w_j} - p_{(B,j)} \right| \leq \xi$$

$$\left| \frac{w_j}{w_W} - p_{(j,W)} \right| \leq \xi$$

$$\sum_{j=1}^{n} w_j = 1$$

$$w_j \geq 0 \quad \forall j \tag{5.14}$$

in which ξ = the maximum absolute difference of estimated values of the pairwise comparisons with their computed values. It goes without saying that the smaller values for ξ indicate a more consistent judgment by the decision-maker. Also, note that in the off chance that the decision-maker makes fully consistent comparisons ξ would be equal to zero. Eventually, solving the described problem in Eq. (5.14) would reveal the optimal solution which is a set of arrays $(w_1^*, w_2^*, \dots, w_j^*, \dots, w_n^*)$, and, resultantly, ξ can be obtained. It is worth mentioning that, although the BWM is essentially designed to estimate the weights of criteria in an MADM problem, the explained process could be modified to obtain the value of alternatives with respect to each given criterion.

5.3.5 Step 5: Measuring the Inconsistency of Decision-Makers Judgments

MADM methods that are pairwise comparison-oriented may suffer from the logical inconsistencies that are rooted in the decision-makers inaccurate judgments. Consequently, the final step of the decision-making process ought to be the logical evaluation of the assessments made by the decision-maker. As a pairwise comparison-based method, the BWM also requires an inaccuracy measurement procedure through which the accuracy of the decision-making process is checked. To that end, Rezaei (2015) proposed a novel approach to measure the inconsistencies that was altered specifically for the unique characteristic of the BWM.

Given the features of the BWM a comparison is fully consistent, if and only if, the following condition holds (Rezaei 2015):

$$p_{(B,i)} \times p_{(i,W)} = p_{(B,W)} \quad \forall j \tag{5.15}$$

in which $p_{(B,W)}$ = the preference of the best criterion over the worst criterion. Notice for each given $p_{(B,W)}$ the following statement applies (Rezaei 2015):

$$p_{(i,j)} \in \{1, 2, \dots, p_{(B,W)}\} \tag{5.16}$$

According to Eq. (5.15), the largest error y would occurs if $p_{(B,j)} = p_{(j,W)} = p_{(B,W)}$. In such circumstances, based on Eq. (5.14), the decision-maker's absolute error in judgment would be, say ξ^*. This indicates that the decision-maker has overestimated both $p_{(B,j)}$ and $p_{(j,W)}$, and underestimated $p_{(B,W)}$ by ξ^*. Consequently, the following equation can be obtained (Rezaei 2015):

$$[p_{(B,j)} - \xi^*] \times [p_{(j,W)} - \xi^*] = [p_{(B,W)} + \xi^*] \tag{5.17}$$

Given that $p_{(B,j)} = p_{(j,W)} = p_{(B,W)}$, Eq. (5.17) can be rearranged as follows (Rezaei 2015):

$$(\xi^*)^2 - [1 + 2p_{(B,W)}] \times \xi^* + [p_{(B,W)}]^2 - p_{(B,W)} = 0 \tag{5.18}$$

Table 5.2 The inconsistency index (ξ^*) of 1–9 scale.

$p_{(B,W)}$	1	2	3	4	5	6	7	8	9
ξ^*	0.00	0.44	1.00	1.63	2.30	3.00	3.73	4.47	5.23

Equation (5.18) allows the decision-maker to compute ξ^* or the inconsistency index, which is the largest error that can be made through the decision-making process via the BWM. Rezaei (2015) solved the aforementioned problem for a pairwise comparison that has been made on a 1–9 scale. The results are summarized in Table 5.2.

Lastly, the BWM inconsistency ratio (*BIR*) is computed as follows (Rezaei 2015):

$$BIR = \frac{\xi}{\xi^*} \tag{5.19}$$

It goes without saying that the more consistent the pairwise comparisons are, the smaller the calculated *BIR*s can be. Naturally, if the computed *BIR* is to be considered negligible by the decision-maker, the results of the BWM are logically validated. Finally, the logically validated set of computed weights $(w_1^*, w_2^*, \dots, w_j^*, \dots, w_n^*)$ is used to aggregate the overall preference of alternatives (Eq. (5.2)). The BWM was originally designed to evaluate and assign the proper weights to the decision-making's criteria set. Yet, the entire process can be altered to score the alternatives' values with respect to each criterion $[v_{(i,j)}]$.

5.4 Conclusion

This chapter was dedicated to the BWM, a compensatory, pairwise comparison-oriented MADM method, that reflects the decision-maker's preferences through an alternative/criterion weighting mechanism which aggregates the alternatives' values so that the most suitable alternative emerge as the solution to the MADM problem at hand. A solid logical background and the relative ease of use makes the BWM a primary candidate to cope with real-world MADM problems.

References

Ahmad, W.N.K.W., Rezaei, J., Sadaghiani, S., and Tavasszy, L.A. (2017). Evaluation of the external forces affecting the sustainability of oil and gas supply chain using best worst method. *Journal of Cleaner Production* 153: 242–252.

Annema, J.A., Mouter, N., and Razaei, J. (2015). Cost-benefit analysis (CBA), or multi-criteria decision-making (MCDM) or both: politicians' perspective in transport policy appraisal. *Transportation Research Procedia* 10: 788–797.

Banihabib, M.E., Hashemi-Madani, F.S., and Forghani, A. (2017). Comparison of compensatory and non-compensatory multi criteria decision making models in water resources strategic management. *Water Resources Management* 31 (12): 3745–3759.

Chang, Y.H. and Yeh, C.H. (2001). Evaluating airline competitiveness using multiattribute decision making. *Omega* 29 (5): 405–415.

Chitsaz, N. and Azarnivand, A. (2017). Water scarcity management in arid regions based on an extended multiple criteria technique. *Water Resources Management* 31 (1): 233–250.

Churchman, C.W. and Ackoff, R.L. (1954). An approximate measure of value. *Journal of the Operations Research Society of America* 2 (2): 172–187.

Dyer, J.S. (1990). Remarks on the analytic hierarchy process. *Management Science* 36 (3): 249–258.

Guo, S. and Zhao, H. (2017). Fuzzy best-worst multi-criteria decision-making method and its applications. *Knowledge-Based Systems* 121: 23–31.

Gupta, H. and Barua, M.K. (2016). Identifying enablers of technological innovation for Indian MSMEs using best–worst multi criteria decision making method. *Technological Forecasting and Social Change* 107: 69–79.

Gupta, H. and Barua, M.K. (2017). Supplier selection among SMEs on the basis of their green innovation ability using BWM and fuzzy TOPSIS. *Journal of Cleaner Production* 152: 242–258.

Hafezalkotob, A. and Hafezalkotob, A. (2017). A novel approach for combination of individual and group decisions based on fuzzy best-worst method. *Applied Soft Computing* 59: 316–325.

Herman, M.W. and Koczkodaj, W.W. (1996). A Monte Carlo study of pairwise comparison. *Information Processing Letters* 57 (1): 25–29.

Jeffreys, I. (2004). The use of compensatory and non-compensatory multi-criteria analysis for small-scale forestry. *Small-scale Forest Economics, Management and Policy* 3 (1): 99–117.

Ma, J., Fan, Z.P., and Huang, L.H. (1999). A subjective and objective integrated approach to determine attribute weights. *European Journal of Operational Research* 112 (2): 397–404.

Mou, Q., Xu, Z., and Liao, H. (2016). An intuitionistic fuzzy multiplicative best-worst method for multi-criteria group decision making. *Information Sciences* 374: 224–239.

Pamučar, D., Petrović, I., and Ćirović, G. (2017). Modification of the best-worst and MABAC methods: a novel approach based on interval-valued fuzzy-rough numbers. *Expert Systems with Applications* 91: 89–106.

Ren, J., Liang, H., and Chan, F.T. (2017). Urban sewage sludge, sustainability, and transition for Eco-City: multi-criteria sustainability assessment of technologies based on best-worst method. *Technological Forecasting and Social Change* 116: 29–39.

Rezaei, J. (2015). Best-worst multi-criteria decision-making method. *Omega* 53: 49–57.

Rezaei, J. (2016). Best-worst multi-criteria decision-making method: some properties and a linear model. *Omega* 64: 126–130.

Rezaei, J., Wang, J., and Tavasszy, L. (2015). Linking supplier development to supplier segmentation using best-worst method. *Expert Systems with Applications* 42 (23): 9152–9164.

Rezaei, J., Nispeling, T., Sarkis, J., and Tavasszy, L. (2016). A supplier selection life cycle approach integrating traditional and environmental criteria using the best-worst method. *Journal of Cleaner Production* 135: 577–588.

Rezaei, J., Hemmes, A., and Tavasszy, L. (2017). Multi-criteria decision-making for complex bundling configurations in surface transportation of air freight. *Journal of Air Transport Management* 61: 95–105.

Saaty, T.L. (1977). A scaling method for priorities in hierarchical structures. *Journal of Mathematical Psychology* 15 (3): 234–281.

Saaty, T.L. (1980). *The Analytic Hierarchy Process*. New York, NY: McGraw-Hill Education.

Saaty, T.L. (1985). Decision making for leaders. *IEEE Transactions on Systems, Man, and Cybernetics* 3: 450–452.

Saaty, T.L. (1986). Axiomatic foundation of the analytic hierarchy process. *Management Science* 32 (7): 841–855.

Saaty, T.L. (1988). What is the analytic hierarchy process? In: *Mathematical Models for Decision Support* (eds. G. Mitra, H.J. Greenberg, F.A. Lootsma, et al.), 109–121. Berlin: Springer.

Saaty, T.L. (1990). How to make a decision: the analytic hierarchy process. *European Journal of Operational Research* 48 (1): 9–26.

Saaty, T.L. (1994). Highlights and critical points in the theory and application of the analytic hierarchy process. *European Journal of Operational Research* 74 (3): 426–447.

Saaty, T.L. (1996). *Decision Making with Dependence and Feedback: The Analytic Network Process*. Pittsburgh, PA: RWS Publications.

Saaty, T.L. (2004). Fundamentals of the analytic network process: dependence and feedback in decision-making with a single network. *Journal of Systems Science and Systems Engineering* 13 (2): 129–157.

Saaty, T.L. (2005). *Theory and Applications of the Analytic Network Process: Decision Making with Benefits, Opportunities, Costs, and Risks*. Pittsburgh, PA: RWS Publications.

Saaty, T.L. (2006). The analytic network process. In: *Decision Making with the Analytic Network Process* (eds. T.L. Saaty and L.G. Vargas), 1–26. Boston, MA: Springer.

Saaty, T.L. (2008). Decision making with the analytic hierarchy process. *International Journal of Services Sciences* 1 (1): 83–98.

Saaty, T.L. and Vargas, L. (2006). *Decision Making with the Analytic Network Process: Economics, Political, Social and Technological Applications with Benefits, Opportunities, Costs, and Risks*. New York, NY: Springer.

Salimi, N. and Rezaei, J. (2016). Measuring efficiency of university-industry Ph.D. projects using best-worst method. *Scientometrics* 109 (3): 1911–1938.

Thurstone, L.L. (1927). A law of comparative judgment. *Psychological Review* 34 (4): 273–286.

Torabi, S.A., Giahi, R., and Sahebjamnia, N. (2016). An enhanced risk assessment framework for business continuity management systems. *Safety Science* 89: 201–218.

Yang, Q., Zhang, Z., You, X., and Chen, T. (2016). Evaluation and classification of overseas talents in China based on the BWM for intuitionistic relations. *Symmetry* 8 (11): 137.

Yu, P.L. (1990). *Forming Winning Strategies: An Integrated Theory of Habitual Domains*. Heidelberg, Germany: Springer Science and Business Media Publication.

6

TOPSIS

6.1 Introduction

Based on the basic principle of multiattribute decision-making (MADM), the decision-maker can use the similarity between the feasible alternatives and the preferential result and/or incongruity of the alternatives to the undesirable outcome in decision-making. The aforementioned notion is, chiefly, the core principle of the reference-dependent theory (Kahneman and Tversky 1979). According to the reference-dependent theory, the decision-maker evaluates the feasible alternatives in terms of gains and losses relative to a predetermined subjective reference point(s) (Kahneman and Tversky 1984, 2000; Kahneman et al. 1991; Quattrone and Tversky 1988; Hardie et al. 1993; Highhouse and Johnson 1996). In the MADM viewpoint, these reference points are represented by the ideal and/or inferior alternatives (Tzeng and Huang 2011). Note that the definition of reference points, the similarity measurement techniques, and the computational assumptions are what distinguish the MADM methods that are established upon reference-dependent theory.

The technique for order preferences by similarity to an ideal solution (TOPSIS) is an MADM solving method that is rooted in the basic principles of reference-dependence theory. The pioneering implementation of TOPSIS as an MADM method can be traced back to Hwang and Yoon (1981). The method's flourishment was largely indebted to the works of Yoon (1987), Chen and Hwang (1992), and Hwang et al. (1993). In essence, the TOPSIS method finds an alternative that has the shortest distance from the ideal alternative and, also, the farthest distance from the inferior alternative (Opricovic and Tzeng 2004), a trait that makes this method a suitable risk-avoidance MADM method (Jahan et al. 2012). In other words, the TOPSIS method finds a feasible alternative that would be considered the most beneficial by the decision-maker, and which also avoids selecting the solution that would be most costly for the stakeholders of

A Handbook on Multi-Attribute Decision-Making Methods, First Edition.
Omid Bozorg-Haddad, Babak Zolghadr-Asli, and Hugo A. Loáiciga.

the decision-making problem, thus making the method a reliable risk-avoidance technique (Aghajani-Mir et al. 2016).

TOPSIS method has been successfully implemented in various cases, and the results have revealed the great potential of this method as an MADM method. Climatic studies (Zeyaeyan et al. 2017), drilling management (Ravikumar et al. 2015), energy planning (Kumar et al. 2017), expedition planning (Opricovic and Tzeng 2004), financial management (Seçme et al. 2009), material processing (Shukla et al. 2017), material screening (Jahan et al. 2010), manufacturing management (Sivapirakasam et al. 2011), robot selection (Chu and Lin 2003), soil waste management (Aghajani-Mir et al. 2016), tourism planning (Zhang et al. 2011), transportation systems evaluation (Aydogan 2011), warfare selection (Dağdeviren et al. 2009), waste disposal management (Ekmekçioğlu et al. 2010), and water resources management (Mani et al. 2019) are merely few examples of effective application of TOPSIS method. This method has also been successfully linked with other mathematical framework, such as: Grey-TOPSIS method (Chen and Tzeng 2004), fuzzy TOPSIS (Wang and Lee 2007), analytic hierarchy process (AHP)-TOPSIS (Lin et al. 2008), nonlinear programming (Li 2010), Delphi-TOPSIS (Joshi et al. 2011), and decision-making trial and evaluation laboratory (DEMATEL)-TOPSIS (Baykasoğlu et al. 2013). A detailed stepwise description of TOPSIS methods is provided in Section 6.2.

6.2 Stepwise Description of the TOPSIS Method

At this junction, it is beneficial to recall the basic scheme of a decision-matrix. Let D denote the decision-matrix, described as follows (Yu 1990):

$$D = \begin{matrix} & \begin{matrix} c_1 & \cdots & c_n \end{matrix} \\ \begin{matrix} a_1 \\ \vdots \\ a_m \end{matrix} & \begin{bmatrix} v_{(1,1)} & \cdots & v_{(1,n)} \\ \vdots & \ddots & \vdots \\ v_{(m,1)} & \cdots & v_{(m,n)} \end{bmatrix} \end{matrix} \tag{6.1}$$

in which a_i = the predetermined, feasible ith alternative; c_j = the predefined jth criterion determined by the decision-maker; $v_{(i,j)}$ = the value of the ith alternative with regard to the jth criterion; m = the number of feasible alternatives; and n = the number of criteria.

As stated earlier, a decision-maker attempts to aggregate the preference of an alternative with regard to all predefined criteria, to choose the most suitable alternative that would best represent the interest of the stakeholders of the MADM problem. The TOPSIS method is a compensatory method that would enable the decision-makers to cope with such situations. In order to implement the TOPSIS method, the decision-maker must make sure that the predefined criteria are independent of one another and that the preference values ought to be monotonically increasing or decreasing (Kumar et al. 2017). It is also advised to use this method when the decision-maker is assured of the presence of a sufficient and adequate number of criteria that best describe the interest of the stakeholders (Greene et al. 2011).

The procedure of the TOPSIS method is described by the following steps:

6.2.1 Step 1: Establishing the Formation of the Decision-making Problem

In this step, the decision-maker mathematically expresses the decision-making problem through the decision-matrix. It goes without saying that the integrity of the final results would heavily rely on the accuracy of this step. In other words, a well-defined decision-matrix that precisely represents the stakeholder's interest is the key ingredient for an acceptable decision-making.

6.2.2 Step 2: Normalizing the Element of the Decision-matrix

In practice, it is common for real-world decision-making problems to be composed of criteria with a different range, units of measurement, and scales. To cope with this challenge, the decision-maker must transform the elements of the decision-matrix into a dimensionless, equally ranged data, through a mathematical procedure, better known as normalization. The described mathematical procedure can be expressed with various formulations. However, the following three forms are the most common approaches to normalize the decision-matrix when the TOPSIS method is employed:

Form I: The following equation is used with positively valued alternatives when the larger the value, the better the situation, or negatively valued alternatives, when the smaller the value, the better the situation (Tzeng and Huang 2011):

$$r_{(i,j)} = \frac{v_{(i,j)}}{\sqrt{\sum_{i=1}^{m} [v_{(i,j)}]^2}} \tag{6.2}$$

in which $r_{(i,j)}$ = the normalized performance value for the ith alternatives with respect to the jth criterion.

Form II: This normalization process transforms linearly all the performance values so that the relative order of magnitude of the ratings remains equal. The procedure is formulated as follows (Yoon 1987; Chang and Yeh 2001):

- *For positive criteria*:

$$r_{(i,j)} = \frac{v_{(i,j)}}{v_j^+} \tag{6.3}$$

- *For negative criteria*:

$$r_{(i,j)} = \frac{1/v_{(i,j)}}{1/v_j^+} = \frac{v_j^+}{v_{(i,j)}} \tag{6.4}$$

in which v_j^+ = the components of the ideal alternative with regard to the jth criterion.

Form III: In this normalizing procedure, ideal and inferior alternatives are used to normalize the performance values, and it is expressed as follows (Hwang et al. 1993; Ma et al. 1999):

- *For positive criteria*:

$$r_{(i,j)} = \frac{v_{(i,j)} - v_j^-}{v_j^+ - v_j^-} \tag{6.5}$$

- *For negative criteria*:

$$r_{(i,j)} = \frac{v_j^- - v_{(i,j)}}{v_j^- - v_j^+} \tag{6.6}$$

in which v_j^- = the components of the inferior alternatives with regard to the jth criterion.

6.2.3 Step 3: Computing the Weighted Normalized Preference Values

As far as MADM is concerned, the decision-maker ought to mathematically express the importance of each evaluation criteria. Let w_j denote the importance value of the jth criterion. In this step, the decision-maker represents each of the feasible alternatives, as a weighted normalized vector, as follows:

$$x_{(i,j)} = w_j \times r_{(i,j)} \tag{6.7}$$

in which $x_{(i,j)}$ = the weighted normalized performance value of the ith alternative with regard to the jth criterion. Regarding the weight assignment procedure the following must hold:

$$\sum_{j=1}^{n} w_j = 1 \tag{6.8}$$

6.2.4 Step 4: Defining the Reference Alternatives

The TOPSIS method is based on comparing each feasible solution with reference alternatives, namely, the ideal and inferior solutions. The ideal alternative is an arbitrarily defined vector, which describes the aspired solution to the given problem that may or may not be a realistic solution to the given MADM problem, while the inferior alternative, is an arbitrarily defined solution that represents the most undesirable option for the given MADM. One could use the upper and lower boundaries of the feasible range for *j*th criterion to compose these arbitrarily defined alternatives. In such cases, if the criterion is positively valued, where the larger the value, the better the situation, the upper boundary constitutes the ideal alternative, and the lower boundary is used to compose the inferior alternative. Conversely, for the negatively valued criteria, where smaller the value, better the situation, the lower boundary is used to compose the ideal alternative and the upper boundary becomes the inferior alternative. These alternatives are as follows (Hwang and Yoon 1981):

$$a^+ = (x_1^+, x_2^+, \ldots, x_j^+, \ldots, x_n^+) \tag{6.9}$$

$$a^- = (x_1^-, x_2^-, \ldots, x_j^-, \ldots, x_n^-) \tag{6.10}$$

in which a^+ and a^- = the ideal and inferior alternatives, respectively; and x_j^+ and x_j^- = the weighted value of the ideal and inferior alternatives with respect to the *j*th criterion, respectively. The TOPSIS methods equate the ideal alternative to the positive ideal solution (PIS), and the inferior alternative is referred to as the negative ideal solution (NIS).

6.2.5 Step 5: Calculation of the Separation Measure

In this step every, given alternative is compared to the reference points, namely, the ideal and inferior alternatives. The described procedure, which in TOPSIS terms is known as the separation measurement, is expressed as follows (Hwang and Yoon 1981):

$$D_j^+ = \sqrt{\sum_{j=1}^{n} [x_{(i,j)} - x_j^+]^2} \tag{6.11}$$

and

$$D_j^- = \sqrt{\sum_{j=1}^{n} [x_{(i,j)} - x_j^-]^2} \tag{6.12}$$

in which D_j^+ and D_j^- = the separation measurements of the *j*th criterion with respect to the ideal and inferior alternatives.

Equations (6.11, 6.12) measure the Euclidean distance of the *j*th criterion to the reference points, namely, the ideal and inferior alternatives. However, it should be noted that the *p*-norm distance (Minkowski distance of order *p*) can also be implemented instead (Tzeng and Huang 2011). In that regard, the following equations express a more general form to compute the separation measurements (Tzeng and Huang 2011):

$$D_j^+ = \sqrt[\frac{1}{p}]{\sum_{j=1}^{n} [x_{(i,j)} - x_j^+]^p} \quad 1 \leq p < \infty \tag{6.13}$$

and

$$D_j^- = \sqrt[\frac{1}{p}]{\sum_{j=1}^{n} [x_{(i,j)} - x_j^-]^p} \quad 1 \leq p < \infty \tag{6.14}$$

6.2.6 Step 6: Computing the Relative Closeness to the Ideal Solution

In this step, the decision-maker measures the relative closeness of each given alternative to the ideal solution. The aforementioned notion, which can also be described as calculating the similarities of a given alternative with the ideal solution, is expressed as follows (Hwang and Yoon 1981):

$$C_j^+ = \frac{D_j^-}{D_j^+ + D_j^-} \tag{6.15}$$

in which C_j^+ = the relative closeness of the jth alternative to the ideal solution ($C_j^+ \in [0, 1]$). Note that the greater values of C_j^+ imply the existence of more similarities between the jth criterion and the ideal solution.

6.2.7 Step 7: Ranking the Alternatives

The last step sorts the feasible alternatives in descending order according to the computed values of the relative closeness. The alternative with the greatest relative closeness value is the most desirable solution, while the alternative with the lowest value for relative closeness represents the least desirable solution (Hwang and Yoon 1981).

6.3 A Common Misinterpretation of TOPSIS Results

Equation (6.15) works as the aggregation function in the TOPSIS method, which, in essence, enables the decision-makers to estimate the overall preference of each given alternative. Note that if $C_r^+ > C_k^+$, then the decision-maker can assume that the rth alternative would be preferable to the kth one. This situation occurs if (Opricovic and Tzeng 2004; Tzeng and Huang 2011):

(a) $D_r^+ < D_k^+$ and $D_r^- > D_k^-$ (i.e. the rth alternative is separated from the inferior solution, while the kth alternative is separated from the ideal solution); or

(b) $D_r^+ > D_k^+$, $D_r^- > D_k^-$, and $D_r^+ < \frac{D_k^+ \times D_r^-}{D_k^-}$ (i.e. compared to the kth alternative the rth alternative is more separated from both reference points, yet the separation from the inferior solution will neutralize the negative impact of the dissimilarities of the rth alternative and the ideal solution).

Decision under the circumstances described in situation (a) is as clear as it can get, where the rth alternative is chosen as the better solution; however, situation (b) implies the kth alternative is demonstrating more similarity to the ideal solution, but due to the fact that TOPSIS does not consider the relative importance of the separation measurements (i.e. in the formulation of relative closeness both separation measurements are assigned equal weights) the TOPSIS method would choose the rth alternative (Opricovic and Tzeng 2004). This situation might be problematic in coping with practical MADM problems (Tzeng and Huang 2011), yet one might argue that the TOPSIS method, deliberately, ignores the relative importance of separation measurements by implying that the decision-maker must seek the most suitable solution by finding an alternative most similar to the ideal solution, while avoids possible risks in the decision-making process by avoiding similarities between the chosen alternative and the inferior solution.

6.4 Conclusion

The TOPSIS method, which is based on the foundations of the reference-dependent theory, finds a feasible alternative with the shortest distance to the ideal alternative, and the greatest distance from the inferior alternative. To do so, the weighted normalized vectors of each alternative are used to compute the distance of each given alternative from the reference points, namely, the ideal and inferior alternatives. In the TOPSIS terms, the aforementioned procedure is referred to as the separation measurements. The computed distances are then used to quantify the similarities of each given alternative to the ideal situation. Through this process, which is better known as computing, the relative closeness of alternatives to the ideal solution, the decision-maker aggregates the preference of alternatives for computing an overall preference value for each given alternative. Lastly, the overall scores are used to rank and opt the most desirable alternative. The TOPSIS method is based on the assumption of independence of evaluation criteria, and a monotonically increasing or decreasing values for preference values is the other requirement for employing this method to cope with MADM problems.

References

Aghajani-Mir, M., Ghazvinei-Tehrani, P., Sulaiman, N.M.N. et al. (2016). Application of TOPSIS and VIKOR improved versions in a multi criteria decision analysis to develop an optimized municipal solid waste management model. *Journal of Environmental Management* 166: 109–115.

Aydogan, E.K. (2011). Performance measurement model for Turkish aviation firms using the rough-AHP and TOPSIS methods under fuzzy environment. *Expert Systems with Applications* 38 (4): 3992–3998.

Baykasoğlu, A., Kaplanoğlu, V., DurmuşOğlu, Z.D., and ŞAhin, C. (2013). Integrating fuzzy DEMATEL and fuzzy hierarchical TOPSIS methods for truck selection. *Expert Systems with Applications* 40 (3): 899–907.

Chang, Y.H. and Yeh, C.H. (2001). Evaluating airline competitiveness using multiattribute decision making. *Omega* 29 (5): 405–415.

Chen, S.J. and Hwang, C.L. (1992). *Fuzzy Multiple Attribute Decision Making: Methods and Applications*. Heidelberg, Germany: Springer Publication Company.

Chen, M.F. and Tzeng, G.H. (2004). Combining grey relation and TOPSIS concepts for selecting an expatriate host country. *Mathematical and Computer Modelling* 40 (13): 1473–1490.

Chu, T.C. and Lin, Y.C. (2003). A fuzzy TOPSIS method for robot selection. *The International Journal of Advanced Manufacturing Technology* 21 (4): 284–290.

Dağdeviren, M., Yavuz, S., and Kılınç, N. (2009). Weapon selection using the AHP and TOPSIS methods under fuzzy environment. *Expert Systems with Applications* 36 (4): 8143–8151.

Ekmekçioğlu, M., Kaya, T., and Kahraman, C. (2010). Fuzzy multicriteria disposal method and site selection for municipal solid waste. *Waste Management* 30 (8): 1729–1736.

Greene, R., Devillers, R., Luther, J.E., and Eddy, B.G. (2011). GIS-based multiple-criteria decision analysis. *Geography Compass* 5 (6): 412–432.

Hardie, B.G., Johnson, E.J., and Fader, P.S. (1993). Modeling loss aversion and reference dependence effects on brand choice. *Marketing Science* 12 (4): 378–394.

Highhouse, S. and Johnson, M.A. (1996). Gain/loss asymmetry and riskless choice: loss aversion in choices among job finalists. *Organizational Behavior and Human Decision Processes* 68 (3): 225–233.

Hwang, C.L. and Yoon, K. (1981). Methods for multiple attribute decision making. In: *Multiple Attribute Decision Making: Lecture Notes in Economics and Mathematical Systems* (eds. C.L. Hwang and K. Yoon), 58–191. Heidelberg, Germany: Springer Publication Company.

Hwang, C.L., Lai, Y.J., and Liu, T.Y. (1993). A new approach for multiple objective decision making. *Computers and Operations Research* 20 (8): 889–899.

Jahan, A., Ismail, M.Y., Sapuan, S.M., and Mustapha, F. (2010). Material screening and choosing methods: a review. *Materials and Design* 31 (2): 696–705.

Jahan, A., Mustapha, F., Sapuan, S.M. et al. (2012). A framework for weighting of criteria in ranking stage of material selection process. *The International Journal of Advanced Manufacturing Technology* 58 (1): 411–420.

Joshi, R., Banwet, D.K., and Shankar, R. (2011). A Delphi-AHP-TOPSIS based benchmarking framework for performance improvement of a cold chain. *Expert Systems with Applications* 38 (8): 10170–10182.

Kahneman, D. and Tversky, A. (1979). Prospect theory: an analysis of decision under risk. *Econometrica: Journal of the Econometric Society*: 263–291.

Kahneman, D. and Tversky, A. (1984). Choices, values, and frames. *American Psychologist* 39 (4): 341.

Kahneman, D. and Tversky, A. (eds.) (2000). *Choices, Values, and Frames*. Cambridge, UK: Cambridge University Press.

Kahneman, D., Knetsch, J.L., and Thaler, R.H. (1991). Anomalies: the endowment effect, loss aversion, and status quo bias. *The Journal of Economic Perspectives* 5 (1): 193–206.

Kumar, A., Sah, B., Singh, A.R. et al. (2017). A review of multi criteria decision making (MCDM) towards sustainable renewable energy development. *Renewable and Sustainable Energy Reviews* 69: 596–609.

Li, D.F. (2010). TOPSIS-based nonlinear-programming methodology for multiattribute decision making with interval-valued intuitionistic fuzzy sets. *IEEE Transactions on Fuzzy Systems* 18 (2): 299–311.

Lin, M.C., Wang, C.C., Chen, M.S., and Chang, C.A. (2008). Using AHP and TOPSIS approaches in customer-driven product design process. *Computers in Industry* 59 (1): 17–31.

Ma, J., Fan, Z.P., and Huang, L.H. (1999). A subjective and objective integrated approach to determine attribute weights. *European Journal of Operational Research* 112 (2): 397–404.

Mani, M., Bozorg-Haddad, O., and Loáiciga, H.A. (2019). A new framework for the optimal management of urban runoff with low-impact development stormwater control measures considering service-performance reduction. *Journal of Hydroinformatics* 21 (5): 727–744.

Opricovic, S. and Tzeng, G.H. (2004). Compromise solution by MCDM methods: a comparative analysis of VIKOR and TOPSIS. *European Journal of Operational Research* 156 (2): 445–455.

Quattrone, G.A. and Tversky, A. (1988). Contrasting rational and psychological analyses of political choice. *American Political Science Review* 82 (3): 719–736.

Ravikumar, H., Arun, P.L., and Thileepan, S. (2015). Analysis in drilling of Al6061/20% SiCp composites using grey Taguchi based TOPSIS (GT-TOPSIS). *International Journal of ChemTech Research* 8 (12): 292–303.

Seçme, N.Y., Bayrakdaroğlu, A., and Kahraman, C. (2009). Fuzzy performance evaluation in Turkish banking sector using analytic hierarchy process and TOPSIS. *Expert Systems with Applications* 36 (9): 11699–11709.

Shukla, A., Agarwal, P., Rana, R.S., and Purohit, R. (2017). Applications of TOPSIS algorithm on various manufacturing processes: a review. *Materials Today: Proceedings* 4 (4): 5320–5329.

Sivapirakasam, S.P., Mathew, J., and Surianarayanan, M. (2011). Multi-attribute decision making for green electrical discharge machining. *Expert Systems with Applications* 38 (7): 8370–8374.

Tzeng, G.H. and Huang, J.J. (2011). *Multiple Attribute Decision Making: Methods and Applications*. Boca Raton, FL: CRC Press.

Wang, Y.J. and Lee, H.S. (2007). Generalizing TOPSIS for fuzzy multiple-criteria group decision-making. *Computers and Mathematics with Applications* 53 (11): 1762–1772.

Yoon, K. (1987). A reconciliation among discrete compromise solutions. *Journal of the Operational Research Society* 38: 277–286.

Yu, P.L. (1990). *Forming Winning Strategies: An Integrated Theory of Habitual Domains*. Heidelberg, Germany: Springer Science and Business Media Publication.

Zeyaeyan, S., Fattahi, E., Ranjbar, A., and Vazifedoust, M. (2017). Classification of rainfall warnings based on the TOPSIS method. *Climate* 5 (2): 33.

Zhang, H., Gu, C.L., Gu, L.W., and Zhang, Y. (2011). The evaluation of tourism destination competitiveness by TOPSIS and information entropy: a case in the Yangtze River Delta of China. *Tourism Management* 32 (2): 443–451.

7

VIKOR

7.1 Introduction

The very nature of multiattribute decision-making (MADM) problems entails the decision-makers to make their judgments in an environment with conflict of interest. On the one hand, the stakeholders' conflicting interest may be the root of this challenging aspect of MADM problems. Chiefly, in such cases, which in technical terms are referred to as "zero-sum games," a stakeholder's profit is tied to the loss of others (Osborne and Rubinstein 1994; Myerson 2013). On the other hand, the conflict of interest might be rooted in the evaluation criteria, which are the signifiers that are determined by the decision-maker to evaluate the desirability of each feasible alternatives available for each given problem. In such cases, improving the performance of an alternative with regard to a specific criterion would cause the degradation of alternative's performance with respect to at least another criterion. In other words, the decision-maker attempts to find a solution with regard to a set of evaluating criteria, where no alternative exists that clearly dominate the other feasible alternatives.

MADM can be considered as a two-stage process, where first, the goal of the decision-making is defined (Duckstein and Opricovic 1980). In this initial stage, the decision-maker reflects the stakeholders' main goal by defining a set of evaluating criteria. The evaluation criteria are indicators that reflect the interest of the stakeholders representing technical and political preferences (Yu 1973). The decision-maker must consider a set of feasible alternatives for the MADM problem at hand. Note that the feasibility of these under consideration alternatives can be tested by mathematical and physical models. In the second stage, the decision-maker chooses what is considered the most suitable alternative (Duckstein and Opricovic 1980). MADM methods assist the decision-maker in overcoming the challenge of choosing one of the predefined alternatives in an environment that can be often characterized by several noncommensurable

A Handbook on Multi-Attribute Decision-Making Methods, First Edition.
Omid Bozorg-Haddad, Babak Zolghadr-Asli, and Hugo A. Loáiciga.

and conflicting evaluation criteria, where no solution satisfying all criteria simultaneously may be found.

To illustrate the aforementioned notion, consider an MADM problem with two positive evaluation criteria, say c_1 and c_2. First, employing multiobjective techniques (see Chapter 1), the decision-maker searches the decision-space to determine a set of feasible, noninferior, solutions that cannot dominate one another, nor can be dominated by other solutions. Note that in technical terms, the aforementioned set of solution is referred to as the Pareto Front (PF; Bozorg-Haddad et al. 2017; Zolghadr-Asli et al. 2017). Given that both evaluation criteria are positive, where the larger the value the better the situation, the decision-maker can determine the ideal (a^+) and inferior (a^-) alternatives. These arbitrarily defined alternatives describe the desired and the most undesirable solution to the given problem, respectively. In light of the MADM, the decision-maker selects a set of feasible alternatives that are those that seem promising from the stakeholders' point of view. It goes without saying that these underconsideration alternatives are members of the nondominated set of solutions. As long as compromising is concerned in the MADM process the decision-maker is searching for an alternative (a^c) where the stakeholders' preferences resolve the conflicting nature of the evaluation criteria (Opricovic 1998). The described situation is demonstrated in Figure 7.1.

Accordingly, there is a number of compromising-oriented MADM methods available, in which the decision makers' preferences are used to choose the

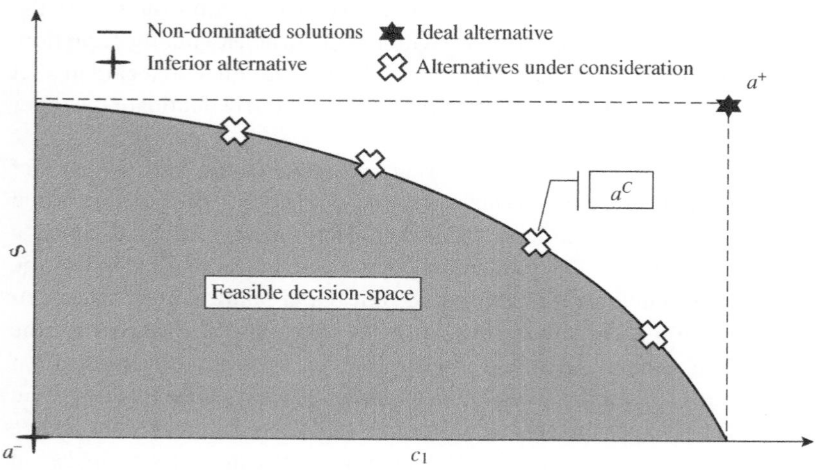

Figure 7.1 The general scheme of an MADM problem with two positive criteria c_1 and c_2.

compromised alternative from a set of nondominated solutions (Hwang and Yoon 1981; Yoon 1987; Chen and Hwang 1992). The VIKOR method, which stands for VlseKriterijumska Optimizacija I Kompromisno Resenje (in *Serbian*, multicriteria optimization and compromise solution (Liou et al. 2011)), is one of these compromising-oriented MADM methods (Opricovic 1998). The foundation of the VIKOR method was established by Yu (1973) and Zeleny (1982) works. Yu (1973) introduced compromise solutions based on the idea of finding a feasible solution that is as close as possible to an ideal solution. Zeleny (1982) stated that according to human rationality alternatives that are closer to the ideal solution are preferred to those that are farther away. The combination of the aforementioned ideas inspired Opricovic (1998) to introduce the VIKOR method to cope with MADM problems.

As far as the human rationality in the decision-making process is concerned, it is safe to assume that the ideal solution minimizes conflict (Zeleny 1982). Though as stated earlier, the existence of an ideal solution might be in question, for the set of nondominated, feasible, alternatives might not include that arbitrarily defined ideal solution. The general idea is a feasible alternative with the most similarity to the ideal solution is the least likely solution with conflict of interest, making it a comprise solution. The idea that quickly springs to mind is to measure the distance between the given feasible alternatives and the ideal solution. In light of compromise-oriented reasoning Yu (1973) introduced a distance function called the group regret for a decision, a regret that the ideal cannot be chosen. Duckstein and Opricovic (1980) later expanded the idea of the addressed distance function into the following general form:

$$L_{(p,i)} = \left\{ \sum_{j=1}^{n} \left[w_j \times \left(\frac{v_j^+ - v_{(i,j)}}{v_j^+ - v_j^-} \right) \right]^p \right\}^{1/p} \quad 1 \leq p \leq \infty \tag{7.1}$$

in which $L_{(p,i)}$ = the p-norm derived distance between the ith alternative and the ideal alternative; w_j = the assigned weight to the jth criterion; n = the number of evaluation criteria; $v_{(i,j)}$ = the performance value of the ith alternative with respect to the jth criterion; v_j^+ and v_j^- = the performance value of the ideal and inferior alternatives, respectively, with regard to the jth criterion. Here, $L_{(1,i)}$ represents the sum of all individual regrets and $L_{(\infty,i)}$ stand for the maximum regret that an individual could have (Opricovic and Tzeng 2002, 2004, 2007). Note that the term compromise is hereby referred to an agreement established by mutual concessions. Consequently, alternatives obtained by minimizing $L_{(1,i)}$ and $L_{(\infty,i)}$ can be interpreted as those with maximum group utility and minimum individual regret, respectively (Tzeng and Huang 2011).

The VIKOR method employs two deviations of the L_p-metric introduced in Eq. (7.1), where $p = 1$ and $p = \infty$ are employed to aggregate the performance value of alternatives and to select a compromise solution, denoted by a^c, where this opted alternative is considered to be the feasible solution that has the most similarity, or the closest distance, to the arbitrarily defined ideal solution (a^+).

The VIKOR method has been numerously employed to solve MADM problems, and its applications include but are not limited to: agricultural management (Aktan and Samut 2013), airline agencies' business strategies planning (Liou et al. 2011), energy resources (Debbarma et al. 2017), expedition planning (Opricovic and Tzeng 2004), financial management (Wu et al. 2017), land-use strategic planning (Chang and Hsu 2009), medical and healthcare system (Zeng et al. 2013; Chang 2014), military operations (Sennaroglu and Celebi 2018), policy, social and education (Gul et al. 2016), reconstruction planning for postnatural disasters (Opricovic and Tzeng 2002), site selection for hydropower systems (Opricovic and Tzeng 2007), soil waste management (Aghajani-Mir et al. 2016), water resources management (Ameri et al. 2018; Simab et al. 2018), and sustainable energy planning (Kumar et al. 2017). In the following section, a stepwise description of the VIKOR method is provided.

7.2 Stepwise Description of the VIKOR Method

Recall the basic scheme of a decision-matrix. Let D denote the decision-matrix, described as follows (Yu 1990):

$$D = \begin{matrix} & \begin{matrix} c_1 & \cdots & c_n \end{matrix} \\ \begin{matrix} a_1 \\ \vdots \\ a_m \end{matrix} & \begin{bmatrix} v_{(1,1)} & \cdots & v_{(1,n)} \\ \vdots & \ddots & \vdots \\ v_{(m,1)} & \cdots & v_{(m,n)} \end{bmatrix} \end{matrix} \tag{7.2}$$

in which a_i = the ith predetermined, feasible, alternative; c_j = the jth predefined criterion determined by the decision-maker; and m = the number of feasible alternatives. The following is a stepwise description of the VIKOR method.

7.2.1 Step 1: Modeling the Decision-Making Problem

The decision-maker expresses mathematically the decision-making problem through the decision-matrix. At this level, the VIKOR method compels the decision-maker to define the ideal and inferior alternatives. The ideal alternative (a^+) is an arbitrarily defined vector, which describes the desired solution to the given problem, that may or may not be achievable, while the inferior alternative (a^-) is an arbitrarily defined solution that represents the most undesirable option for the given MADM problem. There are two main methods to compose the ideal and inferior alternatives. One can use the best and worst values represented in the jth column of the decision-matrix to compose the jth component of the ideal and inferior alternatives, respectively. On the other hand, one could also use the upper and lower boundaries of the feasible range for jth criterion to compose these arbitrarily defined alternatives. In such cases, if the criterion is positively valued, then the larger the value, the better the situation, and the upper boundary becomes the ideal alternative, while the lower boundary becomes the inferior alternative. Conversely, for negative criteria the smaller the value, the better the situation means the lower boundary and the upper boundary are, respectively, chosen as the ideal and the inferior alternatives.

7.2.2 Step 2: Normalizing the Element of the Decision-Matrix

In practice, it is common for real-world decision-making problems to involve criteria defined over different ranges, units, and scales. To cope with this challenge the decision-maker must transform the elements of the decision-matrix into a dimensionless, equally ranged, data, through normalization, which can take several formulations. However, the following form is commonly recommended for the VIKOR method (Hwang et al. 1993; Ma et al. 1999):

- *For positive criteria*:

$$r_{(i,j)} = \frac{v_{(i,j)} - v_j^-}{v_j^+ - v_j^-} \tag{7.3}$$

- *For negative criteria*:

$$r_{(i,j)} = \frac{v_j^- - v_{(i,j)}}{v_j^- - v_j^+} \tag{7.4}$$

in which $r_{(i,j)}$ = the normalized preference value of the ith alternative with respect to the jth criterion.

7.2.3 Step 3: Compute the "Group Satisfaction" and "Individual Regret" Parameters

Equation (7.1) implies the group satisfaction and individual regret parameters are computed as follows (Opricovic and Tzeng 2002, 2004, 2007):

$$S_i = \sum_{j=1}^{n} w_j \times r_{(i,j)} \tag{7.5}$$

$$R_i = \underset{j}{Max}[w_j \times r_{(i,j)}] \tag{7.6}$$

in which S_i and R_i = the group satisfaction and individual regret of the ith alternative, respectively; and w_j = the weight of the jth criterion. Note that the weights must be assigned such that:

$$\sum_{j=1}^{n} w_j = 1 \tag{7.7}$$

It is noteworthy that the group satisfaction and individual regret are deviations of the L_p-metric introduced in Eq. (7.1), where $p = 1$ and $p = \infty$, respectively. Group satisfaction and individual regret parameters represent the distance between the compromise solution and the ideal alternative (Figure 7.1); hence, they can be interpreted as the average and maximum gaps of the improvement priority, respectively (Tzeng and Huang 2011).

7.2.4 Step 4: Computing the VIKOR Parameter

The VIKOR parameter is computed as follows (Opricovic and Tzeng 2002, 2004, 2007):

$$Q_i = \left(\upsilon \times \frac{S_i - \underset{i}{Min}\, S_i}{\underset{i}{Max}\, S_i - \underset{i}{Min}\, S_i} \right) + \left[(1 - \upsilon) \times \frac{R_i - \underset{i}{Min}\, R_i}{\underset{i}{Max}\, R_i - \underset{i}{Min}\, R_i} \right] \tag{7.8}$$

in which Q_i = the VIKOR parameter for the ith alternative; and υ = the weight of the strategies, which has a (0, 1] range (Opricovic and Tzeng 2007). The decision-maker determines the type of decision-making strategy by assigning values to the weights of strategies; In such a case, $\upsilon > 0.5$ represents the "voting by majority rule," $\upsilon \approx 0.5$ is making decision "by consensus," and $\upsilon < 0.5$ describe decision making "with veto" (Opricovic and Tzeng 2002, 2004, 2007). In real-world MADM problems, assuming $\upsilon = 0.5$ is the most common practice (Opricovic and Tzeng 2002, 2004, 2007; Chang and Hsu 2009; Tzeng and Huang 2011).

7.2.5 Step 5: Ranking the Alternatives

The decision-making ranks the alternatives sorting by the values of group satisfaction (S), individual regret (R), and the VIKOR parameter (Q) in decreasing order. The results produce three ranking lists.

7.2.6 Step 6: Determining the Compromise Solution

The best-ranked alternative by measure Q, denoted by a' can be considered as a compromise solution (a^c) if the following conditions hold true (Opricovic and Tzeng 2002, 2004, 2007):

Condition I. Acceptable advantage:

$$Q[a''] - Q[a'] \geq \frac{1}{m-1} \tag{7.9}$$

in which a'' = the second best (minimum) Q; $Q[a']$ and $Q[a'']$ = the value of the VIKOR parameter for the first and second position in ranking listed by Q, respectively.

Condition II. Acceptable stability in decision-making: The alternative a' must also be the best ranked by the group satisfaction (S) and/or individual regret (R) parameters.

If either of the above conditions is not satisfied, the VIKOR method proposes a set of compromise solutions as follows:

(I) Alternatives a' and a'', if only the second condition does not apply; or
(II) Alternatives $a', a'', \ldots, a^{(k)}$, if only the first condition does not apply, in which k is the maximum number (by the rank in the decreasingly-order sorted alternatives with respect to Q) calculate with the following equation (Opricovic and Tzeng 2002):

$$Q[a^{(k)}] - Q[a'] < \frac{1}{m-1} \tag{7.10}$$

The VIKOR method determines the comprise solution(s) by taking the decision-making strategy into account. The proposed compromise solution(s) yields the maximum group satisfaction (S) and the minimum individual regret (R). These compromise solutions form the basis for negotiations involving the decision-makers' preferences. Hence, the VIKOR method is most suitable for situations in which the decision-maker is either not fully aware or not able to express the stakeholders' preferences at the beginning of the decision-making procedure (Tzeng and Huang 2011).

7.3 Conclusion

The nature of MADM problem dictates the decision-maker must choose an alternative that cannot fully satisfy all the evaluation criteria. In other words, the conflicting nature of the evaluation criteria disables the alternatives to fully outperform the other solution with respect to all the evaluation criteria. Hence, the decision-maker must cope with a set of feasible alternatives that dominate the suboptimal solutions, though these nondominated set of solutions cannot outperform each other. As far as the human behavior is concerned, the decision-maker is most likely to settle for a feasible alternative that behaves most similar to the ideal solution. In light of conflict resolution, the VIKOR method focuses on ranking and selecting from a set of alternatives in the presence of conflicting criteria. The VIKOR method determines a compromise solution that provide the maximum group satisfaction and minimizes the individual regret.

References

Aghajani-Mir, M., Ghazvinei-Tehrani, P., Sulaiman, N.M.N. et al. (2016). Application of TOPSIS and VIKOR improved versions in a multi criteria decision analysis to develop an optimized municipal solid waste management model. *Journal of Environmental Management* 166: 109–115.

Aktan, H.E. and Samut, P.K. (2013). Agricultural performance evaluation by integrating fuzzy AHP and VIKOR methods. *International Journal of Applied Decision Sciences* 6 (4): 324–344.

Ameri, A.A., Pourghasemi, H.R., and Cerda, A. (2018). Erodibility prioritization of sub-watersheds using morphometric parameters analysis and its mapping: a comparison among TOPSIS, VIKOR, SAW, and CF multi-criteria decision making models. *Science of the Total Environment* 613: 1385–1400.

Bozorg-Haddad, O., Solgi, M., and Loáiciga, H.A. (2017). *Meta-Heuristic and Evolutionary Algorithms for Engineering Optimization*. Hoboken, NJ: Wiley.

Chang, T.H. (2014). Fuzzy VIKOR method: a case study of the hospital service evaluation in Taiwan. *Information Sciences* 271: 196–212.

Chang, C.L. and Hsu, C.H. (2009). Multi-criteria analysis via the VIKOR method for prioritizing land-use restraint strategies in the Tseng-Wen reservoir watershed. *Journal of Environmental Management* 90 (11): 3226–3230.

Chen, S.J. and Hwang, C.L. (1992). *Fuzzy Multiple Attribute Decision Making: Methods and Applications*. Heidelberg, Germany: Springer Publication Company.

Debbarma, B., Chakraborti, P., Bose, P.K. et al. (2017). Exploration of PROMETHEE II and VIKOR methodology in a MCDM approach for ascertaining the optimal performance-emission trade-off vantage in a hydrogen-biohol dual fuel endeavour. *Fuel* 210: 922–935.

Duckstein, L. and Opricovic, S. (1980). Multiobjective optimization in river basin development. *Water Resources Research* 16 (1): 14–20.

Gul, M., Celik, E., Aydin, N. et al. (2016). A state of the art literature review of VIKOR and its fuzzy extensions on applications. *Applied Soft Computing* 46: 60–89.

Hwang, C.L. and Yoon, K. (1981). Methods for multiple attribute decision making. In: *Multiple Attribute Decision Making: Lecture Notes in Economics and Mathematical Systems* (eds. C.L. Hwang and K. Yoon), 58–191. Heidelberg, Germany: Springer Publication Company.

Hwang, C.L., Lai, Y.J., and Liu, T.Y. (1993). A new approach for multiple objective decision making. *Computers and Operations Research* 20 (8): 889–899.

Kumar, A., Sah, B., Singh, A.R. et al. (2017). A review of multi criteria decision making (MCDM) towards sustainable renewable energy development. *Renewable and Sustainable Energy Reviews* 69: 596–609.

Liou, J.J., Tsai, C.Y., Lin, R.H., and Tzeng, G.H. (2011). A modified VIKOR multiple-criteria decision method for improving domestic airlines service quality. *Journal of Air Transport Management* 17 (2): 57–61.

Ma, J., Fan, Z.P., and Huang, L.H. (1999). A subjective and objective integrated approach to determine attribute weights. *European Journal of Operational Research* 112 (2): 397–404.

Myerson, R.B. (2013). *Game Theory: Analysis of Conflict*. Cambridge, MA: Harvard University Press.

Opricovic, S. (1998). Multicriteria optimization of civil engineering systems. Ph.D. thesis. Faculty of Civil Engineering, Belgrade, Serbia.

Opricovic, S. and Tzeng, G.H. (2002). Multicriteria planning of post-earthquake sustainable reconstruction. *Computer-Aided Civil and Infrastructure Engineering* 17 (3): 211–220.

Opricovic, S. and Tzeng, G.H. (2004). Compromise solution by MCDM methods: a comparative analysis of VIKOR and TOPSIS. *European Journal of Operational Research* 156 (2): 445–455.

Opricovic, S. and Tzeng, G.H. (2007). Extended VIKOR method in comparison with outranking methods. *European Journal of Operational Research* 178 (2): 514–529.

Osborne, M.J. and Rubinstein, A. (1994). *A Course in Game Theory*. Cambridge, MA: MIT Press.

Sennaroglu, B. and Celebi, G.V. (2018). A military airport location selection by AHP integrated PROMETHEE and VIKOR methods. *Transportation Research Part D: Transport and Environment* 59: 160–173.

Simab, M., Javadi, M.S., and Nezhad, A.E. (2018). Multi-objective programming of pumped-hydro-thermal scheduling problem using normal boundary intersection and VIKOR. *Energy* 143: 854–866.

Tzeng, G.H. and Huang, J.J. (2011). *Multiple Attribute Decision Making: Methods and Applications*. Boca Raton, FL: CRC Press.

Wu, M., Li, C., Fan, J. et al. (2017). Assessing the global productive efficiency of Chinese banks using the cross-efficiency interval and VIKOR. *Emerging Markets Review* 34: 77–86.

Yoon, K. (1987). A reconciliation among discrete compromise solutions. *Journal of the Operational Research Society* 38: 277–286.

Yu, P.L. (1973). A class of solutions for group decision problems. *Management Science* 19 (8): 936–946.

Yu, P.L. (1990). *Forming Winning Strategies: An Integrated Theory of Habitual Domains*. Heidelberg, Germany: Springer Science and Business Media Publication.

Zeleny, M. (1982). *Multiple Criteria Decision Making*. New York, NY: McGraw-Hill Publication.

Zeng, Q.L., Li, D.D., and Yang, Y.B. (2013). VIKOR method with enhanced accuracy for multiple criteria decision making in healthcare management. *Journal of Medical Systems* 37 (2): 9908.

Zolghadr-Asli, B., Bozorg-Haddad, O., and Loáiciga, H.A. (2017). Discussion of 'optimization of phenol removal using Ti/PbO_2 anode with response surface methodology' by C. García-Gómez, J. A. Vidales-Contreras, J. Nápoles-Armenta, and P. Gortáres-Moroyoqui. *Journal of Environmental Engineering* 143 (9): 07017001.

8

ELECTRE

8.1 Introduction

Too often in real-world decision-making, the decision-makers are faced with a situation in which the interests of the stakeholders can only be represented with conflicting set of evaluation criteria, while there is more than one plausible solution that the decision-makers must take under consideration. In most cases no single, obvious, solution can emerge, for these alternatives cannot fully dominate one another in terms of all the evaluation criteria. To overcome this conundrum, the decision-maker must be represented with a solid, logically supported, mathematical framework, provided by the multi-attribute decision-making (MADM) methods. As far as MADM is concerned, the aforementioned dilemma is mathematically expressed as evaluating a set of feasible alternatives, denoted by $A = \{a_1, a_2, \ldots, a_i, \ldots, a_m\}$, where a_i is the ith alternative and m is the number of alternatives under consideration, in terms of a set of predefined evaluation criteria, denoted by $C = \{c_1, c_2, \ldots, c_j, \ldots, c_n\}$, where c_j represents the jth criteria and n denotes the number of evaluation criteria (Yu 1990). Logically, the solution under such circumstances would be the alternative with the most desirable overall performance.

In light of MADM, the decision-makers are provided with a vast range of viable, logic-oriented, frameworks that enable them to perform sound decision-making and secure the interests of stakeholders. One of the schools of thoughts in MADM is referred to as the outranking methods. The basic principle is to omit those alternatives that can be dominated by the other plausible solutions. This leaves the decision-maker with those alternatives that cannot be outranked by others, and thus, can be represented as the most desirable alternatives available to that given problem.

The Elimination et choix traduisant la realité (ELECTRE) family of methods (translates to *elimination and choice expressing reality*) arose in the mid-1960s and flourished by the early 1970s. ELECTRE is one the finest examples of the

A Handbook on Multi-Attribute Decision-Making Methods, First Edition.
Omid Bozorg-Haddad, Babak Zolghadr-Asli, and Hugo A. Loáiciga.

outranking-oriented MADM methods. The members of this family include commonly practiced methods such as ELECTRE I (Benayoun et al. 1966), ELECTRE II (Roy and Bertier 1971), ELECTRE III (Roy 1978), and ELECTRE IV (Roy and Hugonnard 1982), which are rooted in the same core ideology; yet, they differ from one another on how to tackle the challenges of MADM problems, as discussed later in this chapter. However, one of the main features that binds these methods as members of the same family is the twofold stage outranking procedure, namely, aggregation and exploitation (Figueira et al. 2013).

The aggregation phase is the first of the two-state procedure applied by the ELECTRE method to perform the outranking of feasible alternatives. The aggregation phase resorts to the concordance and discordance concepts to compare pairs of alternatives with regard to their performance in terms of the set of evaluation criteria. The implementation of this stage may differ in the ELECTRE methods. For instance, according to the mathematical procedure of ELECTRE I, the alternatives are compared against one another. Evidently, such procedure may not necessarily lead to a complete ranking of the alternatives, but, rather, end with a list of alternatives that cannot fully dominate one another. In fact, the aforementioned notion describes what is known as the choice problematic. On the other hand, in ELECTRE II, III, and IV the alternatives are compared with a reference alternative. The aforementioned procedure that could lead to a complete ranking of the alternatives is referred to as the ranking problematic (Figueira et al. 2013; Govindan and Jepsen 2016).

The second stage of the outranking procedure of the ELECTRE family of methods is to assess the outranking relationships that exists between the set of feasible alternatives. Through the exploitation stage and based on the pair comparisons made on the previous stage, the alternatives are labeled as preferable, indifferent, or incomparable. When an alternative is preferred to another, the former can fully dominate the latter, however, this might not always be the case, because there might be an instance when an alternative cannot outrank the other in terms of all the evaluation criteria. In such a case, these alternatives are indifferent, whereby in terms of the stakeholders' perspective, they are of the same nature. Alternatively, they are considered to be incomparable, where no decisive statement can be made about the outranking relationship of such alternatives (Figueira et al. 2013; Govindan and Jepsen 2016).

The other key distinguishing features of the ELECTRE family is that, akin to the preference ranking organization method for enrichment evaluations (PROMETHEE) methods, this family of methods enables decision-makers to actively participate and collaborate with the methods' solution selection procedure. This mechanism relies on the determination of arbitrarily defined thresholds for each given criterion by the decision-makers and is discussed in the following sections. The next section reviews the history of the ELECTRE family of MADM methods, followed by a description of methodologies in subsequent sections.

8.2 A Brief History of the ELECTRE Family of Methods

In 1965, the société d'économie et de mathématiques appliquées (SEMA), a European consulting company, was striving for a concrete and reliable framework to cope with complex, real-world, MADM problems. Resultantly, méthode d'analyse, de recherche, et de sélection d'activités nouvelles (MARSAN), which was a deviation of weighted sum method (WSM) was presented to the company's board by the commissioned research committee (Figueira et al. 2005). Nevertheless, preliminary results of the method seemed not to appeal to the executive levels of the company, for, its engineers recognized major drawbacks in the taxonomy of the method. By that time, Bernard Roy and his colleges were brought to the project and commissioned to overcome the limitations of the aforementioned mathematical framework. Within the same year, the ELECTRE method, which in the upcoming years would become known as the ELECTRE I was theorized by the commissioned research team. However, it was not until 1966 that the method would appear in a documented form as a company's research report (Benayoun et al. 1966). Several members of the commissioned research team that laid the foundation of the ELECTRE method applied it to cope with MADM problems (e.g. Buffet et al. 1967). Yet, it was the work of Roy (1968) that put the spotlight on the ELECTRE method. From that point onward, based on the requirements of the scholars, researchers, and decision-makers, the core principles of ELECTRE I were revised and extended, accordingly. The aforementioned notion eventually led to the formation of one the most influential family of MADM methods. Aside from the first version of the method (ELECTRE I), the most noteworthy members of this family are ELECTRE II (Roy and Bertier 1971), ELECTRE III (Roy 1978), and ELECTRE IV (Roy and Hugonnard 1982). A more detailed background on the family of ELECTRE methods can be found in Figueira et al. (2005) and Roy and Vanderpooten (1996a,1996b).

The methods of the ELECTRE family share the same core principles and are founded on the base of a common ideology. Nevertheless, they differ in their applications. ELECTRE I, for instance, is applicable to what is referred to as the choice problematic, where the main objective of the decision-makers is not choosing one singular solution, but rather selecting the smallest set of best alternatives. ELECTRE II, III, and IV, on the other hand, feature as their preliminary objective deriving a ranking of the feasible alternatives from the best alternative to the worst one. The aforementioned notion is referred to as the ranking problematic. In order to embark upon such a task, ELECTRE II relies on a concept known as the true criteria, whereas both ELECTRE III and IV use the concept of quasi-criteria. ELECTRE III and ELECTRE IV differ on a number of traits, yet, their main difference is that the latter does not use or employ the concept of weighted criteria. In fact, ELECTRE IV is the only member of the ELECTRE family with such a characteristic (Govindan and Jepsen 2016).

Stepwise descriptions of the main members of the ELECTRE family, namely, ELECTRE I–IV, are presented, along with a history of their applications.

8.3 ELECTRE I

Benayoun et al. (1966) introduced the first member of the ELECTRE family of methods. ELECTRE I does not attempt to find a single solution to an MADM problem, but rather a set that contains alternatives that can outrank other feasible alternatives even though there might not be definitive evidence indicating they can outperform each other. This, in technical terms, is the description of a kernel set of solutions. To derive such a set, ELECTRE I employs the concept of concordance and discordance indexes. In fact, the aforementioned indexes are the core ideology to map out the outranking relationships among the alternatives applied by the other members of the ELECTRE family of methods.

The concordance index, denoted by $CI(a, b)$, measures how much an alternative under consideration, say a, is at least as desirable as the other alternative, say b. This notion can be mathematically expressed as follows:

$$CI(a,b) = \frac{\sum_{j\in\Psi_{(a,b)}} w_j}{\sum_{j=1}^{n} w_j} \tag{8.1}$$

in which w_j = the importance weight of the jth criterion, and $\Psi_{(a,b)}$ = the set of evaluation criteria for which the preference of alternative a is at least as desirable as alternative b. Note that the concordance index ranges from 0 to 1.

The discordance index, denoted by $DI(a, b)$, on the other hand, quantifies the degree to which the comparing alternative (b), is strictly preferred to the alternative under consideration (a), and can be computable as follows:

$$DI(a,b) = \frac{\max\limits_{j\in\Lambda_{(a,b)}} \{[r_{(b,c_j)} - r_{(a,c_j)}]\}}{\max\limits_{x,y\in A} \{[r_{(x,c_j)} - r_{(y,c_j)}]\}} \tag{8.2}$$

in which $r_{(a,c_j)}$ = the normalized performance value of alternative a with respect to the jth criterion, and $\Lambda_{(a,b)}$ = the set of evaluation criteria for which the comparing alternative b is strictly preferred to alternative a. Note that the discordance index also ranges from 0 to 1. The basic principles of the set theory dictate the following expression:

$$A = \psi_{(a,b)} + \Lambda_{(a,b)} \tag{8.3}$$

The performance values of alternatives must be expressed in a dimensionless form ranging from 0 to 1, which requires normalizing the expressed values for alternatives, say the ith alternative with regard to the evaluation criteria, say the jth criterion $[v_{(a_i,c_j)}]$. This is obtained with the following equation:

$$r_{(a_i,c_j)} = \frac{v_{(a_i,c_j)}}{\sum_{j=1}^{n} v_{(a_i,c_j)}} \tag{8.4}$$

Equation (8.4) normalizes the performance values, yet there are other normalizing approaches. A detailed discussion regarding this matter is found in Chapter 2.

Next, the decision-maker must conduct a comparison between the paired alternatives, to see whether an alternative (a) can outperform the comparison alternative (b). In ELECTRE I terms, such a situation can be symbolized by aOb, which indicates that alternative a can outperform alternative b. If the conditions could not be obtained, that is if alternative a cannot outperform alternative b, then $a \emptyset b$ would be used to symbolize such a situation. In light of the aggregation stage of ELECTRE I, the following rule would be the guideline for such comparisons:

$$aOb, \text{ iff } CI(a,b) \geq CI^* \text{ and } DI(a,b) \leq DI^* \tag{8.5}$$

in which CI^* and DI^* = the concordance and discordance levels, respectively, which are arbitrarily defined thresholds by the decision-makers. The concordance level makes sure that the strength of the concordance index is considerable, while the discordance level represents the threshold level that surpassing it by the discordance index invalidates the outperforming relationship among the alternatives. It is recommended that the value of the concordance level falls within the range of $[0.5, 1 - \underset{j}{Min}(w_j)]$ (Figueira et al. 2005).

A central principle to bear in mind is that the hypothetical alternative a outperforming alternative b (aOb) does not necessarily mean that alternative a outranks alternative b, because alternative b may also outperform alternative a. Table 8.1 presents a guideline to the exploitation stage of the ELECTRE I method.

Table 8.1 The guideline for the exploitation stage of ELECTRE I.

Outperforming relations	bOa	$b \emptyset a$
aOb	a and b are **indifferent**	a **outranks** b
$a \emptyset b$	b **outranks** a	a and b are **incomparable**

The ELECTRE I method has been successfully employed in banking (Amiri et al. 2008), ecotourism planning (Ok et al. 2011), eutrophication assessment (Moriki and Karydis 1994), facility layout (Ashayeri and Rongen 1997), human resources management (Wu and Chen 2011), investment planning (de Almeida 2007), land reclamation (Nijkamp 1975), machine selection (Ramos et al. 2010), production management (Vahdani et al. 2013), supplier selection (Hatami-Marbini and Tavana 2011), water resources management (David and Duckstein 1976), and wastewater management (Tecle et al. 1988). Additionally, this method has been linked with other logical frameworks and mathematical algorithms to expand its capabilities. Compromised programming (Duckstein and Opricovic 1980), cooperative game theory (Gershon and Duckstein 1983), fuzzy logic theory (Wu and Chen 2011), and geographical information systems (GISs) (Floc'hlay and Plottu 1998) are few examples of applications.

ELECTRE I is a valid MADM method with recognized potential; yet, it may not find a set of solutions for some particular MADM problems. Furthermore, there may be cases when decision-makers must rank the feasible alternatives from best to worst. The ELECTRE II was introduced to achieve such ranking.

8.4 ELECTRE II

ELECTRE II's (Roy and Bertier 1971) preliminary objective is to derive the complete ranking of alternatives by overcoming the challenge of indifference relations among alternatives and preventing circuits in the set of solutions (Hokkanen et al. 1995). To that end, the concepts of strong and weak outranking relations were added to the decision-making procedure. In addition, few procedural frameworks of the ELECTRE method were adjusted to make it more compatible with these newly defined concepts. The resulting ELECTRE II was a promising MADM method that ranks all the alternatives.

Since then ELECTRE II demonstrated a great potential in coping with real-world MADM problems. Application in biochemical engineering (Fichefet et al. 1984), farm forestry management (Jeffreys 2004), investment strategies (Alexopoulos et al. 2012), machine selection (Ramos et al. 2010), municipal design (Frenette et al. 2010), policy making (Bona et al. 1979), portfolio selection (Martel et al. 1988), sediment management (Alvarez-Guerra et al. 2009), software evaluation (Vlahavas et al. 1999), supplier selection (Alencar et al. 2010), tourism planning (Andrades-Caldito et al. 2013), and water resources development plans (Gershon et al. 1982) are just a few examples of the successful implementation of ELECTRE II method. Furthermore, this method has been linked with other mathematical and conceptual framework to extend its capabilities (e.g. cooperative game theory (Gershon and Duckstein 1983)).

ELECTRE II is centered around the concept of outranking. In light of the terminology of ELECTRE II, the set of evaluation criteria is decomposed into three, nonoverlapping, subsets that for a set of positively valued evaluation criteria is defined as follows:

$$C^{+}(a,b) = \{c_j \mid r_{(a,c_j)} > r_{(b,c_j)}\} \tag{8.6}$$

$$C^{=}(a,b) = \{c_j \mid r_{(a,c_j)} = r_{(b,c_j)}\} \tag{8.7}$$

$$C^{-}(a,b) = \{c_j \mid r_{(a,c_j)} < r_{(b,c_j)}\} \tag{8.8}$$

The principles of set theory dictate the following condition must hold:

$$C = C^{+}(a,b) + C^{=}(a,b) + C^{-}(a,b) \forall a, b \in A \tag{8.9}$$

With regard to the newly defined subsets of the evaluation criteria the following variables are defined:

$$W^{+}(a,b) = \sum_{j \in C^{+}(a,b)} w_j \tag{8.10}$$

$$W^{=}(a,b) = \sum_{j \in C^{=}(a,b)} w_j \tag{8.11}$$

$$W^{-}(a,b) = \sum_{j \in C^{-}(a,b)} w_j \tag{8.12}$$

Note that, according to Eq. (8.9), the following holds:

$$W^{+}(a,b) + W^{=}(a,b) + W^{-}(a,b) = \sum_{j=1}^{n} w_j \quad \forall a, b \in A \tag{8.13}$$

Consequently, for every pair of feasible alternatives, say *a* and *b*, the concordance index (Eq. (8.1)), is redefined as follows:

$$CI(a,b) = \frac{W^{+}(a,b) + W^{=}(a,b)}{W^{+}(a,b) + W^{=}(a,b) + W^{-}(a,b)} \tag{8.14}$$

Similarly, the discordance index (Eq. (8.2)) is expressed by the following redefined equation:

$$DI(a,b) = \frac{\underset{j \in C^{-}(a,b)}{Max}\{[r_{(b,c_j)} - r_{(a,c_j)}]\}}{\underset{x,y \in A}{Max}\{[r_{(x,c_j)} - r_{(y,c_j)}]\}} \tag{8.15}$$

In this stage, however, unlike its predecessor ELECTRE I, this method requires the decision-makers to define two levels of concordance and discordance, namely strong and weak thresholds. For the concordance levels, these arbitrarily defined thresholds must meet the following condition:

$$0 \le CI^{*}_{weak} \le CI^{*} \le CI^{*}_{strong} \le 1 \tag{8.16}$$

in which CI^*_{weak} and CI^*_{strong} = the weak and strong concordance levels, respectively. Any two arbitrary defined numbers that satisfy the conditions introduced in Eq. (8.16) can be represented as the weak and strong concordance levels. Nevertheless, it is recommended for these concordance levels to fall in the range $[0.5, 1 - \underset{j}{Min}(w_j)]$ (Figueira et al. 2005).

Likewise, the weak and strong discordance levels are defined by the decision-makers so that the following is obtained:

$$0 \leq DI^*_{strong} \leq DI^* \leq DI^*_{weak} \leq 1 \tag{8.17}$$

in which DI^*_{weak} and DI^*_{strong} = the weak and strong discordance levels, respectively.

The final step of the aggregation stage of ELECTRE II requires evaluating the outperforming of paired alternatives. As stated earlier, an additional constraint was added to the evaluation process so that the circuit effects are omitted. Consequently, for alternative a to strongly outperform alternative b (aSb), the following must hold:

$$aSb, \text{ iff } CI(a,b) \geq CI^*_{strong} \text{ and } DI(a,b) \leq DI^*_{strong} \text{ and } CI(a,b) \geq CI(b,a) \tag{8.18}$$

and for the alternative a to weakly outperform alternative b ($a\text{W}b$), the following condition must hold:

$$a\text{W}b, \text{ iff } CI(a,b) \geq CI^*_{weak} \text{ and } DI(a,b) \leq DI^*_{weak} \text{ and } CI(a,b) \geq CI(b,a) \tag{8.19}$$

The exploitation stage of ELECTRE II, through which the relations of the alternatives are evaluated, is a two-step iterative process (Hokkanen et al. 1995). The first step requires the decision-makers to rank the alternatives in a descending order. The aforementioned step is achieved by the following steps (Hokkanen et al. 1995):

I. Derive the nondominated set Θ, which cannot be strongly outperformed by any feasible alternative in A.
II. Determine the first class of alternatives, denoted by Θ' in a descending ranked list, in which none of its members can be weakly outperformed by the other feasible alternatives in Θ.
III. Remove the ranked alternatives in Θ' and return to step II until all the alternatives in Θ are fully ranked.
IV. Return to step I and repeat the process for the remaining members of the feasible alternatives in $A\text{–}\Theta$, until all alternatives are ranked in a descending order.

The second step requires the decision-makers to form an ascending ranked list of alternatives, which can be obtained through the following stepwise instruction (Hokkanen et al. 1995):

I. Derive the dominated set Ξ, which cannot strongly outperform any feasible alternative in A.
II. Determine the first class of alternatives, denoted by Ξ' in an ascending ranked list, in which none of its members can weakly outperform the other feasible alternatives in Ξ.
III. Remove the ranked alternatives in Ξ' and return to step II until all the alternatives in Ξ are fully ranked.
IV. Return to step I and repeat the process for the remaining members of the feasible alternatives in $A-\Xi$, until all alternatives are ranked in an ascending order.

The interaction of the descending and the ascending ranked list of alternatives is resolved by assigning the final ranking position of each alternative as the average of its position in the two ranked lists (Hokkanen et al. 1995).

To this point, all the introduced members of the ELECTRE family employ the true preference values in their methodology. However, ELECTRE III introduces the concept of quasi-criteria, which enables the decision-makers to account for the uncertainties arising from the lack of knowledge and ill-information regarding the problem at hand, a common trait of most real-word MADM problems (Roy and Vincke 1984).

8.5 ELECTRE III

Recall ELECTRE I provides the partial ranks of alternatives, while the complete ranked list of alternatives is the out-product of ELECTRE II. These two members of the ranking family share a basic perspective in dealing with MADM problems, which is using the "true" criteria for their evaluation procedures. This notion indicates that any difference in the performance as measured by $r_{(a_i,c_j)}$ implies a corresponding preference of these alternatives. Introduction of the quasi-criterion by Roy (1978), which was an alternative to the basic perspective of ELECTRE I and II, laid the foundation for the new member of this outranking family of methods, namely, ELECTRE III.

ELECTRE III shares the basic procedural framework with ELECTRE II, yet these methods differ in one major feature, which is the employment of quasi-criteria by ELECTRE III. The performance evaluation is the basis for alternative selection in both methods. Yet, according to ELECTRE III, the difference between the performance of alternatives does not necessarily indicate that an alternative can and should outrank others. In other words, in the interpretation of the differences in performance values, one must consider that these are relative notions with regard to the expectations of the decision-makers. The quasi-criterion, as the major contribution of ELECTRE III, is a viable, pragmatic answer to the aforementioned notion. The quasi-criteria is a type of threshold upon which the decision-makers decide whether a difference in the performance values is meaningful and must be accounted for or, alternatively, it is not meaningless and, thus, must be neglected.

ELECTRE III defines three relationships for a pair of alternatives, say a and b, as follows:

$$r_{(b,c_j)} + \kappa_j[r_{(b,c_j)}] < r_{(a,c_j)} \Leftrightarrow aSb \tag{8.20}$$

$$r_{(b,c_j)} + \varpi_j[r_{(b,c_j)}] < r_{(b,c_j)} < r_{(a,c_j)} + \kappa_j[r_{(b,c_j)}] \Leftrightarrow a\text{W}b \tag{8.21}$$

$$r_{(b,c_j)} < r_{(a,c_j)} < r_{(b,c_j)} + \varpi_j[r_{(b,c_j)}] \Leftrightarrow aIb \tag{8.22}$$

in which $\kappa_j[]$ = the preference threshold function for the jth criterion, and $\varpi_j[]$ = the indifference threshold function for the jth criterion. In defining the preference and indifference threshold functions, for a situation where $r_{(b,c_j)} < r_{(a,c_j)}$ the following three constraints must be encountered for (Tzeng and Huang 2011):

$$r_{(b,c_j)} + \kappa_j[r_{(b,c_j)}] < r_{(a,c_j)} + \kappa_j[r_{(a,c_j)}] \tag{8.23}$$

$$r_{(b,c_j)} + \varpi_j[r_{(b,c_j)}] < r_{(a,c_j)} + \varpi_j[r_{(a,c_j)}] \tag{8.23}$$

$$\varpi_j[r_{(a_i,c_j)}] < \kappa_j[r_{(a_i,c_j)}]\forall i,j \tag{8.24}$$

Roy (1978) recommended the following linear formulations for the preference and indifference thresholds:

$$\kappa_j[r_{(a,c_j)}] = \eta_\kappa r_{(a,c_j)} + \omega_\kappa \tag{8.25}$$

$$\varpi_j[r_{(a,c_j)}] = \eta_\varpi r_{(a,c_j)} + \omega_\varpi \tag{8.26}$$

in which η_κ and η_ϖ = the slope of the preference and indifference threshold functions, respectively; and ω_κ and ω_ϖ = the intercept of the preference and indifference threshold functions, respectively. The slope and intercepts for the preference and indifference functions are calibrated by the decision-makers (Roy et al. 1986).

The notions of concordance and discordance indexes must be adjusted, also. Consequently, the concordance index for a hypothetical pair of alternatives, say a and b, are quantified as follows (Roy 1978):

$$CI(a,b) = \frac{\sum_{j=1}^{n}[w_j \times CI_j(a,b)]}{\sum_{j=1}^{n} w_j} \tag{8.27}$$

in which $CI_j(a, b)$ = the concordance value for the pair of alternatives a and b, with regard to the jth criterion, which is defined as follows (Belton and Stewart 2002):

$$CI_j(a,b) = \begin{cases} 1 & \text{if} \quad r_{(b,c_j)} \leq r_{(a,c_j)} + \varpi_j[r_{(a,c_j)}] \\ \frac{r_{(a,c_j)} - r_{(b,c_j)} + \kappa_j[r_{(a,c_j)}]}{\kappa_j[r_{(a,c_j)}] - \varpi_j[r_{(a,c_j)}]} & \text{if } r_{(a,c_j)} + \varpi_j[r_{(a,c_j)}] < r_{(b,c_j)} < r_{(a,c_j)} + \kappa_j[r_{(a,c_j)}] \\ 0 & \text{if} \quad r_{(a,c_j)} + \kappa_j[r_{(a,c_j)}] \leq r_{(b,c_j)} \end{cases} \tag{8.28}$$

In light of the new notions introduced in ELECTRE III, the discordance value for the alternatives a and b with regard to the jth criterion $[DI_j(a, b)]$ are defined as follows (Belton and Stewart 2002):

$$DI_j(a,b) = \begin{cases} 1 & \text{if} \quad r_{(a,c_j)} + \tau_j[r_{(a,c_j)}] \leq r_{(b,c_j)} \\ \frac{r_{(b,c_j)} - r_{(a,c_j)} - \kappa_j[r_{(a,c_j)}]}{\tau_j[r_{(a,c_j)}] - \kappa_j[r_{(a,c_j)}]} & \text{if } r_{(a,c_j)} + \kappa_j[r_{(a,c_j)}] < r_{(b,c_j)} < r_{(a,c_j)} + \tau_j[r_{(a,c_j)}] \\ 0 & \text{if} \quad r_{(b,c_j)} \leq r_{(a,c_j)} + \kappa_j[r_{(a,c_j)}] \end{cases} \tag{8.29}$$

in which $\tau_j[]$ = the veto threshold function for the jth criterion. The following formulation for the veto function was recommended (Roy 1978):

$$\tau_j[r_{(a,c_j)}] = \eta_\tau r_{(a,c_j)} + \omega_\tau \tag{8.30}$$

in which η_τ = the slope of the veto threshold function, and ω_τ = the intercept of the veto of the threshold function. In defining the quasi-criteria (preference, indifference, and veto threshold functions), the following constraint must be held:

$$\varpi_j[] < \kappa_j[] < \upsilon_j[] \forall j \tag{8.31}$$

In the final step of the aggregation stage ELECTRE III proposes the concept of the credibility index. The credibility of alternative a with regard to alternative b, denoted by $Cr(a, b)$, is expressed as follows (Roy 1978):

$$Cr(a,b) = \begin{cases} CI(a,b) \text{ if } DI_j(a,b) \leq CI(a,b) & \forall j \\ CI(a,b) \times \prod_{j \in J(a,b)} \left[\frac{1 - DI_j(a,b)}{1 - CI(a,b)}\right] & \text{else} \end{cases} \tag{8.32}$$

in which $J(a, b)$ = the set of criteria, in which $DI_j(a, b) > CI(a, b)$ is calculated.

The interpretation of the credibility index must be carefully made before making any conclusions. The best interpretation of the credibility index is as an indicator of the order of magnitude of the support for the claim that alternative a can outperform alternative b (Roy and Bouyssou 1993). In other words, the notion of

$Cr(a, b) > Cr(c, d)$ should not necessarily be interpreted as a sign that there is stronger evidence that a outperforms b than that of c outperforming d. The imprecise nature of the credibility index makes such conclusions futile unless there is a strong evidence in support of such notion (Belton and Stewart 2002). In that regard, assume that $Cr(a, b) = \lambda$. Accordingly, the conclusion that alternative a can outperform alternative b may be viewed as more firmly grounded than that of alternative c outperforming alternative d if $Cr(c, d) \leq \lambda - \iota$, where $\iota = 0.3 - 0.15\lambda$ (Roy and Bouyssou 1993; Belton and Stewart 2002). This notion helps decision-makers in determining the rank mapping required in the exploitation stage of the ELECTRE III method. The decision-maker attempts to determine whether alternative a is λ-preferred to alternative b. This can be mathematically tested as follows (Roy and Bouyssou 1993; Belton and Stewart 2002):

$$(1 - \iota) \times Cr(a, b) > Cr(b, a) \text{ and } Cr(a, b) > \lambda \tag{8.33}$$

The exploitation stage of ELECTRE III through which the relations of the alternatives are evaluated is a two-step iterative process (Belton and Stewart 2002; Tzeng and Huang 2011). The first step requires decision-makers to rank the alternatives in a descending order. The aforementioned step is achieved by the following stepwise instruction (Belton and Stewart 2002; Tzeng and Huang 2011):

I. Determine the maximum value of the credibility index, $\lambda_{max} = \text{Max}\, Cr(a, b)$, where the maximization is taken over the current set of feasible alternatives (A).
II. Set $\lambda = \lambda_{max} - (0.3 - 0.15\lambda_{max})$.
III. For each alternative determine its λ-strength, namely the number of alternatives in the current set to which it is λ-preferred.
IV. For each alternative determine its λ-weakness, namely the number of alternatives in the current set which are λ-preferred.
V. Compute the qualification of each alternative, which is its λ-strength minus its λ-weakness.
VI. The set of alternatives having the largest qualification is called the first distillate, Θ'.
VII. In cases where Θ' has more than one member, return to step I and repeat the process on the set Θ' until all its members have been classified.
VIII. Return to step I and repeat the process for the remaining members of the set of feasible alternatives ($A - \Theta'$), until all alternatives are ranked in a descending order.

The second step requires the decision-makers to form an ascending ranked list of alternatives, which can be obtained through the following steps (Belton and Stewart 2002; Tzeng and Huang 2011):

I. Determine the maximum value of the credibility index, $\lambda_{max} = \text{Max}\, Cr(a, b)$, where the maximization is taken over the current set of feasible alternatives.
II. Set $\lambda = \lambda_{max} - (0.3 - 0.15\lambda_{max})$.
III. For each alternative, determine its λ-strength, namely the number of alternatives in the current set to which it is λ-preferred.
IV. For each alternative, determine its λ-weakness, namely the number of alternatives in the current set which are λ-preferred to.
V. Compute the qualification of each alternative, which is its λ-strength minus its λ-weakness.
VI. The set of alternatives having the lowest qualification is called the first distillate, Ξ'.
VII. In cases where Ξ' has more than one member, return to step I and repeat the process on the set Ξ' until all its members have been classified.
VIII. Return to step I and repeat the process for the remaining members of the set of feasible alternatives $(A-\Xi')$, until all alternatives are ranked in a descending order.

The final ranking position of each alternative is assigned as the average of its position in these separate lists (Belton and Stewart 2002; Tzeng and Huang 2011).

ELECTRE III has been applied in many fields such as banking (Rigopoulos et al. 2008), economic assessment (Augusto et al. 2008), ecotourism planning (Ok et al. 2011), energy management (Barda et al. 1990), facility layout (Aiello et al. 2006), groundwater management (Duckstein et al. 1994), human resources management (Certa et al. 2009), irrigation systems (Raju et al. 2000), market forecasting (Xu and Ouenniche 2012), public transportation operation (Roy et al. 1986), water supply systems (Roy et al. 1992), and wastewater management (Carriço et al. 2012) and revealed its great potential to cope with real-world MADM problems. In addition, ELECTRE III has been linked with other mathematical frameworks to expand its capabilities (e.g. fuzzy logic theory (Czyżak and Skowiiński 1996), genetic algorithm (GA; Leyva-Lopez and Fernandez-Gonzalez 2003), GIS (Proulx et al. 2007), Monte-Carlo method (El Hanandeh and El-Zein 2010)).

In spite of its capacities, ELECTRE III decision-makers often find it difficult to justify the complexity of this method. In addition, this method heavily relies on the decision-makers' ability to calibrate the methodology with regard to the specific characteristics of the MADM problem at hand. However, the aforementioned notions can be the source through which considerable errors would beset the decision-making process. ELECTRE IV (Roy and Hugonnard 1982) was introduced as an answer to overcome these shortcomings.

8.6 ELECTRE IV

ELECTRE III has proven to be an effective framework that enables the decision-makers to cope with real-world MADM problems; yet, there were cases in which the decision-makers could not justify the complexity of this method. Weight assignment to each evaluation criteria, for example, was one of those procedures that could greatly influence the final outcome. ELECTRE III provides no guidance for this procedure, and weight assignment had been completely left to the decision-makers. ELECTRE IV (Roy and Hugonnard 1982) assumes equal weights for the evaluation criterion, making the weight assignment a nonissue. Furthermore, ELECTRE IV categorizes the relations among alternatives into five classes of dominance. For a pair of alternatives a and b, these relations are defined from the most powerful domination to the weakest, as follows (Roy and Hugonnard 1982; Tzeng and Huang 2011):

I. *Quasi-Dominance*: Alternative a has a quasi-dominance over alternative b, if and only if, the following could be obtained:
   - For every criterion, alternative a is either preferred or indifferent to alternative b; and
   - The number of criteria for which the performance of alternative b is better than that of alternative a (b staying indifferent to a) is strictly inferior to the number of criteria for which the performance of alternative a is better than that of alternative b.

II. *Canonic Dominance*: Alternative a has a canonic dominance over alternative b, if and only if, the following could be obtained:
   - For no criterion, alternative b is strictly preferred to alternative a;
   - The number of criteria for which alternative b is weakly preferred to alternative a is inferior or equal to the number of criteria for which alternative a is strictly preferred to alternative b; and
   - The number of criteria for which the performance of alternative b is better than that of alternative a is strictly inferior to the number of criteria for which the performance of alternative a is better than that of alternative b.

III. *Pseudo-Dominance*: Alternative a has a pseudo-dominance over alternative b, if and only if, the following could be obtained:
   - For no criterion, alternative b is strictly preferred to alternative a; and
   - The number of criteria for which alternative b is weakly preferred to alternative a is inferior or equal to the number of criteria for which alternative a is strictly or weakly preferred to alternative b.

IV. *Subdominance*: Alternative a has a subdominance over alternative b, if and only if, the following could be obtained:
  - For no criterion, alternative b is strictly preferred to alternative a.

V. *Veto dominance*: Alternative a has a veto dominance over alternative b, if and only if, the following could be obtained:
  - Either for no criterion alternative b is strictly preferred to alternative a, or alternative b is strictly preferred to alternative a for only one criterion, but this criterion does not veto the outranking of alternative b by alternative a; and
  - Alternative a is strictly preferred to alternative b for at least half of the evaluation criteria.

Notice that apart from the weighting assignments to the evaluation criteria, the procedure of ELECTRE IV is identical to ELECTRE III's.

ELECTRE IV has proven itself as an effective MADM method that can help the decision-makers with the process of sound decision-making in a wide range of fields, that include energy management (Climaco et al. 1990), environmental protection planning (Silva et al. 2010), financial management (Gomes and Rangel 2009), irrigation systems (Raju et al. 2000), public transportation operation (Roy and Hugonnard 1982), supplier selection (Alencar and de Almeida 2008), wastewater management (Hokkanen and Salminen 1997).

8.7 Conclusion

Sparked in the mid-1960s and bloomed by the early 1970s, the family of ELECTRE methods uses the concept of outranking to evaluate and rank a set of feasible alternatives. Four main members of this family of compensatory, outranking-oriented methods, are ELECTRE I, which can present the decision-makers with a partial preorder of alternatives, ELECTRE II, which leads to the complete ranked list of alternatives, ELECTRE III, which employs quasi-criterion for coping with real-world MADM problems, and ELECTRE IV, which was a simplified version of ELECTRE III. The family of ELECTRE methods is based on a two-stage procedure, namely, aggregation and exploitation. In the first stage, these methods attempt to evaluate the relations between all the possible paired alternatives in terms of determining whether these alternatives can outperform one another. In light of the established relations among the alternatives, the second stage of decision-making derives the ranked list of alternatives by separating the dominating alternatives from the dominated ones. Those methods that would lead to a partially ranked list of alternatives are ideal to deal with MADM problems that are referred to as choice problematic (e.g. ELECTRE I). On the other hand, methods that derive the complete ranking of alternatives cope with situations called ranking problematic (e.g. ELECTRE II, III, and IV). Through time and numerous applications, this family of methods has proven its potential to solve complex, real-world, MADM problems.

References

Aiello, G., Enea, M., and Galante, G. (2006). A multi-objective approach to facility layout problem by genetic search algorithm and ELECTRE method. *Robotics and Computer-Integrated Manufacturing* 22 (5–6): 447–455.

Alencar, L.H. and de Almeida, A.T. (2008). Multicriteria decision group model for the selection of suppliers. *Pesquisa Operacional* 28 (2): 321–337.

Alencar, L.H., de Almeida, A.T., and Morais, D.C. (2010). A multicriteria group decision model aggregating the preferences of decision-makers based on ELECTRE methods. *Pesquisa Operacional* 30 (3): 687–702.

Alexopoulos, S., Siskos, Y., Tsotsolas, N., and Hristodoulakis, N. (2012). Evaluating strategic actions for a Greek publishing company. *Operational Research* 12 (2): 253–269.

de Almeida, A.T. (2007). Multicriteria decision model for outsourcing contracts selection based on utility function and ELECTRE method. *Computers and Operations Research* 34 (12): 3569–3574.

Alvarez-Guerra, M., Viguri, J.R., and Voulvoulis, N. (2009). A multicriteria-based methodology for site prioritisation in sediment management. *Environment International* 35 (6): 920–930.

Amiri, M., Nosratian, N.E., Jamshidi, A., and Kazemi, A. (2008). Developing a new ELECTRE method with interval data in multiple attribute decision making problems. *Journal of Applied Sciences* 8 (22): 4017–4028.

Andrades-Caldito, L., Sánchez-Rivero, M., and Pulido-Fernández, J.I. (2013). Differentiating competitiveness through tourism image assessment: an application to Andalusia (Spain). *Journal of Travel Research* 52 (1): 68–81.

Ashayeri, J. and Rongen, J.M. (1997). Central distribution in Europe: a multi-criteria approach to location selection. *The International Journal of Logistics Management* 8 (1): 97–109.

Augusto, M., Lisboa, J., Yasin, M., and Figueira, J.R. (2008). Benchmarking in a multiple criteria performance context: an application and a conceptual framework. *European Journal of Operational Research* 184 (1): 244–254.

Barda, O.H., Dupuis, J., and Lencioni, P. (1990). Multicriteria location of thermal power plants. *European Journal of Operational Research* 45 (2–3): 332–346.

Belton, V. and Stewart, T. (2002). *Multiple Criteria Decision Analysis: An Integrated Approach*. Boston, USA: Springer Publishing Agency.

Benayoun, R., Roy, B., and Sussman, B. (1966). ELECTRE: Une méthode pour guider le choix en présence de points de vue multiples. In: *Note de travail 49, SEMA-METRA International*. Paris, France: Direction Scientifique.

Bona, B., Merighi, D., and Ostanello, A. (1979). A model of public resources allocation for social investments on urban districts: the case of a Northern Italian metropolitan area. *IEEE Transactions on Systems, Man, and Cybernetics* 9 (9): 459–464.

Buffet, P., Gremy, J.P., Marc, M., and Sussmann, B. (1967). Peut-on choisir en tenant compte de critères multiples? Une méthode (ELECTRE) et trois applications. *Revue Metra* 6 (2): 283–316.

Carriço, N., Covas, D.I.C., Almeida, M.C. et al. (2012). Prioritization of rehabilitation interventions for urban water assets using multiple criteria decision-aid methods. *Water Science and Technology* 66 (5): 1007–1014.

Certa, A., Enea, M., Galante, G., and La Fata, C.M. (2009). Multi-objective human resources allocation in R&D projects planning. *International Journal of Production Research* 47 (13): 3503–3523.

Climaco, J., Martins, A.G., and Almeida, A.D. (1990). On the use of multicriteria optimisation for electric energy planning. *International Journal of Global Energy Issues* 2 (3): 194–203.

Czyżak, P. and Skowiiński, R. (1996). Possibilistic construction of fuzzy outranking relation for multiple-criteria ranking. *Fuzzy Sets and Systems* 81 (1): 123–131.

David, L. and Duckstein, L. (1976). Multi-criterion ranking of alternative long-range water resource systems. *Journal of the American Water Resources Association* 12 (4): 731–754.

Duckstein, L. and Opricovic, S. (1980). Multiobjective optimization in river basin development. *Water Resources Research* 16 (1): 14–20.

Duckstein, L., Treichel, W., and Magnouni, S.E. (1994). Ranking ground-water management alternatives by multicriterion analysis. *Journal of Water Resources Planning and Management* 120 (4): 546–565.

El Hanandeh, A. and El-Zein, A. (2010). The development and application of multi-criteria decision-making tool with consideration of uncertainty: the selection of a management strategy for the bio-degradable fraction in the municipal solid waste. *Bioresource Technology* 101 (2): 555–561.

Fichefet, J., Leclercq, J.P., Beyne, P., and Rousselet-Piette, F.F. (1984). Microcomputer-assisted identification of bacteria and multicriteria decision models. *Computers and Operations Research* 11 (4): 361–372.

Figueira, J., Greco, S., and Ehrgott, M. (2005). *Multiple Criteria Decision Analysis: State of the Art Surveys*. New York, NY: Springer.

Figueira, J.R., Greco, S., Roy, B., and Słowiński, R. (2013). An overview of ELECTRE methods and their recent extensions. *Journal of Multi-Criteria Decision Analysis* 20 (1–2): 61–85.

Floc'hlay, B. and Plottu, E. (1998). Democratic evaluation: from empowerment evaluation to public decision-making. *Evaluation* 4 (3): 261–277.

Frenette, C.D., Beauregard, R., Abi-Zeid, I. et al. (2010). Multicriteria decision analysis applied to the design of light-frame wood wall assemblies. *Journal of Building Performance Simulation* 3 (1): 33–52.

Gershon, M. and Duckstein, L. (1983). Multiobjective approaches to river basin planning. *Journal of Water Resources Planning and Management* 109 (1): 13–28.

Gershon, M., Duckstein, L., and McAniff, R. (1982). Multiobjective river basin planning with qualitative criteria. *Water Resources Research* 18 (2): 193–202.

Gomes, L.F.A.M. and Rangel, L.A.D. (2009). Using ELECTRE IV in the promotion of social and economic development: a case study in Rio de Janeiro. *Foundations of Computing and Decision Sciences* 34 (3): 155–172.

Govindan, K. and Jepsen, M.B. (2016). ELECTRE: a comprehensive literature review on methodologies and applications. *European Journal of Operational Research* 250 (1): 1–29.

Hatami-Marbini, A. and Tavana, M. (2011). An extension of the ELECTRE I method for group decision-making under a fuzzy environment. *Omega* 39 (4): 373–386.

Hokkanen, J. and Salminen, P. (1997). ELECTRE III and IV decision aids in an environmental problem. *Journal of Multi-Criteria Decision Analysis* 6 (4): 215–226.

Hokkanen, J., Salminen, P., Rossi, E., and Ettala, M. (1995). The choice of a solid waste management system using the ELECTRE II decision-aid method. *Waste Management and Research* 13 (2): 175–193.

Jeffreys, I. (2004). The use of compensatory and non-compensatory multi-criteria analysis for small-scale forestry. *Small-Scale Forest Economics, Management and Policy* 3 (1): 99–117.

Leyva-Lopez, J.C. and Fernandez-Gonzalez, E. (2003). A new method for group decision support based on ELECTRE III methodology. *European Journal of Operational Research* 148 (1): 14–27.

Martel, J.M., Khoury, N.T., and Bergeron, M. (1988). An application of a multicriteria approach to portfolio comparisons. *Journal of the Operational Research Society* 39 (7): 617–628.

Moriki, A. and Karydis, M. (1994). Application of multicriteria choice-methods in assessing eutrophication. *Environmental Monitoring and Assessment* 33 (1): 1–18.

Nijkamp, P. (1975). A multicriteria analysis for project evaluation: economic-ecological evaluation of a land reclamation project. *Papers in Regional Science* 35 (1): 87–111.

Ok, K., Okan, T., and Yilmaz, E. (2011). A comparative study on activity selection with multi-criteria decision-making techniques in ecotourism planning. *Scientific Research and Essays* 6 (6): 1417–1427.

Proulx, F., Rodriguez, M.J., Sérodes, J., and Bouchard, C. (2007). A methodology for identifying vulnerable locations to taste and odour problems in a drinking water system. *Water Science and Technology* 55 (5): 177–183.

Raju, K.S., Duckstein, L., and Arondel, C. (2000). Multicriterion analysis for sustainable water resources planning: a case study in Spain. *Water Resources Management* 14 (6): 435–456.

Ramos, J.M., García, D.L., Gómez-Bravo, F., and Morón, A.B. (2010). Application of multicriteria decision-making techniques to manoeuvre planning in nonholonomic robots. *Expert Systems with Applications* 37 (5): 3962–3976.

Rigopoulos, G., Psarras, J., and Askounis, D. (2008). Fuzzy assignment procedure based on categories boundaries. *American Journal of Applied Sciences* 5 (7): 844–851.

Roy, B. (1968). Classement et choix en présence de points de vue multiples. *Revue Franjaise D'Informatique et de Recherche Opérationnelle* 2 (8): 57–75.

Roy, B. (1978). ELECTRE III: Un algorithme de classement fondé sur une représentation floue des préférences en présence de critères multiples. *Cahiers du Centre d'Etudes de Recherche Opérationnelle* 20 (1): 3–24.

Roy, B. and Bertier, P. (1971). La méthode ELECTRE II. In: *Note de travail 142, SEMA-METRA, Metra International*. Paris, France: Direction Scientifique.

Roy, B. and Bouyssou, D. (1993). *Aide multicritère à la décision: Méthodes et cas*. Paris, France: Economica.

Roy, B. and Hugonnard, J.C. (1982). Ranking of suburban line extension projects on the Paris metro system by a multicriteria method. *Transportation Research Part A: General* 16 (4): 301–312.

Roy, B. and Vanderpooten, D. (1996a). The European school of MCDA: emergence, basic features and current works. *Journal of Multi-Criteria Decision Analysis* 5 (1): 22–38.

Roy, B. and Vanderpooten, D. (1996b). Response to F.A. Lootsma's comments on our paper 'The European school of MCDA: emergence, basic features and current works'. *Journal of Multi-Criteria Decision Analysis* 5 (2): 165–166.

Roy, B. and Vincke, P. (1984). Relational systems of preference with one or more pseudo-criteria: some new concepts and results. *Management Science* 30 (11): 1323–1335.

Roy, B., Présent, D.M., and Silhol, D. (1986). A programming method for determining which Paris metro stations should be renovated. *European Journal of Operational Research* 24 (2): 318–334.

Roy, B., Slowinski, R., and Treichel, W. (1992). Multicriteria programming of water supply systems for rural areas. *Journal of the American Water Resources Association* 28 (1): 13–31.

Silva, V.B., Morais, D.C., and De Almeida, A.T. (2010). Prioritizing complex issues of hydrographic basin committees by group decision approach. *Brazilian Journal of Operations & Production Management* 7 (1): 123–139.

Tecle, A., Fogel, M., and Duckstein, L. (1988). Multicriterion selection of wastewater management alternatives. *Journal of Water Resources Planning and Management* 114 (4): 383–398.

Tzeng, G.H. and Huang, J.J. (2011). *Multiple Attribute Decision Making: Methods and Applications*. Boca Raton, FL: CRC Press.

Vahdani, B., Mousavi, S.M., Tavakkoli-Moghaddam, R., and Hashemi, H. (2013). A new design of the elimination and choice translating reality method for multi-criteria group decision-making in an intuitionistic fuzzy environment. *Applied Mathematical Modelling* 37 (4): 1781–1799.

Vlahavas, I., Stamelos, I., Refanidis, I., and Tsoukiàs, A. (1999). ESSE: an expert system for software evaluation. *Knowledge-Based Systems* 12 (4): 183–197.

Wu, M.C. and Chen, T.Y. (2011). The ELECTRE multicriteria analysis approach based on Atanassov's intuitionistic fuzzy sets. *Expert Systems with Applications* 38 (10): 12318–12327.

Xu, B. and Ouenniche, J. (2012). Performance evaluation of competing forecasting models: a multidimensional framework based on MCDA. *Expert Systems with Applications* 39 (9): 8312–8324.

Yu, P.L. (1990). *Forming Winning Strategies: An Integrated Theory of Habitual Domains*. Heidelberg, Germany: Springer Science and Business Media Publication.

9
PROMETHEE

9.1 Introduction

The multiattribute decision-making (MADM) methods are frameworks through which decision-makers can depict and mathematically express the intentions of the stakeholders in the form of an evaluation criteria set. Eventually, the decision-makers attempt to select the most suitable path of actions among the other feasible alternatives available to the given MADM problem. The chosen solution should best reflect the stakeholders' interests.

Outranking-oriented methods are one of the major branches of MADM, in which the decision-makers are presented with a framework through which the evaluation criteria are used to map an outranking relation among the set of feasible alternatives. The alternatives are compared to each other and the one that fully dominates the others would emerge as the final solution to the MADM problem at hand. In most cases, these methods are of iterative nature and this notion adds to the computing costs of decision-making, especially in cases where the decision-making process involves many feasible alternatives and evaluation criteria. Or there may be cases in which the methods do not lead to a full outranking list of alternatives. Nevertheless, given the simple nature of the computation algorithms and evaluation taxonomies, and their capability to be hybridize with other mathematical frameworks and algorithms, scholars and decision-makers greatly favor these methods. The family of preference ranking organization methods for enrichment evaluation (PROMETHEE) is a leading outranking-oriented MADM techniques.

Theorized by Brans (1982) and further developed by Vincke and Brans (1985), the family of PROMETHEE is among the best-known outranking methods, which, thanks to their simplistic computational procedure have turned into one the first choices of pragmatic scholars and decision-makers when faced with real-world MADM problems. PROMETHEE I and PROMETHEE II, for instance, are used for partial and complete ranking of feasible alternatives (Brans 1982; Vincke and

A Handbook on Multi-Attribute Decision-Making Methods, First Edition.
Omid Bozorg-Haddad, Babak Zolghadr-Asli, and Hugo A. Loáiciga.

Brans 1985). PROMETHEE III, on the other hand, can be employed for interval ranking of alternatives by emphasizing on indifference, while the PROMETHEE IV enables the decision-makers to cope with situations where the set of viable solutions is of a continuous form (Brans et al. 1986; Mladineo et al. 1987). To this day, the expansion and development of new branches for the family of PROMETHEE continues (Behzadian et al. 2010; Chen 2014).

One of the main distinguishing features of the PROMETHEE family is that, unlike most MADM methods, this branch of outranking-oriented techniques requires additional data from the decision-makers (Tzeng and Huang 2011). This means the decision-makers' knowledge regarding the MADM problem at hand reflects the methods' capability of finding the final solution. In other words, there are parameters in the family of the PROMETHEE that must be calibrated by the decision-makers. It should be noted that there are other MADM methods, including but not limited to the pairwise comparison methods (e.g. analytic hierarchy process [AHP], analytic network process [ANP], and best–worst method [BWM]), that rely on the subjective judgments of the experts and decision-makers in terms of the implicit measuring scales that constitute the core principle of such methods. The basic structure of the PRMETHEE family is shaped and tailored from such subjective yet viable assessments.

The aforementioned notion may be interoperated by some that such mechanism in an MADM method could be the window through which the inept judgments of the decision-makers might enter the decision-making and jeopardize the integrity of the final emerging solutions. However, one must bear in mind that this mechanism would also enable the decision-makers to tune the method accordingly so that it could reflect the requirement and the particular characteristics of the unique MADM case at hand (e.g. the nature of the feasible alternatives and evaluation criteria, requirements of the decision-maker, and/or the stakeholders main objective). The fact that tuning the family of PROMETHEE has been limited to a few parameters bears on the merits of this branch of methods. These characteristics render the solutions by these methods more reliable in that one could benefit from the expertise and experience of the decision-makers in the process of solution finding for an MADM problem.

The following sections present the basic principles of the family of PROMETHEE, including a stepwise description of the PROMETHEE I through IV.

9.2 Common Ground of the PROMETHEE Family

Recall the basic structure of an MADM problem. In light of the MADM, the decision-maker evaluates the set of feasible paths of actions while attempting to secure the stakeholders' interest, which in turn would be represented in the form of a set of (often conflicting) criteria. Consequently, an MADM problem can be represented via a set of feasible alternatives denoted by $\{a_1, a_2, \ldots, a_i, \ldots, a_m\}$, where a_i represents the ith alternative, a set of evaluation criteria denoted by $\{c_1, c_2, \ldots, c_j, \ldots, c_n\}$, where c_j is the jth criteria. It goes without saying that the best-performing alternative with regard to the set of evaluation criteria would, naturally, emerge as the final solution to the MADM problem at hand.

According to the PROMETHEE family one can depict the MADM procedure through the following mathematical framework:

$$Max\{v_{(i,1)}, v_{(i,2)}, \ldots, v_{(i,j)}, \ldots, v_{(i,n)} \mid i = 1, \ldots, m\} \tag{9.1}$$

in which $v_{(i,j)}$ = the performance of the ith feasible alternative (a_i) with regard to the jth evaluation criterion (c_j), n = number of evaluation criteria, and m = number of feasible alternatives. Note that the assumption that all the aforementioned performance evaluation functions [$v_{(i,j)}$] are of a positive nature, that is the larger the value, the better the performance is, hence, the decision-maker attempts to maximize the alternatives performance. In case of negative criteria or minimizing rather than maximizing, where the lower the value the better the performance, the decision-maker could simply transform and generate a new performance function by simply multiplying the previous one by −1.

Common scenes dictate that if the following holds for two hypothetical alternatives, say a and b:

$$v_{(a,j)} \geq v_{(b,j)} \quad \forall j \tag{9.2}$$

and at least one strict inequality, one can then safely deduce that the alternative a dominates and, thus, outperform the alternative b. Consequently, in this hypothetical case, the alternative a is more desirable than the alternative b.

The PROMETHEE family' main framework is composed of three stages, which are as follows:

9.2.1 Stage 1: Construction of the Generalized Criteria

In most MADM problems, the decision-maker evaluates the desirability of feasible alternatives with respect to a set of usually conflicting, criteria, each of which may be of different nature and units of measurement. The first step of any sound decision-making method is to represent the result of these evaluations in a unified form given that these evaluations must eventually be aggregated so that an overall preference value could be assigned to each of these feasible alternatives. Recall most MADM methods cope with these challenges by resorting to the normalizing procedures. The family of PROMETHEE employs a different mechanism. In a nutshell, these methods attempt to generate a generalized criterion by considering a concept called the preference function.

Let $A = \{a_1, a_2, \ldots, a_i, \ldots, a_m\}$ represent the finite set of feasible alternatives that are available for the MADM problem at hand. The assumption, hereby, is for the decision-maker to measure and express the performance of the ith alternative with respect to the jth criterion $[v_{(i,j)}]$. Yet, given the diverse nature of these criteria in terms of its essence and units the overall performance of the alternatives cannot be computed, just yet. To overcome this challenge, the family of PROMETHEE proposes employing an exclusively defined preference function (f_j), which, in essence, indicates the degree to which one alternative is preferred to other. For a hypothetical case, where alternatives a and b are evaluated, the aforementioned notion is mathematically expressed as follows:

$$f_j(a, b) = f_j(d_{ab|j}) \tag{9.3}$$

in which $f_j(a, b)$ = the degree to which the alternative a is preferred over the alternative b while the jth criterion is under consideration, and $d_{ab|j}$ = the distance of the performance value of the a and b alternatives with respect to the jth criterion, and can be computed as follows:

$$d_{ab|j} = v_{(a,j)} - v_{(b,j)} \tag{9.4}$$

The family of PROMETHEE provides some options through which the decision-maker can define the preference function. As stated earlier, these functions are induced with a few parameters that requires the decision-maker to expertly tune them while considering the particular characteristics of each given criterion. Notice that this unique feature of the PROMETHEE family enables the decision-makers to employ their expertise and valuable experiences to bring the most out of the well-customized MADM method. Table 9.1 lists the available forms of preference functions (Brans et al. 1986; Tzeng and Huang 2011).

The functions listed in Table 9.1 require calibration of at most three major parameters, namely, p, q, and σ. The definition of these parameters is presented in Table 9.2.

By employing the exclusively costumed preference functions, the alternatives' evaluations are made in a dimensionless form that ranges from 0 to 1. This means the decision-makers strive for aggregating the overall preference of the alternatives. The preference index is the instrument to tackle such task, and it is mathematically expressed as follows:

$$\pi(a, b) = \sum_{j=1}^{n} w_j \times f_j(a, b) \tag{9.5}$$

in which $\pi(a, b)$ = the preference index of the alternative a over alternative b, and w_j = the importance of the jth criterion. The following condition is met by the weights:

$$\sum_{j=1}^{n} w_j = 1 \tag{9.6}$$

Table 9.1 The recommended preference functions for the family of PROMETHEE methods.

Name of the preference function	Mathematical representation	Graphical representation	Parameter(s)
Usual function	$f(d) = \begin{cases} 0 & d = 0 \\ 1 & \text{else} \end{cases}$	$f(d)$, 1, d	—
Quasi-function	$f(d) = \begin{cases} 0 & \mid d \mid \leq q \\ 1 & \text{else} \end{cases}$	$f(d)$, 1, $-q$, q, d	q
V-shape function	$f(d) = \begin{cases} \frac{\mid d \mid}{p} & \mid d \mid \leq p \\ 1 & \text{else} \end{cases}$	$f(d)$, 1, $-p$, p, d	p
Level function	$f(d) = \begin{cases} 0 & \mid d \mid \leq q \\ \frac{1}{2} & q < \mid d \mid \leq p \\ 1 & \text{else} \end{cases}$	$f(d)$, 1, 1/2, $-p$ $-q$, q p, d	q, p
Linear function	$f(d) = \begin{cases} 0 & \mid d \mid \leq q \\ \frac{\mid d \mid - q}{p - q} & q < \mid d \mid \leq p \\ 1 & \text{else} \end{cases}$	$f(d)$, 1, $-p$ $-q$, q p, d	q, p
Gaussian function	$f(d) = 1 - \exp\left(-\frac{d^2}{2\sigma^2}\right)$	$f(d)$, $-\sigma$, σ, d	σ

Table 9.2 The definition of the parameters used in the tuning of the PROMETHEE family.

Name of the parameter	Symbol	Description
Difference threshold	q	The largest value of d below which the decision-maker considers there is indifference
Strict preference threshold	p	The lowest value of d above which the decision-maker considers there is strict preference
Standard deviation	σ	The standard deviation of a normal distribution

9.2.2 Stage 2: Mapping the Outrank Relation on the Set of Feasible Alternatives

The family of the PROMETHEE provides the decision-makers with a framework through which the overall performance of alternatives can be accounted for. This stage's main objective is to find a mechanism that depicts the superiorities of the alternatives over one another. To this end, the notion of inflow and outflow rates is promoted by the family of PROMETHEE. Accordingly, each alternative, say the hypothetical alternative a, is correlated with leaving and entering flow values, denoted by $\phi^+(a)$ and $\phi^-(a)$, respectively. These variables are computed as follows:

$$\phi^+(a) = \sum_{j=1}^{n} \pi(a, c_j) \quad c_j \neq a \tag{9.7}$$

$$\phi^-(a) = \sum_{j=1}^{n} \pi(c_j, a) \quad c_j \neq a \tag{9.8}$$

Consequently, the net flow, denoted by $\phi(a)$, is the difference between the leaving and the entering flows (Eq. (9.9)). It goes without saying that the higher the value of the net flow, the more desirable an alternative is

$$\phi(a) = \phi^+(a) - \phi^-(a) \tag{9.9}$$

9.2.3 Stage 3: Evaluation the Relation Among the Feasible Alternatives

The final stage of the family of PROMETHEE's methodology enquires an evaluation procedure through which the most desirable alternative would emerge as the final solution to the MADM problem at hand. In light of the PROMETHEE terminology, four relations exist among a pair of given alternatives, say a and b, which are summarized in Table 9.3.

Table 9.3 The types of conditions for pairs of alternatives in the family of PROMETHEE methods.

Symbol	Required condition
aP^+b	$\phi^+(a) > \phi^+(b)$
aI^+b	$\phi^+(a) = \phi^+(b)$
aP^-b	$\phi^-(a) < \phi^-(b)$
aI^-b	$\phi^-(a) = \phi^-(b)$

Based on the leaving flow, three relations can be formed between two given alternatives: either a or b is preferred over one another, or these alternatives are indifferent to each other. The same analogy may also be said if the entering flow of the two given alternatives is considered. Notice the family of PROMETHEE would explore these relationships to arrange the set of feasible alternatives. In fact, the techniques and assumptions are where the different methods of the family of PROMETHEE are distinguished from one another. The following sections shed light on the mechanism that each PROMETHEE method uses to derive the ranked list of feasible alternatives.

9.3 PROMETHEE I

The PROMETHEE I preliminary task is to derive a partial preorder of the feasible alternatives available to an MADM problem. Employing the introduced relationships in Table 9.3 the status of a pair of alternatives is labeled by the PROMETHEE I as: (i) either of the alternatives can outrank the other (P^I), (ii) the alternatives are indifferent to each other (I^I), or (iii) the alternatives are incomparable to one another (R^I). The conditional assessments employed by the PROMETHEE I are summarized in Table 9.4.

Table 9.4 Conditional assessments used in the PROMETHEE I method.

Status' symbol	Requiring condition	Description
aP^Ib	(I) aP^+b and aP^-b; or (II) aP^+b and aI^-b; or (III) aI^+b and aP^-b	The alternative a outranks alternative b
aI^Ib	aI^+b and aI^-b	The alternatives a and b are indifferent to one another
aR^Ib	Otherwise	No conclusive comments can be made about the relationship of the alternative a and b

The PROMETHEE I has been successively used in numerous instances including but not limited to: Computer-aided diagnoses (Du Bois et al. 1989), energy plants site selection (Mladineo et al. 1987), environmental management (Briggs et al. 1990), investment planning (Albadvi et al. 2007), manufacture planning (Petrović et al. 1988), sport agendas (Olson 2001), transportation planning (Elevli and Demirci 2004), and water resources planning and management (Özelkan and Duckstein 1996). This method has been also successfully merged with the fuzzy logic theory (Geldermann and Rentz 2005).

The PROMETHEE I leads to the partial ranking of feasible alternatives; hence, through this method there may exist alternatives that cannot be fully ranked. In essence, PROMETHEE II attempts to overcome this plausible shortcoming.

9.4 PROMETHEE II

Using the net flow of the discrete, feasible alternatives introduced in Eq. (9.9), the PROMETHEE II arrives at a complete preorder list. The conditional assessments employed by the PROMETHEE II are summarized in Table 9.5.

The PROMETHEE II has been employed to cope with MADM problems in agricultural management (Palma et al. 2007), environmental management (Petraš 1997), greenhouse gas emission agendas (Vaillancourt and Waaub 2004), hydropower plants site selection (Mladineo et al. 1987), motor vehicle industry (Beynon and Wells 2008), groundwater remediation programming (Khelifi et al. 2006), irrigation planning (Raju et al. 2000), sediment management projects (Linkov et al. 2006), stock trading (Albadvi et al. 2007), waste management (Kapepula et al. 2007), and water resources planning and management (Abu-Taleb and Mareschal 1995). Additionally, the following hybrid forms of PROMETHEE II has also proven to be beneficial in coping with real-world, complex MADM problems: Fuzzy (Le Téno and Mareschal 1998), PROMETHEE II-AHP hybrid (Babic and Plazibat 1998), PROMETHEE II-artificial neural network (ANN) hybrid (Zhang et al. 2006).

The complete ranked list of the alternatives may be considered as an advantage in most pragmatic cases. Yet based on a strictly theoretical point of view, the

Table 9.5 Conditional assessments used in the PROMETHEE II method.

Status' symbol	Requiring condition	Description
$aP^{II}b$	$\phi(a) > \phi(b)$	The alternative a outranks alternative b
$aI^{II}b$	$\phi(a) = \phi(b)$	The alternatives a and b are indifferent to one another

partial preorder can carry vital information for it considers both leaving and entering flows (Tzeng and Huang 2011; Eppe and De Smet 2014). In other words, the main assumption behind the PROMETHEE II is that negative effects of the entering flow are compensated with the positive impacts of the leaving flow. While this is a valid strategy to overcome the conundrum of partial ranking lists in practical MADM problems, theoretically speaking, that may not be a necessarily an accurate statement.

On a different perspective, one could employ intervals to compare and represent the outranking relations among the feasible alternatives. The aforementioned notion is the core ideology behind the PROMETHEE III, which is discussed in Section 9.5.

9.5 PROMETHEE III

According to the PROMETHEE III the preference of each given alternative, say alternative a, is to be viewed as an interval denoted by $[\alpha_a, \beta_a]$, where α_a and β_a represent the beginning and the end of such interval, respectively, and is computed as follows:

$$\alpha_a = \overline{\phi}(a) - \Omega\sigma_a \tag{9.10}$$

$$\beta_a = \overline{\phi}(a) + \Omega\sigma_a \tag{9.11}$$

$$\sigma_a = \sqrt{\frac{1}{n}\sum_{j=1}^{n}[\pi(a, c_j) - \pi(c_j, a) - \overline{\phi}(a)]^2} \tag{9.12}$$

in which Ω = the parameter of PROMETHEE III, which in general is a nonzero and positive value, σ_a = the standard deviation of the alternative a, and $\overline{\phi}(a)$ = the center of the preference interval that has been defined for alternative a, and is calculated as follows:

$$\overline{\phi}(a) = \frac{1}{n}\sum_{j=1}^{n}[\pi(a, c_j) - \pi(c_j, a)] = \frac{1}{n}\phi(a) \tag{9.13}$$

It is seen in Eqs. (9.10)–(9.13) that $[\alpha_a, \beta_a]$ is an interval centered about the net mean flow $[\overline{\phi}(a)]$ whose length is proportional to the standard deviation of the numbers $[\pi(a, c_j) - \pi(c_j, a)]$ and depends on the method's parameter selection (Ω). Evidently, the smaller the number of Ω, the greater the number of strict outranking. In an extreme case, for instance, $\Omega = 0$, the results of the PROMETHEE III and II are identical. Hence, the PROMETHEE III is a generalization of the PROMETHEE II. To avoid a considerable number of indifference relationships among the alternatives, it may be requested that the mean length of the intervals

Table 9.6 Conditional assessments used in the PROMETHEE III method.

Status' symbol	Required condition	Description
$aP^{III}b$	$\alpha_a > \beta_b$	The alternative a can outrank alternative b
$aI^{III}b$	$\alpha_a \leq \beta_b$ and $\alpha_b \leq \alpha_a$	The alternatives a and b are indifferent to one another

be less than the mean distance between two successive mean flow, which leads, to a value of about 0.15 for Ω (Tzeng and Huang 2011).

Deriving the outranking is based on the information whose summary is listed in Table 9.6.

The PROMETHEE III has been employed in wastewater management (Kapepula et al. 2007), and proven to be a promising MADM method. A few researchers have generated hybrid versions of this method using fuzzy logic to expand its capabilities (Fernández-Castro and Jiménez 2005).

To this point, all the introduced members of the family of PROMETHEE have been shown to assist the decision-maker where a discrete feasible set of alternative is involved. PROMETHEE IV was developed to promote decision-making with a continuous set of alternatives.

9.6 PROMETHEE IV

PROMETHEE IV is an extended version of the PROMETHEE II to the case of continuous sets of alternatives. The revised definition of leaving and entering flows can be expressed as follows:

$$\phi^+(a) = \int_A \pi(a, b)db \tag{9.14}$$

$$\phi^-(a) = \int_A \pi(b, a)db \tag{9.15}$$

in which A = the set of continuous feasible alternatives. Note that the rest of the method's procedure is identical to the PROMETHEE IIs.

The PROMETHEE IV is one of the most underrated members of the PROMETHEE family, and in fact, except for a few notable examples in civil engineering (Albuquerque 2015) and tourism planning (Albuquerque and Montenegro 2016) this method has not been widely applied to decision-making for empirical cases of MADM (Albuquerque and Montenegro 2016). This, however, does not deny the potential of PROMETHEE IV.

9.7 Conclusion

The family of PROMETHEE is categorized as one of the outranking-oriented MADM methods, which thanks to a rare combination of low computational effort and reliable results has become widely popular among decision-making researchers and practitioners. Among the many branches of this family are PROMETHEE I which produces a partial ranking of the alternatives; PROMETHEE II yields a complete ranking of alternatives; PROMETHEE III employs the concept of intervals for alternative evaluation; and PROMETHEE IV applies to a continuous set of feasible alternatives form the main body of this family's tree. The PROMETHEE family is based on three stages: (i) construction of the generalized criteria, (ii) mapping the outrank relation on the set of feasible alternatives, and (iii) evaluating the relations among the feasible alternatives. The third stage is where the branches of the family usually diverge. Through these stages, the alternatives' performance evaluation represent in a generalized form, the preference function. Note that based on the unique character of the MADM problem at hand, this function must be tuned by the decision-maker for each given evaluation criteria. This distinguishing feature of the PROMETHEE family enables the decision-makers to customize the MADM method so that it best reflects the expertise and experiences of those who are involved in the process of decision-making. Next, the unit dimensionless, same-ranged performance evaluations of criteria are aggregated for each given alternative through the preference index. The concept of leaving, entering, and net flows are employed to map the outranking relationship among the alternatives. Lastly, the family of PROMETHEE contains a group of promising techniques that can be employed to cope with a wide range of real-world MADM problems.

References

Abu-Taleb, M.F. and Mareschal, B. (1995). Water resources planning in the Middle East: application of the PROMETHEE V multicriteria method. *European Journal of Operational Research* 81 (3): 500–511.

Albadvi, A., Chaharsooghi, S.K., and Esfahanipour, A. (2007). Decision making in stock trading: an application of PROMETHEE. *European Journal of Operational Research* 177 (2): 673–683.

Albuquerque, P.H.M. (2015). PROMETHEE IV as a decision analyst's tool for site selection in civil engineering. In: *Decision Models in Engineering and Management* (ed. P. Guarnieri), 257–267. Cham, Germany: Springer.

Albuquerque, P.H.M. and Montenegro, M.R. (2016). PROMETHEE IV through kernel density estimation. *Communications in Statistics – Theory and Methods* 45 (18): 5355–5362.

Babic, Z. and Plazibat, N. (1998). Ranking of enterprises based on multicriterial analysis. *International Journal of Production Economics* 56: 29–35.

Behzadian, M., Kazemzadeh, R.B., Albadvi, A., and Aghdasi, M. (2010). PROMETHEE: a comprehensive literature review on methodologies and applications. *European Journal of Operational Research* 200 (1): 198–215.

Beynon, M.J. and Wells, P. (2008). The lean improvement of the chemical emissions of motor vehicles based on preference ranking: a PROMETHEE uncertainty analysis. *Omega* 36 (3): 384–394.

Brans, J.P. (1982). L'ingénierie de la decision. Elaboration d'instruments d'aide a la decision: Methode PROMETHEE. In: *L'aide a la Decision: Nature, Instruments et Perspectives D'avenir* (eds. R. Nadeau and M. Landry), 183–214. Québec, Canada: Presses de Universite Laval.

Brans, J.P., Vincke, P., and Mareschal, B. (1986). How to select and how to rank projects: the PROMETHEE method. *European Journal of Operational Research* 24 (2): 228–238.

Briggs, T., Kunsch, P.L., and Mareschal, B. (1990). Nuclear waste management: an application of the multicriteria PROMETHEE methods. *European Journal of Operational Research* 44 (1): 1–10.

Chen, T.Y. (2014). A PROMETHEE-based outranking method for multiple criteria decision analysis with interval type-2 fuzzy sets. *Soft Computing* 18 (5): 923–940.

Du Bois, P., Brans, J.P., Cantraine, F., and Mareschal, B. (1989). MEDICIS: an expert system for computer-aided diagnosis using the PROMETHEE multicriteria method. *European Journal of Operational Research* 39 (3): 284–292.

Elevli, B. and Demirci, A. (2004). Multicriteria choice of ore transport system for an underground mine: application of PROMETHEE methods. *Journal of the South African Institute of Mining and Metallurgy* 104: 251–256.

Eppe, S. and De Smet, Y. (2014). Approximating PROMTHEE II's net flow scores by piecewise linear value functions. *European Journal of Operational Research* 233 (3): 651–659.

Fernández-Castro, A.S. and Jiménez, M. (2005). PROMETHEE: an extension through fuzzy mathematical programming. *Journal of the Operational Research Society* 56 (1): 119–122.

Geldermann, J. and Rentz, O. (2005). Multi-criteria analysis for technique assessment: case study from industrial coating. *Journal of Industrial Ecology* 9 (3): 127–142.

Kapepula, K.M., Colson, G., Sabri, K., and Thonart, P. (2007). A multiple criteria analysis for household solid waste management in the urban community of Dakar. *Waste Management* 27 (11): 1690–1705.

Khelifi, O., Lodolo, A., Vranes, S. et al. (2006). A web-based decision support tool for groundwater remediation technologies selection. *Journal of Hydroinformatics* 8 (2): 91–100.

Le Téno, J.F. and Mareschal, B. (1998). An interval version of PROMETHEE for the comparison of building products' design with ill-defined data on environmental quality. *European Journal of Operational Research* 109 (2): 522–529.

Linkov, I., Satterstrom, F.K., Kiker, G. et al. (2006). From comparative risk assessment to multi-criteria decision analysis and adaptive management: recent developments and applications. *Environment International* 32 (8): 1072–1093.

Mladineo, N., Margeta, J., Brans, J.P., and Mareschal, B. (1987). Multicriteria ranking of alternative locations for small scale hydro plants. *European Journal of Operational Research* 31 (2): 215–222.

Olson, D.L. (2001). Comparison of three multicriteria methods to predict known outcomes. *European Journal of Operational Research* 130 (3): 576–587.

Özelkan, E.C. and Duckstein, L. (1996). Analysing water resources alternatives and handling criteria by multi criterion decision techniques. *Journal of Environmental Management* 48 (1): 69–96.

Palma, J., Graves, A.R., Burgess, P.J. et al. (2007). Integrating environmental and economic performance to assess modern silvoarable agroforestry in Europe. *Ecological Economics* 63 (4): 759–767.

Petraš, J.C. (1997). Ranking the sites for low-and intermediate-level radioactive waste disposal facilities in Croatia. *International Transactions in Operational Research* 4 (4): 237–249.

Petrović, R., S̄enborn, A., and Vujos̄ević, M. (1988). Multicriteria ranking of spares allocations. *Naval Research Logistics (NRL)* 35 (6): 707–717.

Raju, K.S., Duckstein, L., and Arondel, C. (2000). Multicriterion analysis for sustainable water resources planning: a case study in Spain. *Water Resources Management* 14 (6): 435–456.

Tzeng, G.H. and Huang, J.J. (2011). *Multiple Attribute Decision Making: Methods and Applications*. Boca Raton, FL: CRC Press.

Vaillancourt, K. and Waaub, J.P. (2004). Equity in international greenhouse gases abatement scenarios: a multicriteria approach. *European Journal of Operational Research* 153 (2): 489–505.

Vincke, J.P. and Brans, P. (1985). A preference ranking organization method: the PROMETHEE method for MCDM. *Management Science* 31 (6): 647–656.

Zhang, G., Ni, Y., Churchill, J., and Kokot, S. (2006). Authentication of vegetable oils on the basis of their physico-chemical properties with the aid of chemometrics. *Talanta* 70 (2): 293–300.

10

Superiority and Inferiority Ranking (SIR)

10.1 Introduction

Multiattribute decision-making (MADM) is the process of pursuing the selection of a solution from a set of feasible alternatives when the stakeholders' interest can only be portrayed through a set of, often conflicting, evaluation criteria. As far as the sound decision-making is concerned, often, the decision-makers are faced with a diversified set of evaluation criteria, which is composed of tangible and intangible variables, expressed in terms of cardinal and ordinal values, respectively. Nevertheless, in light of MADM methods, the decision-makers are presented with logically supported and mathematically expressed frameworks, which, eventually, enables them to protect the interests of the stakeholders in the process of decision-making. Outranking-oriented methods are one of the well-known, pragmatic, branches of MADM methods, which attempt to overcome the challenges of real-world decision-making problems.

In essence, the outranking-oriented MADM methods' solution selection procedure is centered about a two-stage process, namely, aggregation and exploitation (Figueira et al. 2013), through which the dominating and dominated alternatives become separated. The first stage is where outranking-oriented MADM methods explore the inner relations among the paired alternatives in terms of whether an alternative is preferred to the comparing one, they are indifferent to one another, or they are incomparable with each other. With regard to the established relations in the first stage, the second stage is where the decision-makers are enabled to exploit the overall ranks of the feasible alternatives. Notice that, depending on the mathematical procedures and logical assumptions of the outranking-oriented MADM methods, either partial or complete ranking of alternatives can emerge as the final outcome of this stage.

During the mid-1990s and based on the fuzzy bags theory Rebai (1993, 1994) introduced the mathematical and philosophical foundations of new MADM notions, namely, superiority, inferiority, and noninferiority scores. These notions

A Handbook on Multi-Attribute Decision-Making Methods, First Edition.
Omid Bozorg-Haddad, Babak Zolghadr-Asli, and Hugo A. Loáiciga.

promoted a novel outranking-oriented MADM method called superiority and inferiority ranking (SIR) method. Theorized by Xu (2001), the SIR method represents a new school of thought in MADM, that is, the outranking-oriented MADM methods. The SIR method employs the borrowed concepts of superiority, inferiority, and noninferiority scores to form superiority and inferiority flows. These values are the key features to establish the relations among the paired alternatives. In light of the exploitation stage, the SIR method enables the decision-makers to extract either the partial or complete ranked lists of feasible alternatives using the previously established relations among the paired alternatives. What distinguishes this method from the rest of outranking-oriented MADM methods, however, is the ability of this method to cope with both cardinal and ordinal values. Furthermore, this method can be seen as an artful combination of some generalized versions of well-known MADM methods, i.e. weighted sum method (WSM; Churchman and Ackoff 1954), weighted product method (WPM; Chang and Yeh 2001). The technique for order preferences by similarity to an ideal solution (TOPSIS; Hwang and Yoon 1981; Yoon 1987; Chen and Hwang 1992; Hwang et al. 1993), elimination et Choix traduisant la realité (ELECTRE; Benayoun et al. 1966; Roy and Bertier 1971; Roy 1978; Roy and Hugonnard 1982) and preference ranking organization methods for enrichment evaluation (PROMETHEE; Brans 1982; Vincke and Brans 1985; Brans et al. 1986; Mladineo et al. 1987) blends and amplifies the strengths of the aforementioned MADM methods (Tam et al. 2004). This, in turn, provides the decision-makers with a verity of options to calibrate and tune the method based on the unique characteristics of the MADM problem at hand and the requirements of the stakeholders.

Despite the fact that SIR method is a relatively new MADM method, it has received positive feedbacks from scholars, researchers, and decision-makers. In addition, the preliminary results demonstrated the method's potential to cope with real-world MADM problems. Some applications of this method include, but not limited to, business management (Marzouk 2008), construction engineering (Tam et al. 2004), procurement management (Marzouk et al. 2013), supplier selection (Chai et al. 2012), and supply chain management (Liu 2010). Furthermore, this method has also been successfully linked with the fuzzy logic theory (Chai et al. 2012), in an attempt to expand its capabilities.

The following section lays out the mathematical foundations of SIR method. A stepwise description of this method is also presented.

10.2 Foundational Bases of the SIR Method

An informed decision to be made with a MADM problem requires consideration of the following information:

(1) The set of alternatives, denoted by $A = \{a_i \mid i = 1, 2, \ldots, m\}$, where a_i is the ith alternative and m is the number of alternatives under consideration;
(2) The set of evaluation criteria, denoted by $C = \{c_j \mid j = 1, 2, \ldots, n\}$, where c_j represents the jth criterion and n is the number of evaluation criteria;
(3) The anticipated value or what is referred to in technical terms as the performance of alternative with regard to each evaluation criterion. Let $v_{(i,j)}$ represent the value of the ith alternative with respect to the jth criterion; and
(4) The decision-makers' priorities regarding the evaluation criteria, denoted by $W = \{w_j \mid j = 1, 2, \ldots, n\}$. Based on the stakeholders of the MADM problem, each w_j ought to reflect the importance of the corresponding criterion.

The aforementioned information sets are usually presented in a matrix form, commonly referred to as the decision-matrix (D), which can be mathematically expressed as follows:

$$D = \begin{array}{c} \\ a_1 \\ \vdots \\ a_m \end{array} \begin{array}{c} \begin{array}{ccc} c_1 & \cdots & c_n \end{array} \\ \begin{bmatrix} v_{(1,1)} & \cdots & v_{(1,n)} \\ \vdots & \ddots & \vdots \\ v_{(m,1)} & \cdots & v_{(m,n)} \end{bmatrix} \end{array} \tag{10.1}$$

In addition to the decision-matrix, in some cases, the decision-maker composes arbitrary alternatives, namely, ideal (a^+) and inferior (a^-) alternatives. The ideal alternative is an arbitrarily defined vector, which describes the aspired solution to the given problem that in practice may or may not be achievable, while the inferior alternative is an arbitrarily defined solution that represents the most undesirable option for the given MADM. There are basically two main methods to compose the ideal and inferior alternatives. One can use the best and worst values represented in the jth column of the decision-matrix to compose the jth component of the ideal and inferior alternatives, respectively. On the other hand, one could also use the upper and lower boundaries of the feasible range for the jth criterion to compose these arbitrarily defined alternatives. In such cases, if the criterion is considered to be positive, where the larger the value, the better the situation, the upper boundary is used for the ideal alternative and the lower boundary is used to compose the inferior alternative. Conversely, for the negative criterion, where smaller the value, the better the situation, the lower boundary is used to compose the ideal alternative and the upper boundary is used to create the inferior alternative. These alternatives are represented as follows:

$$a^+ = (v_1^+, v_2^+, \ldots, v_j^+, \ldots, v_n^+) \tag{10.2}$$

$$a^- = (v_1^-, v_2^-, \ldots, v_j^-, \ldots, v_n^-) \tag{10.3}$$

in which, v_j^+ and v_j^- = the components of the ideal and inferior alternatives with regard to the jth criterion, respectively.

When it comes to evaluating the relation of a paired feasible alternatives, say alternatives a and b, the fallacious idea that springs to mind is that a preference structure, composed of the preference relation, denoted by aPb (Eq. (10.4)), and the indifference relation, denoted by aIb (Eq. (10.5)), can thoroughly describe the interactions between alternatives. While this is the case for ordinal criteria, when it comes to criteria described with cardinal values, numerous valid concerns could be raised about the aforementioned preference structure. In fact, these concerning voices are those which altered the foundation of a school of thought in MADM, a branch that is commonly referred to as the outranking-oriented methods. The outranking-oriented methods are centered on the basic idea that identifying an alternative presented with a higher preference value should not necessarily lead to the conclusion that such alternative is more preferable. To put it differently, as far as the outranking-oriented MADM methods are concerned, the evaluation process of alternatives are surrounded by imprecisions and uncertainties. Therefore, a small degree of deference between the performance value of cardinal criteria could not eligibly indicate a strict preference among alternatives. Through their perspective, in order to determine whether an alternative can outrank the other feasible solutions one takes the absolute performance values into account and the amplitude of difference between these values should be considered, as well.

$$aPb \text{ iff } v_{(a,j)} > v_{(b,j)} \tag{10.4}$$

$$aIb \text{ iff } v_{(a,j)} = v_{(b,j)} \tag{10.5}$$

Each outranking-oriented MADM method proposes a unique framework through which the decision-makers are enabled to overcome the aforementioned quandary. In that spirit, Rebai (1993, 1994) proposed the concepts of superiority and inferiority scores. Presumably, these scores had the potential to enable the decision-maker to evaluate the plausible relations among the paired alternatives. Xu (2001) explored this idea by employing these values into a newly proposed outranking-oriented method called SIR. This method provided the decision-makers with a framework to account for the magnitude of the difference between the performance values. In essence, this method expands the idea of superiority and inferiority scores using the concept of generalized criteria, a concept introduced by the family of PROMETHEE methods. The computed values are used to compose the superiority and inferiority matrixes. As the last step of the aggregation stage, the decision-makers are then presented with a range of aggregation functions to transform the aforementioned matrixes into superiority and inferiority flows. As for the exploitation stage, the computed flows are then employed to extract the preorder ranked list of alternatives. Notice that based on the requirement of the decision-makers, both complete and partial preorder can emerge as the final outcome of this stage.

The following section contains a stepwise description of the SIR method and the procedure required to employ this method in practice.

10.3 Stepwise Description of the SIR Method

The SIR method can generate the ranked list of the feasible alternatives through the following stepwise procedure:

10.3.1 Step 1: Establishing the Formation of the Decision-Making Problem

In this step, the decision-makers express the MADM problem at hand mathematically, which is defining the four previously described information sets, namely, set of feasible alternatives, set of evaluation criteria, the performance of each alternative with regard to a given criterion, and the criteria's weight vector. It goes without saying that the integrity of the final results would heavily rely on the accuracy of this step. In other words, a well-defined MADM problem that accurately portrays the stakeholders' interest is the key ingredient for a sound decision-making.

10.3.2 Step 2: Computing the Superiority and Inferiority Scores

When it comes to the cardinal values establishing the relation among paired alternatives, the outranking-oriented methods use the magnitude of the difference between the performance of alternatives to determine which alternative represents a more desirable performance with regard to the evaluation criteria. The family of PROMETHEE methods employs the concept of the generalized criteria to overcome this challenge. Accordingly, a generalized criterion can be seen as a specifically designed mathematical function that must be tuned by the decision-maker for each given evaluation criteria. The critical point is that these dimensionless functions have a 0–1 range. Thus, as far as the outranking-oriented MADM methods are concerned, the outcome of these functions can be employed to evaluate the relations among paired alternatives.

Without loss of generality, a MADM problem composed of all positive criteria is, hereby, assumed to demonstrate the remaining mathematical procedures. Consequently, the aforementioned notion is expressed as follows:

$$f_j(a,b) = f_j(d_{ab|j}) \tag{10.6}$$

in which $f_j(a,b)$ = the degree to which the alternative a is preferred over the alternative b while the jth criterion is under consideration; and $d_{ab|j}$ = the distance of the performance value of the a and b alternatives with respect to the jth criterion, which is computed as follows:

$$d_{ab|j} = v_{(a,j)} - v_{(b,j)} \tag{10.7}$$

Notice that the mathematical function introduced in Eq. (10.6) portrays the concept of generalized criterion, a notion that was first theorized by Brans (1982) for the family of PROMETHEE. Eventually, Xu (2001) modified the concepts used in the generalized criteria so that it could meet the requirements needed to be linked with the superiority and inferiority scores that are the core concepts of SIR method. Evidently, the original theorists of this concept described the generalized function as any function from the real numbers to [0,1]. Brans (1982) took one step furthered and recommended six prototype functions that fit the aforementioned description, namely, usual function, quasi-function, V-shape function, level function, linear function, and Gaussian function. The nondecreasing condition was later added to the description of the generalized criteria by Xu (2001) in an attempt to make it more compatible with the requirements of the superiority and inferiority notions. Table 10.1 demonstrates the available forms of modified preference functions (Xu 2001).

Table 10.1 demonstrates that the tuning procedure of the preference functions is through calibration of the three major parameters, namely, p, q, and σ. The definitions of these parameters are presented in Table 10.2.

Using the generalized criteria, the superiority and inferiority indexes are computed as follows:

$$SU(a_i, c_j) = \sum_{k=1}^{m} f_j(a_i, a_k) \tag{10.8}$$

$$IN(a_i, c_j) = \sum_{k=1}^{m} f_j(a_k, a_i) \tag{10.9}$$

in which $SU(a_i, c_j)$ and $IN(a_i, c_j)$ = the superiority and inferiority index for the ith alternatives with regard to the jth criterion, respectively. Given that the preference function is equal to zero for the nonpositive distances, for a positive, cardinal criterion, the superiority and inferiority indexes is restated as follows:

$$SU(a_i, c_j) = \sum_{k=1}^{m} \{f_j(a_i, a_k) \mid v_{(i,j)} > v_{(k,j)}\} \tag{10.10}$$

$$IN(a_i, c_j) = \sum_{k=1}^{m} \{f_j(a_k, a_i) \mid v_{(k,j)} > v_{(i,j)}\} \tag{10.11}$$

Notice that when it comes to the ordinal criteria, a similar procedure takes place with the major difference that for each $v_{(a,j)} > v_{(b,j)}$, one point would be assigned to

Table 10.1 The recommended types of modified preference functions for the SIR method.

Name of the preference function	Mathematical representation	Graphical representation	Parameter(s)
Usual function	$f(d)=\begin{cases}0 & d\le 0\\ 1 & \text{else}\end{cases}$		—
Quasi-function	$f(d)=\begin{cases}0 & d\le q\\ 1 & \text{else}\end{cases}$		Q
V-shape function	$f(d)=\begin{cases}0 & d\le 0\\ \frac{d}{p} & 0<d\le p\\ 1 & \text{else}\end{cases}$		P
Level function	$f(d)=\begin{cases}0 & d\le q\\ \frac{1}{2} & q<d\le p\\ 1 & \text{else}\end{cases}$		q, p
Linear function	$f(d)=\begin{cases}0 & d\le q\\ \frac{d-q}{p-q} & q<d\le p\\ 1 & \text{else}\end{cases}$		q, p
Gaussian function	$f(d)=\begin{cases}0 & d\le 0\\ 1-\exp\left(-\frac{d^2}{2\sigma^2}\right) & \text{else}\end{cases}$		σ

Table 10.2 The definition of the parameters used in the tuning of the SIR method.

Name of the parameter	Symbol	Description
Difference threshold	q	The largest value of d below which the decision-maker considers there is indifference
Strict preference threshold	p	The lowest value of d above which the decision-maker considers there is strict preference
Standard deviation	σ	The standard deviation of a normal distribution

the superiority score of alternative a and another point to the inferiority score of alternative b.

10.3.3 Step 3: Forming the Superiority and Inferiority Matrices

In this step, the decision-makers compose the superiority (SU) and inferiority (IN) matrices using the calculated indexes in the previous step. These matrices are mathematically expressed as follows:

$$SU = [SU(a_i, c_j)]_{m\times n} \tag{10.12}$$

$$IN = [IN(a_i, c_j)]_{m\times n} \tag{10.13}$$

which in their extended versions are represented as follows:

$$SU = \begin{bmatrix} SU(a_1, c_1) & \cdots & SU(a_1, c_j) & \cdots & SU(a_1, c_n) \\ \vdots & \ddots & & & \vdots \\ SU(a_i, c_1) & \cdots & SU(a_i, c_j) & \cdots & SU(a_i, c_n) \\ \vdots & & & \ddots & \vdots \\ SU(a_m, c_1) & \cdots & SU(a_m, c_j) & \cdots & SU(a_m, c_n) \end{bmatrix} \tag{10.14}$$

$$IN = \begin{bmatrix} IN(a_1, c_1) & \cdots & IN(a_1, c_j) & \cdots & IN(a_1, c_n) \\ \vdots & \ddots & & & \vdots \\ IN(a_i, c_1) & \cdots & IN(a_i, c_j) & \cdots & IN(a_i, c_n) \\ \vdots & & & \ddots & \vdots \\ IN(a_m, c_1) & \cdots & IN(a_m, c_j) & \cdots & IN(a_m, c_n) \end{bmatrix} \tag{10.15}$$

The aforementioned matrices convey different information regarding the MADM problem at hand. The superiority matrix determines the intensity to which an alternative is considered preferable than others. On the other hand, the inferiority matrix illustrates that magnitude to which other alternatives might be preferred to the alternative under consideration. As far as deriving the complete preorder of alternatives is concerned, the decision-makers are also encouraged to compute the net matrix (*NM*), which is a matrix composed of arithmetic difference of the superiority and inferiority indexes.

$$NM = SU - IN \tag{10.16}$$

10.3.4 Step 4: Superiority and Inferiority Flows

In this step, this outranking-oriented method attempts to aid the decision-makers in their task to evaluate the relationships among the paired alternatives. Inspired by the PROMETHEE family of methods each alternative is correlated to two variables, namely, superiority and inferiority flows, denoted by $\varphi^{>}(a_i)$ and $\varphi^{<}(a_i)$, respectively. These variables, which are interoperated as the final step of the aggregation stage of outranking-oriented methods, are mathematically expressed as follows:

$$\varphi^{>}(a_i) = \Upsilon[SU(a_i, c_1), \ldots, SU(a_i, c_j), \ldots, SU(a_i, c_n)] \tag{10.17}$$

$$\varphi^{<}(a_i) = \Upsilon[IN(a_i, c_1), \ldots, IN(a_i, c_j), \ldots, IN(a_i, c_n)] \tag{10.18}$$

in which $\Upsilon[] =$ the aggregation function. Naturally, the higher values for the superiority flows and lower values for inferiority flows indicate that an alternative is more desirable.

The choice of the aggregation function can significantly influence the final outcome of the MADM method. Therefore, in light of SIR method, Xu (2001) provided the decision-makers with a variety of mathematical functions that could be employed as the aggregation function. For instance, using a procedure similar to the WSM, the superiority and inferiority flows can be restated as follows:

$$\varphi^{>}(a_i) = \sum_{j=1}^{n} [w_j \times SU(a_i, c_j)] \tag{10.19}$$

$$\varphi^{<}(a_i) = \sum_{j=1}^{n} [w_j \times IN(a_i, c_j)] \tag{10.20}$$

in which $w_j =$ the weight assigned to each evaluation criteria, in a manner that the following is obtained:

$$\sum_{j=1}^{n} w_j \tag{10.21}$$

Note that Xu (2001) demonstrated that by employing Eqs. (10.19, 10.20), the superiority and inferiority flows would coincide with leaving and entering flows of the PROMETHEE method, respectively.

Inspired by TOPSIS method, Xu (2001) also proposed employing the concepts of the ideal and inferior solutions in composing the aggregation function. In that regard, an ideal and inferior solution with regard to the superiority matrix, where the maximization of the performance is the decision-makers' objective, is defined as follows:

$$a_{SU}^{+} = (SU_1^{+}, \ldots, SU_j^{+}, \ldots, SU_n^{+}) \tag{10.22}$$

$$a_{SU}^{-} = (SU_1^{-}, \ldots, SU_j^{-}, \ldots, SU_n^{-}) \tag{10.23}$$

in which a_{SU}^{+} and a_{SU}^{-} = the ideal and inferior solutions with regard to the superiority matrix, respectively; and SU_j^{+} and SU_j^{-} = the jth component of the ideal and inferior solutions vector, respectively, which is defined as follows:

$$SU_j^{+} = \underset{i}{Max}[SU(a_i, c_j)] \tag{10.24}$$

$$SU_j^{-} = \underset{i}{Min}[SU(a_i, c_j)] \tag{10.25}$$

In light of SIR method's terminology, the superiority flow can be redefined as follows:

$$\varphi^{>}(a_i) = \frac{SU^{-}(a_i)}{SU^{+}(a_i) + SU^{-}(a_i)} \tag{10.26}$$

in which $SU^{+}(a_i)$ and $SU^{-}(a_i)$ = the Minkowski distance between the ith alternative and the ideal and inferior solutions with regard to the superiority matrix, respectively, and are mathematically expressed as follows:

$$SU^{+}(a_i) = \left\{ \sum_{j=1}^{n} |w_j \times [SU(a_i, c_j) - SU_j^{+}]|^{\lambda} \right\}^{\frac{1}{\lambda}} \quad 1 \le \lambda < \infty \tag{10.27}$$

$$SU^{-}(a_i) = \left\{ \sum_{j=1}^{n} |w_j \times [SU(a_i, c_j) - SU_j^{-}]|^{\lambda} \right\}^{\frac{1}{\lambda}} \quad 1 \le \lambda < \infty \tag{10.28}$$

Note that the decision-maker can also tune SIR method through assigning the proper value for the λ parameter. For instance, $\lambda = 1$ would result in the block distance, or $\lambda = 2$ is the Euclidean distance between the alternative under consideration and the reference points, which are the ideal and inferior solutions.

In the same manner, the ideal and inferior solutions with regard to the inferiority matrix, where the maximization of the performance is the decision-makers' objective, are defined as follows:

$$a_{IN}^{+} = (IN_1^{+}, \ldots, IN_j^{+}, \ldots, IN_n^{+}) \tag{10.29}$$

$$a_{IN}^{-} = (IN_1^{-}, \ldots, IN_j^{-}, \ldots, IN_n^{-}) \tag{10.30}$$

in which a_{IN}^{+} and a_{IN}^{-} = the ideal and inferior solutions with regard to the inferiority matrix, respectively; and IN_j^{+} and IN_j^{-} = the *j*th component of the ideal and inferior solutions vector, respectively, which are defined as follows:

$$IN_j^{+} = \underset{i}{Max} IN(a_i, c_j) \tag{10.31}$$

$$IN_j^{-} = \underset{i}{Min} IN(a_i, c_j) \tag{10.32}$$

In light of the SIR method's terminology, the inferiority flow is redefined as follows:

$$\varphi^{<}(a_i) = \frac{IN^{-}(a_i)}{IN^{+}(a_i) + IN^{-}(a_i)} \tag{10.33}$$

in which $IN^{+}(a_i)$ and $IN^{-}(a_i)$ = the Minkowski distance between the *i*th alternative and the ideal and inferior solutions with regard to the inferiority matrix, respectively, and are mathematically expressed as follows:

$$IN^{+}(a_i) = \left\{ \sum_{j=1}^{n} |w_j \times [IN(a_i, c_j) - IN_j^{+}]|^{\lambda} \right\}^{\frac{1}{\lambda}} \quad 1 \leq \lambda < \infty \tag{10.34}$$

$$IN^{-}(a_i) = \left\{ \sum_{j=1}^{n} |w_j \times [IN(a_i, c_j) - IN_j^{-}]|^{\lambda} \right\}^{\frac{1}{\lambda}} \quad 1 \leq \lambda < \infty \tag{10.35}$$

Notice that the choice of the aggregation function is by no means exhaustive, and the decision-makers can employ other mathematical functions as they see feet (Xu 2001).

10.3.5 Step 5: Ranking the Set of Feasible Alternatives

The superiority flow measures how a given alternative is globally superior to all other feasible alternatives, while the inferiority flow measures how a given alternative is globally inferior to other plausible solutions. If the partial preorder of the alternatives is required by the decision-maker, the SIR method recommends a procedure similar to the philosophy employed by the ELECTRE family of methods for ranking the set of feasible alternatives. In that regard, first, the decision-makers must extract the decreasing ranked list of alternatives using the superiority flow and the preference structure $\Re_{>} = \{P_{>}, I_{>}\}$, described as follows:

$$aP^{>}b \text{ iff } \varphi^{>}(a) > \varphi^{>}(b) \tag{10.36}$$

$$aI^{>}b \text{ iff } \varphi^{>}(a) = \varphi^{>}(b) \tag{10.37}$$

A similar procedure IS used to extract the ascending ranked list of alternatives using the inferiority flow and the preference structure $\Re_{<} = \{P_{<}, I_{<}\}$, expressed as

Table 10.3 Conditional assessments used in the SIR method.

Status' symbol	Requiring condition	Description
aPb	(I) $aP_{>}b$ and $aP_{<}b$; or (II) $aP_{>}b$ and $aI_{<}b$; or (III) $aI_{>}b$ and $aP_{<}b$	The alternative a can outrank alternative b
aIb	$aI_{>}b$ and $aI_{<}b$	The alternatives a and b are indifferent to one another
aRb	(I) $aP_{>}b$ and $bP_{<}a$; or (II) $bP_{>}a$ and $aI_{<}b$	No conclusive comments can be made about the relationship of the alternative a and b

follows:

$$aP^{<}b \text{ iff } \varphi^{<}(a) < \varphi^{<}(b) \tag{10.38}$$

$$aI^{<}b \text{ iff } \varphi^{<}(a) = \varphi^{<}(b) \tag{10.39}$$

The final partial preorder of alternatives is obtained by combining the aforementioned ranked lists of alternatives using the partial preference structure $\mathfrak{R} = \{P, I, R\}$. This structure would categorize alternatives as a case where one is preferred to the other (aPb), a case where the alternatives are indifferent to one another (aIb), and, lastly, a case where no conclusive statement can be made regarding the comparing alternatives, as in the case when alternatives are incomparable to one another (aRb) (Table 10.3).

Notice the entire process can be done using the net matrix, introduced in Eq. (10.16). In such cases, similar to PROMETHEE II, the complete ranking of the alternatives constitutes the result of the assessment.

10.4 Conclusion

Similar to all compensatory, outranking-oriented MADM techniques, the SIR method is also based on two major stages, that is the aggregation and exploitation stages. Through the aggregation stage, the SIR method combines the concepts of superiority and inferiority scores and the generalized criteria to introduce a novel concept better known as the superiority and inferiority flows. Note that unlike most MADM techniques, the SIR method enables the decision-makers to explore numerous forms of aggregation functions so that the most suitable approach could be tuned for the specific MADM case at hand. In such a procedure, the

SIR method resembles and employs the concepts used in other known MADM methods. In that sense, the SIR method can be thought of as a further extension of some MADM methods, such as WSM, PROMETHEE, and TOPSIS. As for the last stage, the SIR method can generate both partial and complete preorder of alternatives. As a final note, one should bear in mind that in spite the fact that SIR method is a relatively new MADM technique several preliminary studies have demonstrated its potential in coping with real-world MADM problems.

References

Benayoun, R., Roy, B., and Sussman, B. (1966). ELECTRE: Une méthode pour guider le choix en présence de points de vue multiples. In: *Note de travail 49, SEMA-METRA International* (eds. R. Benayoun, B. Roy and B. Sussmann), 89–103. Paris, France: Direction Scientifique.

Brans, J.P. (1982). L'ingénierie de la decision. Elaboration d'instruments d'aide a la decision: Methode PROMETHEE. In: *L'aide a la Decision: Nature, Instruments et Perspectives D'avenir* (eds. R. Nadeau and M. Landry), 183–214. Québec, Canada: Presses de Universite Laval.

Brans, J.P., Vincke, P., and Mareschal, B. (1986). How to select and how to rank projects: the PROMETHEE method. *European Journal of Operational Research* 24 (2): 228–238.

Chai, J., Liu, J.N., and Xu, Z. (2012). A new rule-based SIR approach to supplier selection under intuitionistic fuzzy environments. *International Journal of Uncertainty, Fuzziness and Knowledge-Based Systems* 20 (03): 451–471.

Chang, Y.H. and Yeh, C.H. (2001). Evaluating airline competitiveness using multiattribute decision making. *Omega* 29 (5): 405–415.

Chen, S.J. and Hwang, C.L. (1992). *Fuzzy Multiple Attribute Decision Making: Methods and Applications*. Heidelberg, Germany: Springer Publication Company.

Churchman, C.W. and Ackoff, R.L. (1954). An approximate measure of value. *Journal of the Operations Research Society of America* 2 (2): 172–187.

Figueira, J.R., Greco, S., Roy, B., and Słowiński, R. (2013). An overview of ELECTRE methods and their recent extensions. *Journal of Multi-Criteria Decision Analysis* 20 (1–2): 61–85.

Hwang, C.L. and Yoon, K. (1981). Methods for multiple attribute decision making. In: *Multiple Attribute Decision Making: Lecture Notes in Economics and Mathematical Systems* (eds. C.L. Hwang and K. Yoon), 58–191. Heidelberg, Germany: Springer Publication Company.

Hwang, C.L., Lai, Y.J., and Liu, T.Y. (1993). A new approach for multiple objective decision making. *Computers and Operations Research* 20 (8): 889–899.

Liu, J.N. (2010). A novel multicriteria group decision making approach with intuitionistic fuzzy SIR method. In: *Proceedings of World Automation Congress, 2010*, 1–6. Kobe, Japan, September 19–23: IEEE.

Marzouk, M. (2008). A superiority and inferiority ranking model for contractor selection. *Construction Innovation* 8 (4): 250–268.

Marzouk, M., Shinnawy, N.E., Moselhi, O., and El-Said, M. (2013). Measuring sensitivity of procurement decisions using superiority and inferiority ranking. *International Journal of Information Technology and Decision Making* 12 (03): 395–423.

Mladineo, N., Margeta, J., Brans, J.P., and Mareschal, B. (1987). Multicriteria ranking of alternative locations for small scale hydro plants. *European Journal of Operational Research* 31 (2): 215–222.

Rebai, A. (1993). BBTOPSIS: a bag based technique for order preference by similarity to ideal solution. *Fuzzy Sets and Systems* 60 (2): 143–162.

Rebai, A. (1994). Canonical fuzzy bags and bag fuzzy measures as a basis for MADM with mixed non cardinal data. *European Journal of Operational Research* 78 (1): 34–48.

Roy, B. (1978). ELECTRE III: Un algorithme de classement fondé sur une représentation floue des préférences en présence de critères multiples. *Cahiers du Centre d'Etudes de Recherche Opérationnelle* 20 (1): 3–24.

Roy, B. and Bertier, P. (1971). La méthode ELECTRE II. In: *Note de travail 142, SEMA-METRA, Metra International*. Paris, France: Direction Scientifique.

Roy, B. and Hugonnard, J.C. (1982). Ranking of suburban line extension projects on the Paris metro system by a multicriteria method. *Transportation Research Part A: General* 16 (4): 301–312.

Tam, C.M., Tong, T.K., and Wong, Y.W. (2004). Selection of concrete pump using the superiority and inferiority ranking method. *Journal of Construction Engineering and Management* 130 (6): 827–834.

Vincke, J.P. and Brans, P. (1985). A preference ranking organization method: the PROMETHEE method for MCDM. *Management Science* 31 (6): 647–656.

Xu, X. (2001). The SIR method: a superiority and inferiority ranking method for multiple criteria decision making. *European Journal of Operational Research* 131 (3): 587–602.

Yoon, K. (1987). A reconciliation among discrete compromise solutions. *Journal of the Operational Research Society* 38: 277–286.

11 PAPRIKA

11.1 Introduction

When it comes to real-world decision-making, those in charge often find themselves in a situation where more than one viable and feasible solution can be presented for the problem at hand. In addition, the stakeholders' interests are often expressed through a set of confliction evolution criteria. The decision-makers employ logically supported, mathematically oriented frameworks to evaluate and chose among alternatives. These frameworks are a guide for the decision-makers to ensure a sound, smooth, and informed decision-making process.

The set of evaluation criteria can be composed of both tangible and intangible variables. Note that in a case where the interest of the stakeholders are of intangible nature the performance of an alternative must be expressed with regard to an implicitly defined scale, which in turns employs the experience and expertise of the decision-makers who are involved in the process of decision-making. Often, in such cases, the decision-makers would turn to ordinal values to express the performance of alternatives. Furthermore, even for the cases where multidimensional intangible variables are involved, the decision-makers often find it difficult to justify and cope with the computational efforts required in the process of decision-making where cardinal values are used directly. Instead, the decision-makers often employ an ordinal-oriented scales, which facilitates the assessment of the set of feasible alternatives. At the executive level, where the projects' big picture is of concern, or in cases where a fast decision-making is required, a branch of compensatory multiattribute decision-making (MADM) technique, which is commonly referred to as point counting, performance value, or scoring has proven itself as an effective pragmatic MADM approach.

Scoring-oriented MADM methods represent each evaluation criteria with a set of classes, often, expressed in linguistic terms (e.g. good, mediocre, and bad). Such representation simplify the alternatives evaluation process. However, the task of aggregating the overall performance of alternatives remains as a challenge

A Handbook on Multi-Attribute Decision-Making Methods, First Edition.
Omid Bozorg-Haddad, Babak Zolghadr-Asli, and Hugo A. Loáiciga.

for the decision-makers. In the case of scoring-oriented MADM methods, the decision-makers are presented with a framework to surpass this challenge. The value for each category represents the relative importance and the degree of achievement of a particular performance dimension. Potentially, all pairwise rankings of all possible alternatives (PAPRIKA) is a representative example of this branch of MADM methods.

Theorized by Hansen and Ombler (2008) PAPRIKA presents the decision-makers with an easy-to-use framework to cope with MADM problems that are expressed with ordinal values, where every criterion is placed in mutually exclusive categories. It should be noted that most, if not all, scoring-oriented MADM methods cannot cope with more than two or three criteria, which is the case for most real-world MADM problems. PAPRIKA, implements and combines the concepts that can be traced back to common pairwise comparison and outranking-oriented MADM techniques to rank the set of feasible alternatives based on their desirability on the stakeholders' perspective. It can potentially overcome the aforementioned challenge of high dimensional or multiattribute decision making. PAPRIKA has been successfully employed to cope with MADM problems in the fields of animal and plant breeding (Smith and Fennessy 2011, 2014; Byrne et al. 2012, 2016; Nielsen et al. 2014; Smith et al. 2014), charity giving (Hansen et al. 2014), clinical guidelines development (Griffin et al. 2016; Aggarwal et al. 2017; Pinto et al. 2017), disease diagnosis and classification (Aletaha et al. 2010; Neogi et al. 2010; Johnson 2015; Pope and Johnson 2015; Aringer et al. 2016; Vargas-Santos et al. 2016), environmental resources management (Boyd et al. 2011; Chhun et al. 2013, 2015; Graff and McIntyre 2014), foreign aid investment management (Cunningham et al. 2017), information and communications technology (ICT; Mancini et al. 2015; Al-Isma'ili et al. 2016a,b), marketing research (Lee et al. 2015; Wijland et al. 2016), patient and health technology prioritization (Golan et al. 2011; Georgiadis et al. 2013; Sullivan and Hansen 2017), urban planning (Moura et al. 2017), and waste management (Chang and Gronwald 2016). Most of PAPRIKA's applications were limited to experimental sciences, such as the medical fields. This notion is mainly due to the method's relatively easy mathematical foundation that facilitates coping with MADM problems, and by no means is an indication that this method could not be implemented to cope with more complex, real-world, MADM problems.

The following section represents a stepwise description on how to implement this method to cope with MADM problems.

11.2 Stepwise Description of PAPRIKA

The following is a stepwise description of the PAPRIKA method.

11.2.1 Step 1: Defining the Decision-Making Problem

At this junction, the decision-makers must rephrase the MADM problem at hand in a mathematical framework via a set of feasible, discrete alternatives, denoted by $A = \{a_1, a_2, \ldots, a_i, \ldots, a_m\}$, where a_i represents the ith alternative and m is the number of alternatives, and a set of evaluation criteria, denoted by $C = \{c_1, c_2, \ldots, c_j, \ldots, c_n\}$ in which c_j represents the jth evaluation criterion and n denotes the number of criteria. In MADM methods, the decision-maker expresses each criterion in mutually exclusive categories, where the zth class for the jth criterion is denoted by c_j^z. Assume that each criterion is divided into k mutually exclusive categories and the larger the number of a class, the more desirable it becomes. As far as the scoring-oriented MADM methods is concerned, each alternative can be seen as a vector where each array on this vector represents the performance of the given alternative with regard to the defined evaluation criteria.

11.2.2 Step 2: Identifying the Nondominated Pairs of Alternative

Each feasible alternative located in the discrete decision-space is represented as a vector, where each array corresponds to the score of the alternative with regard to each evaluation criteria, that is the class that best reflects the property of the under consideration alternative with respect to each criterion. Each alternative is categorized either as a dominated or nondominated solution. A nondominated solution is an alternative that in a comparison with other feasible solutions is characterized as a higher ranked category for at least one criterion and as a lower category for at least one other criterion than the other feasible solutions. Conversely, an alternative can be categorized as a dominated solution if the alternative's vector is of a lower category for at least one criterion and not higher with respect to other criteria when compared to other solutions. Clearly, dominated solutions have been clearly outranked by other feasible solutions and thus cannot be selected as the best option. The scoring-oriented MADM methods exploit this notion to derive the ranked lists of alternatives for dominated solutions. Naturally, these solutions are considered to be the least desirable from the stakeholders' perspective and are placed in the bottom layers of the ranked list of alternatives of a given MADM problem. Conversely, a solution that can dominate all other feasible solution is considered as the most desirable solution to the MADM problem at hand.

To rank the nondominated solutions, on the other hand, the decision-makers are instructed to identify all paired nondominated alternatives defined by two criteria at-a-time, that is, all the other criteria's categories are pairwise identical. In view of the joint-factor independence property of compensatory MADM methods (Krantz 1972), which states that the ranking of nondominated pairs is independent of their tied rankings on one or more criteria, the decision-makers are permitted to subtract those criteria in a nondominated pair of alternatives that are in the same category. In technical terms the outcome of the aforementioned process is referred to as the canceled form. The PAPRIKA method classifies all pairs in their canceled forms by their number of criteria, which is referred to as their degree. Notice that the aforementioned ranking mechanism simplifies the computation efforts required to rank the nondominated solutions for scoring-oriented MADM methods due to a phenomenon known as duplicated values. To put it differently, in real-world MADM problems, there is a noticeable overlap due to a considerable duplicated number of paired alternatives when all the nondominated pair of alternatives are represented in their canceled form. Omitting these duplicated entries, which simplifies the computation efforts required to rank the nondominated solutions, leads to identifying the list of unique nondominated paired alternatives. Hansen and Ombler (2008) demonstrated that for an MADM problem portrayed with n evaluation criteria each of which is classified into y mutually exclusive categories the total number of nondominated pairs of alternative with the x degree (TN_x) is calculated as follows:

$$TN_x = C_x^n \times (2^{x-1} - 1) \times (C_2^n)^x \times y^{n-x} \tag{11.1}$$

in which C_α^β = the number of combination of β taken α at-a-time. However, Hansen and Ombler (2008) also proved that the number of unique nondominate pairs with the degree x (UN_x), that is the total number of pairs when replicas are excluded, is as follows:

$$UN_x = C_x^n \times (2^{x-1} - 1) \times (C_2^n)^x \tag{11.2}$$

11.2.3 Step 3: Ranking the Pairs of Nondominated Solutions

To this point, all the nondominated alternatives, which are labeled with different degrees are identified. Extracting the complete preorder of alternatives, and in turn, choosing the most desirable solution to the MADM problem at hand would solely rely on determining the priority between these identified nondominated pairs of alternatives. Given that there is no certain indication to which alternative is considered to be superior, or more desirable to the stakeholders, in a unique nondominated pair of solutions, the PAPRIKA method invokes the decision-makers' subjective assessments. The latter assessments are rooted in cognitive understanding, experts opinions, and decision makers' instincts to explicitly rank the unique nondominated pairs of solutions. Presumably, pairs with just two criteria are intrinsically the least cognitively complex to pairwise rank relative to pairs with more criteria. According to the PAPRIKA method, the decision-maker begins the process of deriving the complete ranking of alternatives by explicitly ranking the second degree identified pairs of unique nondominated solutions. To that end, the decision-makers explicitly rank the pairs by determining which one of these nondominated solutions in the pair is considered to be more desirable to the stakeholders. If an alternative is considered more desirable, say alternative a is preferred to alternative b, the situation is symbolized as $a \succ b$; on the other hand, the decision-maker might consider these alternatives to be indifferent to one another, in which case $a \sim b$ is how the relation among the nondominated pair of alternatives would be labeled.

Notice that while the process of explicitly ranking the identified unique pairs of nondominated solution proceeds some of these pairs are implicitly ranked using the gathered informational from the subjective judgments made explicitly by the decision-makers to rank the previous nondominated pairs of solutions. In fact, central to PAPRIKA is the identification of all nondominated pairs implicitly ranked as corollaries of the explicitly ranked pairs. The process in the PAPRIKA method of identifying those unique pairs of nondominated solutions that can be implicitly ranked is done using a two-stage test. For two hypothetical unique nondominated pair of alternative, say a and b, the hypothesis of $a \succ b$ is tested by examining the existence of a feasible solution to a linear program comprising of the three set of data, that is (i) the predetermined category rankings based on the criteria; (ii) the earlier explicitly ranked pairs of unique nondominate alternatives; and (iii) a hypothetically ranked pair corresponding to the nondominated pair in question, ranked hypothetically as $a \succ b$. If no solution exists for the described linear programming problem, one can safely assume that the pair can be ranked as either $a \prec b$ or $a \sim b$. In either case, the results imply that the pair can be implicitly ranked, thus can be discarded and should not require the decision-maker to explicitly rank them. If, however, there exists a solution to the aforementioned linear programming, the test would proceeded to its second stage, where the existence of a feasible solution to a similar linear program would be tested, except, in this stage the unique nondominated pair of alternative in question is hypothetically ranked as $a \prec b$ instead of $a \succ b$, as the first stage. When no solution emerges for the second linear programming problem given the results from the first stage of the test one can conclude that $a \succ b$ which, in turn indicates that the results are implicitly ranked. In this case, it is not required the decision-makers explicitly rank the alternatives. Instead, if a solution exists, then it is theoretically possible for the decision-maker to explicitly rank the pair as $a \succ b$, $a \prec b$, or $a \sim b$, which in turn, implies that the pair of unique nondominate alternatives under consideration cannot be implicitly ranked as a corollary of the explicitly ranked pairs, thus the decision-makers must explicitly rank the alternatives. With regard to ranking of alternatives, one should realize that fewer explicitly ranked pairs are required when there is indifference rather than strict preference. On the whole, indifferently ranked pairs generate more corollaries than strictly ranked pairs.

One of the main advantages of PAPRIKA over other scoring-oriented MADM method is the degree of freedom it provides for the decision-makers in the process of evaluating the desirability of alternatives. The decision-makers may decline to explicitly rank any given pair of unique nondominated alternatives on the grounds that the lack of knowledge about the precise nature of such pairs under consideration, the problem in hand, or the desires of the stakeholders, disable them to compare that particular pair of alternatives. According to the PAPRIKA method, the decision-makers are enabled to skip evaluating such pairs, therefore excluding them from being explicitly evaluated, on the ground that such a pair would eventually be implicitly evaluated as a corollary of other explicitly ranked pairs using the pieces of information gathered from the other subjective judgments made by the decision-makers.

11.2.4 Step 4: Calculating the Complete Ranking of Alternatives

When it comes to real-world, complex, MADM problems, however, calculating the list of nondominated pairs would be a challenging task for scoring-oriented MADM methods. Likewise, identifying all pairs implicitly ranked as corollaries of the explicitly ranked pairs becomes increasingly intractable as the numbers of criteria and categories increase. In fact, due to these facts, most scoring-oriented MADM methods, which are commonly centered on the idea of using simple pairwise compassion approach to identify the nondominated pairs, are considered to be obsolete and inefficient approaches to help the decision-making to cope with real-world MADM problems (Johnson 1976). The PAPRIKA method, however, is suited with a mathematical and probabilistic-oriented algorithm to overcome this challenge. This algorithm represents the decision-makers with the identified pairs of unique nondominated alternatives to be explicitly ranked, then uses the information to implicitly rank other alternatives.

The process of ranking the alternatives begins with randomly selecting a unique pair of second-degree nondominated alternatives. The selected pair is presented to the decision-maker to be explicitly ranked. Using the two-stage test discussed in the previous step, all the pairs that can be implicitly ranked as corollaries of the subjective judgment made by the decision-makers are identified, ranked, and discarded from the poll of unique nondominated pairs of alternatives. This cycle is repeated until all second-degree pairs have been either explicitly or implicitly ranked. If need be, the decision-maker would then repeat the entire process for the third-degree pairs. This cycle is repeated for successively higher degrees until potentially all nondominated pairs for all degrees have been either explicitly ranked or can be ordered implicitly as corollaries of the explicitly ranked alternatives. Once the decision-maker ceases ranking of the unique nondominated pairs of alternatives linear programming can be employed to solve the system of inequalities and equalities corresponding to the explicitly ranked pairs to obtain the values required to calculate the ranked list of all feasible alternatives.

Given the random nature of electing the paired unique nondominated alternatives that are presented to the decision-makers for an explicit ranking the number of iterations required to derive the final complete preorder of alternatives may differ from case to case. In fact, Hansen and Ombler (2008) explored this issue and concluded that the order in which the decision-maker ranks pairs affects the number of subjective judgments required to be made by the decision-makers to explicitly rank the alternatives. However, determining the optimal order is problematic as it depends on the rankings themselves, which are, obviously, unknown a priori.

The PAPRIKA method is a practical and an efficient scoring-oriented MADM method that is centered around the identification of all unquiet nondominated pairs of alternative, and employment of the subjective judgments made by experts and decision-makers to explicitly rank these identified pairs and, in turn, as corollaries implicitly rank the reaming identified pairs. The iterative, cognitive-supported, mathematical framework used in the PAPRIKA method, which enables the method to overcome the shortcoming in other scoring-oriented MADM methods, one the one hand, and the easy-to-use methodology of the method, on the other, render PAPRIKA an ideal choice for the decision-makers to cope with scoring-oriented MADM problems.

11.3 Conclusion

PAPRIKA is a scoring-oriented MADM method, which is imbedded with an iterative-based, cognitive-supported, mathematical algorithm that enables the decision-makers to extract the complete preorder of all feasible alternatives. Central to the method's algorithm is a three-stage process. At first, the method identifies all the unique nondominated pairs of alternatives. In fact, this pool of alternatives is where the potential solutions to the given MADM pertains are gathered. In the second stage, the judgments of the experts are employed to explicitly rank the identified pairs. The PAPRIKA method applies the gathered information to implicitly rank the other reaming pairs and discard them from the pool of alternatives that is changing over time. This procedure facilitates the process of decision-making by reducing the number of explicit evaluations made by the decision-makers. The aforementioned process continues, iteratively, until potentially all nondominated pairs are ranked. In essence, the number of pairs to be explicitly ranked is minimized by PAPRIKA identifying and eliminating all pairs implicitly ranked as corollaries of the explicitly ranked pairs. In the final stage, PAPRIKA applies linear programming to obtain the values needed to calculate the ranked list of all the feasible alternatives of the scoring-oriented MADM problem at hand. Notice that although multiple solutions to the linear program of inequalities and equalities are possible the resulting values all reproduce the same overall ranking of alternatives.

References

Aggarwal, R., Rider, L.G., Ruperto, N. et al. (2017). 2016 American college of rheumatology/European league against rheumatism criteria for minimal, moderate, and major clinical response in adult dermatomyositis and polymyositis: an international myositis assessment and clinical studies group/paediatric rheumatology international trials organisation collaborative initiative. *Arthritis and Rheumatology* 69 (5): 898–910.

Aletaha, D., Neogi, T., Silman, A.J. et al. (2010). 2010 rheumatoid arthritis classification criteria: an American college of rheumatology/European league against rheumatism collaborative initiative. *Arthritis and Rheumatism* 62 (9): 2569–2581.

Al-Isma'ili, S., Li, M., and Shen, J. (2016a). Cloud computing adoption decision modelling for SMEs: from the PAPRIKA perspective. In: *Frontier Computing* (eds. J.C. Hung, N.Y. Yen and K.-C. Li), 597–615. Singapore: Springer.

Al-Isma'ili, S., Li, M., Shen, J., and He, Q. (2016b). Cloud computing adoption decision modelling for SMEs: a conjoint analysis. *International Journal of Web and Grid Services* 12 (3): 296–327.

Aringer, M., Dörner, T., Leuchten, N., and Johnson, S.R. (2016). Toward new criteria for systemic lupus erythematosus – a standpoint. *Lupus* 25 (8): 805–811.

Boyd, P.W., Law, C.S., and Doney, S.C. (2011). A climate change atlas for the ocean. *Oceanography* 24 (2): 13–16.

Byrne, T.J., Amer, P.R., Fennessy, P.F. et al. (2012). A preference-based approach to deriving breeding objectives: applied to sheep breeding. *Animal* 6 (5): 778–788.

Byrne, T.J., Santos, B.F.S., Amer, P.R. et al. (2016). New breeding objectives and selection indices for the Australian dairy industry. *Journal of Dairy Science* 99 (10): 8146–8167.

Chang, S.Y. and Gronwald, F. (2016). A multi-criteria evaluation of the methods for recycling scrap tires. *The Journal of Solid Waste Technology and Management* 42 (2): 145–156.

Chhun, S., Thorsnes, P., and Moller, H. (2013). Preferences for management of near-shore marine ecosystems: a choice experiment in New Zealand. *Resources* 2 (3): 406–438.

Chhun, S., Kahui, V., Moller, H., and Thorsnes, P. (2015). Advancing marine policy toward ecosystem-based management by eliciting public preferences. *Marine Resource Economics* 30 (3): 261–275.

Cunningham, H., Knowles, S., and Hansen, P. (2017). Bilateral foreign aid: how important is aid effectiveness to people for choosing countries to support? *Applied Economics Letters* 24 (5): 306–310.

Georgiadis, D.R., Mazzuchi, T.A., and Sarkani, S. (2013). Using multi criteria decision making in analysis of alternatives for selection of enabling technology. *Systems Engineering* 16 (3): 287–303.

Golan, O., Hansen, P., Kaplan, G., and Tal, O. (2011). Health technology prioritization: Which criteria for prioritizing new technologies and what are their relative weights? *Health Policy* 102 (2): 126–135.

Graff, P. and McIntyre, S. (2014). Using ecological attributes as criteria for the selection of plant species under three restoration scenarios. *Austral Ecology* 39 (8): 907–917.

Griffin, D.R., Dickenson, E.J., O'donnell, J. et al. (2016). The Warwick Agreement on femoroacetabular impingement syndrome (FAI syndrome): an international consensus statement. *British Journal of Sports Medicine* 50 (19): 1169–1176.

Hansen, P. and Ombler, F. (2008). A new method for scoring additive multi-attribute value models using pairwise rankings of alternatives. *Journal of Multi-Criteria Decision Analysis* 15 (3–4): 87–107.

Hansen, P., Kergozou, N., Knowles, S., and Thorsnes, P. (2014). Developing countries in need: Which characteristics appeal most to people when donating money? *The Journal of Development Studies* 50 (11): 1494–1509.

Johnson, R.M. (1976). Beyond conjoint measurement: a method of pairwise trade-off analysis. *Advances in Consumer Research* 3: 353–358.

Johnson, S.R. (2015). New ACR EULAR guidelines for systemic sclerosis classification. *Current Rheumatology Reports* 17 (5): 32.

Krantz, D.H. (1972). Measurement structures and psychological laws. *Science* 175 (4029): 1427–1435.

Lee, P.Y., Lusk, K., Mirosa, M., and Oey, I. (2015). An attribute prioritization-based segmentation of the Chinese consumer market for fruit juice. *Food Quality and Preference* 46: 1–8.

Mancini, A., Frontoni, E., and Zingaretti, P. (2015). Embedded multisensor system for safe point-to-point navigation of impaired users. *IEEE Transactions on Intelligent Transportation Systems* 16 (6): 3543–3555.

Moura, F., Cambra, P., and Gonçalves, A.B. (2017). Measuring walkability for distinct pedestrian groups with a participatory assessment method: a case study in Lisbon. *Landscape and Urban Planning* 157: 282–296.

Neogi, T., Aletaha, D., Silman, A.J. et al. (2010). The 2010 American college of rheumatology/European league against rheumatism classification criteria for rheumatoid arthritis: phase 2 methodological report. *Arthritis and Rheumatism* 62 (9): 2582–2591.

Nielsen, H.M., Amer, P.R., and Byrne, T.J. (2014). Approaches to formulating practical breeding objectives for animal production systems. *Acta Agriculturae Scandinavica, Section A – Animal Science* 64 (1): 2–12.

Pinto, D., Danilovich, M.K., Hansen, P. et al. (2017). Qualitative development of a discrete choice experiment for physical activity interventions to improve knee osteoarthritis. *Archives of Physical Medicine and Rehabilitation* 98 (6): 1210–1216.

Pope, J.E. and Johnson, S.R. (2015). New classification criteria for systemic sclerosis (scleroderma). *Rheumatic Disease Clinics* 41 (3): 383–398.

Smith, K.F. and Fennessy, P.F. (2011). The use of conjoint analysis to determine the relative importance of specific traits as selection criteria for the improvement of perennial pasture species in Australia. *Crop and Pasture Science* 62 (4): 355–365.

Smith, K.F. and Fennessy, P.F. (2014). Utilizing conjoint analysis to develop breeding objectives for the improvement of pasture species for contrasting environments when the relative values of individual traits are difficult to assess. *Sustainable Agriculture Research* 3 (2): 44.

Smith, K.F., Ludemann, C., Lewis, C.D. et al. (2014). Estimating the value of genetic gain in perennial pastures with emphasis on temperate species. *Crop and Pasture Science* 65 (11): 1230–1237.

Sullivan, T. and Hansen, P. (2017). Determining criteria and weights for prioritizing health technologies based on the preferences of the general population: a New Zealand pilot study. *Value in Health* 20 (4): 679–686.

Vargas-Santos, A.B., Taylor, W.J., and Neogi, T. (2016). Gout classification criteria: update and implications. *Current Rheumatology Reports* 18 (7): 46.

Wijland, R., Hansen, P., and Gardezi, F. (2016). Mobile nudging: youth engagement with banking apps. *Journal of Financial Services Marketing* 21 (1): 51–63.

12

Gray Relational Analysis

12.1 Introduction

The reviewed multiattribute decision-making (MADM) methods assume the decision-makers solved problems known with certainty. In practice, however, this might be a rather unrealistic presumption due to the fact that in most real-world cases, the environment surrounding the decision-making may be uncertain, which in turn makes any attempt to implicate deterministic approaches to capture such environment a moot point. The uncertainty might be rooted in the external world surrounding the decision-making problem, making the decision-maker unable to predict the exact chain of events that leads to the outcome of a problem. In such situations, the occurrence of each given outcome is probabilistic in nature. Probabilistic-oriented methods are the ideal tools to deal with such problems. As stated earlier, these assessments are beyond the scope of this book. Alternatively, these uncertainties might be rooted in an internal source, making the decision-maker unable to precisely express the priorities in an MADM problem. In such circumstances, whether due to a cognitive uncertainty or poor information, the decision-makers' judgments are affected in a manner that an accurate expression of such situations in classical mathematical terms is impossible. Fuzzy logic-oriented methods are the decision-makers' first choice to cope with cognitive uncertainty (Liu et al. 2012). In some instances, the decision-makers are unable to assess the values of alternatives and criteria in a MADM problem. Linguistic rank scales are commonly used in such situations. When decision-making occurs with poor information gray system theory is a suitable method to cope with such situations.

The gray systems theory, introduced by Deng (1982), aims at problems involving small samples and/or partially known information sets, through generating, and extracting useful information from the limited available data. Uncertain systems with small samples and poor information sets exist commonly.

A Handbook on Multi-Attribute Decision-Making Methods, First Edition.
Omid Bozorg-Haddad, Babak Zolghadr-Asli, and Hugo A. Loáiciga.

Therefore, gray systems theory has a wide range of applicability in many fields including agriculture (Wang et al. 2010), economy (Franco-Santos et al. 2007), energy management (Liang et al. 2012), environmental (Qiao et al. 2006), geology (Lv et al. 2012), hydrology (Hao et al. 2007), medical science (Xuerui and Yuguang 2004), meteorology (Yu et al. 2000; Hao et al. 2006), municipal management (Li et al. 2004), sports (Fan 2013), and others.

The essential contents and topics of gray system theory encompass the gray relation space, gray incidence analysis, gray cluster evaluation, gray modeling, gray generating space, gray forecasting, gray control, and gray decision-making (Deng 1989; Liu et al. 2012). The gray rational analysis is a branch of gray system theory which is involved in solving MADM problems. As an emerging MADM tool, the gray rational analysis provides a unique feature that enables the decision-maker to deal with problems that would otherwise be considered as impossible, or at least improbable, to solve due to insufficient available data. Consequently, the gray relational analysis soon caught the attention of scholars and practitioners. A literature of review revealed that from 1996 through 2010 more than 453 studies on gray relational analysis were reported in the fields of engineering (45%), mathematics (20%), computer science (20%), materials science (17%), automation control system (12%), and operations research management science (11%) (Yin 2013). This chapter describes gray system theory, its basic principles, and its application in the field of MADM.

12.2 Gray System Theory: The Foundation and Basic Principles

In 1982 Professor Julong Deng, a fellow of Huazhong University of Science and Technology, Wuhan, China, authored a series of articles that laid the foundation of the gray system theory. From this work, a system with partially available information and/or inaccurate data sets was called a gray system. The word "gray" in this context reflects the absence of sufficient data. Note that in light of this terminology, a "white" system is endowed with fully known information, whereas a "black" system has no information available for the decision-maker (Liu et al. 2012). Gray systems may have inadequate information (e.g. lack of knowledge regarding the system's boundaries, elements, and structure), or exhibit inaccurate data sets, and are thus incomplete, inaccurate, or uncertain to various degrees (Deng 1989; Liu et al. 2012).

The gray system theory is based upon a series of fundamental principles that rest on the following axioms (Liu et al. 2012):

Axiom I. The principle of informational differences: The term "difference" implies the existence of information, where each piece of information must carry some kind of "difference."

Axiom II. The principle of nonuniqueness: Any given problem with incomplete and indeterminate information set cannot have a unique solution.

Axiom III. The principle of minimal information: The gray systems theory is based on making the most out of the minimal amount of available information.

Axiom IV. The principle of recognition base: Information is the foundation on which people identify and comprehend a phenomenon.

Axiom V. The principle of new information priority: each new amount of information is of more value than old pieces of information.

Axiom VI. The principle of absolute grayness: completeness in information is a relative term, however, incompleteness in available information is absolute.

12.3 Gray Relational Modeling

To employ gray relational analysis in a multidimensional problem, one must frame the given problem using the gray relational theory, a process commonly referred to as gray relational modeling. Gray relational modeling involves redefining the mean linkage between one main factor and all other factors in the given system through an instrument, better known as, the gray relational space (Deng 1989). A gray relational space is a binary vector denoted by (X, Γ), in which, the gray relational factor set denoted by X represents a set composed of comparative sequences l_i (for $i = 1, 2, \ldots, m$) and a reference sequence denoted by l_0; and Γ denotes a map set called the gray relational map set. Notice that each given sequence, whether it is a comparison or the reference sequence, is represented through a set of arrays as follows:

$$l_0 = [l_0(1), l_0(2), \ldots, l_0(j), \ldots, l_0(n)] \tag{12.1}$$

$$l_i = [l_i(1), l_i(2), \ldots, l_i(j), \ldots, l_i(n)] \tag{12.2}$$

in which, $l_0(j)$ and $l_i(j)$ = numerals at point j for sequences l_0 and l_i, respectively.

Let $\gamma \in \Gamma$ represent an appointed relational map set, where

$$\gamma[l_0(j), l_i(j)] \in \Re \quad \forall i, j \tag{12.3}$$

Then, $\gamma[l_0(j), l_i(j)]$ is an image at point j from the described series to the real number set with the map γ. The image of the ith comparative sequence (l_i) is obtained as follows (Deng 1989):

$$\gamma(l_0, l_i) = \frac{1}{n}\sum_{j=1}^{n}\gamma[l_0(j), l_i(j)] \quad \forall i \tag{12.4}$$

According to gray system theory, technical terminology $\gamma[l_0(j), l_i(j)]$ = a gray relational coefficient for the ith comparative sequence at the jth point; and $\gamma(l_0, l_i)$ = a gray relational grade if and if the following axioms hold for the gray rational space (Γ):

Axiom 12.1 ***Norm interval***

$$\gamma[l_0(j), l_i(j)] \in (0, 1] \quad \forall j \tag{12.5}$$

where $\gamma[l_0(j), l_i(j)]$ is equal to 1, if and only if $l_0(j)$ is equal to $l_i(j)$. Additionally, $\gamma[l_0(j), l_i(j)]$ is equal to zero if and only if $l_0(j)$ and $l_i(j)$ are members of an empty set $[l_0(j), l_i(j) \in \phi]$.

Axiom 12.2 ***Duality symmetric***

$$\gamma[l_0(j), l_i(j)] = \gamma[l_i(j), l_0(j)] \text{ if and only if } X = \{l_0, l_i\} \tag{12.6}$$

Axiom 12.3 ***Wholeness***

$$\gamma[l_0(j), l_i(j)] \overset{\textit{almost always}}{\neq} \gamma[l_i(j), l_0(j)] \text{ if and only if } X = \{l_i \mid i = 0, 1, \ldots, m\} \quad m > 2 \tag{12.7}$$

Axiom 12.4 ***Approachability***

$\gamma[l_0(j), l_i(j)]$ decreases along with $\Delta_i(j)$ increasing, where:

$$\Delta_i(j) = \mid l_0(j) - l_i(j) \mid \tag{12.8}$$

The following equation expresses the gray relational coefficient which embeds axioms 12.1, 12.2, 12.3, and 12.4 (Deng 1989).

$$\gamma[l_0(j), l_i(j)] = \frac{\underset{i}{Min}\,\underset{j}{Min}\Delta_i(j) + \zeta \underset{i}{Max}\,\underset{j}{Max}\Delta_i(j)}{\Delta_i(j) + \zeta \underset{i}{Max}\,\underset{j}{Max}\Delta_i(j)} \tag{12.9}$$

in which, ζ = distinguishing coefficient, in the range (0,1) (Deng 1989). The purpose of the distinguishing coefficient is to expand or compress the range of the gray relational coefficient. Given that the distinguishing coefficient can influence the determination of the final result, it is beneficial to conduct a survey in which the range of the distinguishing coefficient can be tested according to the unique features of the problem in hand (Kuo et al. 2008). According to the literature, however, in cases where the computational cost is great and/or time is of the essence $\zeta = 0.5$ is commonly applied in gray relational analysis (Deng 1989; Chan and Tong 2007).

12.4 Gray Theory in Relation to MADM

At this juncture, it is beneficial to recall the decision matrix (D):

$$D = \begin{array}{c} \\ a_1 \\ \vdots \\ a_m \end{array} \begin{array}{c} \begin{array}{ccc} c_1 & \cdots & c_n \end{array} \\ \begin{bmatrix} v_{(1,1)} & \dots & v_{(1,n)} \\ \vdots & \ddots & \vdots \\ v_{(m,1)} & \cdots & v_{(m,n)} \end{bmatrix} \end{array} \tag{12.10}$$

in which, a_i = the predetermined, feasible ith alternative; c_j = the predefined jth criterion determined by the decision-maker; $v_{(i,j)}$ = the value of the ith alternative with regard to the jth criterion; m = number of feasible alternatives; and n = number of criteria.

One approach to choose the most suitable alternative in an MADM problem is to aggregate the alternatives' values with regard to each criteria's importance so that an overall score is computed for each given alternative. The aforementioned notion can be mathematically expressed as follows:

$$V_i = \sum_{j=1}^{n} w_j \times v_{(i,j)} \quad \forall j\, w_j \geq 0; \sum w_j = 1 \tag{12.11}$$

in which, V_i = the overall performance of the ith alternative; and w_j = the weight assigned to the jth criterion.

If the decision-maker is aware of the entirety of the problem, then a deterministic MADM approach can be applied to solve the problem at hand. However, this might not be the case in most practical decision-making problems, in which there are elements in the decision-making process that are known only with a degree of certainty. Take the case where the decision-maker is unable to fully express the priorities of alternatives with regard to each of the predefined criteria [$v_{(i,j)}$] due to a poor information set. In such cases, either the lack of information and/or a degree of inaccuracy in the data set could jeopardize the integrity of the alternatives' values with regard to the criteria, and in turn the result of the decision-making process. As far as the uncertainty is concerned, such situations can be remedied with the gray system theory.

According to gray system theory, each alternative is viewed as a sequential series, where each element of the series represents the alternatives' performances with regard to the predefined criteria. However, to fulfill the axioms of the gray relational space, each element of these sequential series must be redefined accordingly. This process, which in technical terms is referred to as gray relational generating, is achieved through the following two equations (Kuo et al. 2008):

$$v^*_{(i,j)} = \frac{v_{(i,j)} - \underset{i}{Min}\, v_{(i,j)}}{\underset{i}{Max}\, v_{(i,j)} - \underset{i}{Min}\, v_{(i,j)}} \tag{12.12}$$

$$v^*_{(i,j)} = \frac{\underset{i}{Max}\, v_{(i,j)} - v_{(i,j)}}{\underset{i}{Max}\, v_{(i,j)} - \underset{i}{Min}\, v_{(i,j)}} \tag{12.13}$$

in which, $v^*_{(i,j)}$ = the gray relational generated value of the ith alternative with regard to the jth criterion. Notice that while Eq. (12.12) is used for the larger-the-better or positive criteria, Eq. (12.13) can be used for the-smaller-the-better or negative criteria.

From the viewpoint of gray relational analysis, one must also define the reference sequence denoted by v_0. Given that through the gray relational generating every element of the comparative sequences is transformed into a 0–1 range, where the most desirable preference is represented by 1, the reference sequence is expressed as follows:

$$v_0 = [v_{(0,1)}, v_{(0,2)}, \ldots, v_{(0,j)}, \ldots, v_{(0,n)}] \quad \forall j, v_{(0,j)} = 1 \tag{12.14}$$

The next step in conducting a gray relational analysis for an MADM problem is to compute the gray relational coefficient for every given element involved in the decision-making process. Bearing in mind the gray relational grade introduced in Eq. (12.9) the gray relational coefficients of the given MADM problem are calculated as follows:

$$\gamma[v_{(0,j)}, v^*_{(i,j)}] = \frac{\underset{i}{Min}\,\underset{j}{Min} \mid v_{(0,j)} - v^*_{(i,j)} \mid + \zeta \underset{i}{Max}\,\underset{j}{Max} \mid v_{(0,j)} - v^*_{(i,j)} \mid}{\mid v_{(0,j)} - v^*_{(i,j)} \mid + \zeta \underset{i}{Max}\,\underset{j}{Max} \mid v_{(0,j)} - v^*_{(i,j)} \mid} \tag{12.15}$$

Lastly, the decision-matrix of the MADM problem is restructured using the gray relational coefficients that are obtained via Eq. (12.15), as follows:

$$D_G = \begin{bmatrix} \gamma[v_{(0,1)}, v^*_{(1,1)}] & \cdots & \gamma[v_{(0,j)}, v^*_{(1,j)}] & \cdots & \gamma[v_{(0,n)}, v^*_{(1,n)}] \\ \vdots & \ddots & & & \vdots \\ \gamma[v_{(0,1)}, v^*_{(i,1)}] & \cdots & \gamma[v_{(0,j)}, v^*_{(i,j)}] & \cdots & \gamma[v_{(0,n)}, v^*_{(i,n)}] \\ \vdots & & & \ddots & \vdots \\ \gamma[v_{(0,1)}, v^*_{(m,1)}] & \cdots & \gamma[v_{(0,j)}, v^*_{(m,j)}] & \cdots & \gamma[v_{(0,n)}, v^*_{(m,n)}] \end{bmatrix} \tag{12.16}$$

in which, D_G = the gray relational coefficient matrix.

Implying a procedure similar to what has been previously exploited in Eq. (12.17) each alternative's gray relational grade, which is the overall value of each given alternative, calculated as follows (Fung 2003):

$$\gamma(v_0, v_i^*) = \sum_{j=1}^{n} w_j \times \gamma[v_{(0,j)}, v_{(i,j)}^*] \quad \forall j\, w_j \geq 0; \sum w_j = 1 \tag{12.17}$$

in which, $\gamma(v_0, v_i^*)$ = the gray relational grade of the ith alternative. Naturally, the higher the gray relational grade, the more preferable the alternative. Also note that while the gray relational analysis assists the decision-maker in expressing the alternatives' values in an uncertain environment, it offers no solution for the criteria weighting mechanism [i.e. assigning weights (w_j) to the criteria]. Presumably, with regard to the unique features of the MADM problem in hand, the decision-maker is free to opt the appropriate weighting mechanism, [e.g. analytical hierarchy process (AHP), analytical network process (ANP), best-worst method (BWM)] (Tzeng and Huang 2011). For more information regarding the weighting mechanism sees the appendix section.

12.5 Conclusion

Making-decision in an uncertain environment is a challenging yet inevitable issue in most practical, real-world, MADM problems. Gray relational analysis, as a branch of gray system theory, offers an elegant and pragmatic solution to address such uncertainties that are rooted in lack of information and/or inaccuracy in data sets. In light of gray system theory, the MADM problem is redefined in a gray relational space. Through this procedure, the decision-maker ought to compare the feasible alternatives of the MADM problem to an ideal solution, better known as the reference sequence. Next, the alternatives are redefined via a mathematical transforming function, called gray relational grade, which in essence, correlates each given alternative to the reference sequence. Finally, the decision-maker is able to aggregate the result and prioritize the feasible solutions of the MADM problem. The gray relational analysis' performance has been tested through a variety of studies, and its potential as an MADM solving method has been proven numerous times.

References

Chan, J.W. and Tong, T.K. (2007). Multi-criteria material selections and end-of-life product strategy: grey relational analysis approach. *Materials and Design* 28 (5): 1539–1546.

Deng, J. (1982). Control problems of grey systems. *Systems and Control Letters* 1 (5): 288–294.

Deng, J. (1989). Introduction to grey system theory. *The Journal of Grey System* 1 (1): 1–24.

Fan, Y. (2013). Statistical analysis based on gray system theory basketball team scores its technical indicators associated. *International Journal of Applied Mathematics and Statistics* 44 (14): 185–192.

Franco-Santos, M., Kennerley, M., Micheli, P. et al. (2007). Towards a definition of a business performance measurement system. *International Journal of Operations and Production Management* 27 (8): 784–801.

Fung, C.P. (2003). Manufacturing process optimization for wear property of fiber-reinforced polybutylene terephthalate composites with grey relational analysis. *Wear* 254 (3): 298–306.

Hao, Y., Yeh, T.C.J., Gao, Z. et al. (2006). A gray system model for studying the response to climatic change: the Liulin karst springs, China. *Journal of Hydrology* 328 (3): 668–676.

Hao, Y., Yeh, T.C.J., Wang, Y., and Zhao, Y. (2007). Analysis of karst aquifer spring flows with a gray system decomposition model. *Groundwater* 45 (1): 46–52.

Kuo, Y., Yang, T., and Huang, G.W. (2008). The use of grey relational analysis in solving multiple attribute decision-making problems. *Computers and Industrial Engineering* 55 (1): 80–93.

Li, J., Yue, Z.Q., and Wong, S.C. (2004). Performance evaluation of signalized urban intersections under mixed traffic conditions by gray system theory. *Journal of Transportation Engineering* 130 (1): 113–121.

Liang, C., Gu, D., Bichindaritz, I. et al. (2012). Integrating gray system theory and logistic regression into case-based reasoning for safety assessment of thermal power plants. *Expert Systems with Applications* 39 (5): 5154–5167.

Liu, S., Forrest, J., and Yang, Y. (2012). A brief introduction to grey systems theory. *Grey Systems: Theory and Application* 2 (2): 89–104.

Lv, Y., Tang, D., Xu, H., and Luo, H. (2012). Production characteristics and the key factors in high-rank coalbed methane fields: a case study on the Fanzhuang Block, Southern Qinshui Basin, China. *International Journal of Coal Geology* 96: 93–108.

Qiao, B., Fang, C.L., and Ban, M.S. (2006). Investigation of the interactive, intimidating relation between urbanization and the environment in an arid area based on grey system theory. *Journal of China University of Mining and Technology* 16 (4): 452–456.

Tzeng, G.H. and Huang, J.J. (2011). *Multiple Attribute Decision Making: Methods and Applications*. Boca Raton, FL: CRC Press.

Wang, Y.B., Wu, P.T., Zhao, X.N. et al. (2010). The optimization for crop planning and some advances for water-saving crop planning in the semiarid loess plateau of China. *Journal of Agronomy and Crop Science* 196 (1): 55–65.

Xuerui, T. and Yuguang, L. (2004). Using grey relational analysis to analyze the medical data. *Kybernetes* 33 (2): 355–362.

Yin, M.S. (2013). Fifteen years of grey system theory research: a historical review and bibliometric analysis. *Expert Systems with Applications* 40 (7): 2767–2775.

Yu, P.S., Chen, C.J., and Chen, S.J. (2000). Application of gray and fuzzy methods for rainfall forecasting. *Journal of Hydrologic Engineering* 5 (4): 339–345.

A
Weight Assignment Approaches

While some multiattribute decision-making (MADM) methods, including the pairwise comparison-oriented methods (e.g. analytic hierarchy process [AHP], Saaty 1977, the analytic network process [ANP], Saaty 2004, and the best–worst method [BWM], Rezaei et al. 2015) are embedded with a mechanism that can assist the decision-maker to obtain the weights of the evaluation criteria, the weight assignment procedure remains as a challenge for most remaining MADM methods. Resultantly, the decision-makers often find the process of assigning weights to the set of evaluation criteria a challenging task for the definition of the assigned weights itself is not precise, nor are the values obtained by the MADM methods. In fact, while the weights can dramatically influence the results of the decision-making process, they lack significant, practical, and physical indicators to guide their choice (Mareschal 1988; Ma et al. 1999).

One always can skip the weight assignment procedure by assuming equal weights for all the evaluation criteria (Chang and Yeh 2001). Yet, unequal weight assignment is still considered to be the most common practice when it comes to applying MADM methods to cope with real-world decision-making problems. According to literatures and researches in the field of MADM various approaches have been proposed to obtain the weights of the evaluation criteria, the majority of which can be classified into subjective approaches and objective approaches (Ma et al. 1999). According to the subjective approaches, the weights of the criteria are assigned based on the information given by the decision-makers. Resultantly, while the weights obtained by subjective approaches reflect the subjective judgment or intuition of the decision-makers, there is always the risk of decision-makers incurring error in judgment that might be rooted in the lack of knowledge or experience, which jeopardizes the integrity of the final outcome of such decision-making approaches. Some fair examples of this approach include the Delphi method (Dalkey and Helmer 1963), eigenvector method (Saaty 1977), weighted least square method (Chu et al. 1979), and the modified Delphi method (Custer et al. 1999).

A Handbook on Multi-Attribute Decision-Making Methods, First Edition.
Omid Bozorg-Haddad, Babak Zolghadr-Asli, and Hugo A. Loáiciga.

The objective approaches, on the other hand, obtain the weights of evaluation criteria using objective information such as by means of the decision matrix. Objective approaches, which often employ some sort of mathematical models as a weight assignment mechanism, neglect the subjective judgment and the decision-makers' intuitions. The entropy method (Shannon 1948; Lotfi and Fallahnejad 2010), multiple objective programming model (Choo and Wedley 1985), and principal element analysis (Fan 1996; Ma et al. 1999) are merely some of the most well-known objective weight assignment approaches. This appendix presents the principles of the weighted least square and multiobjective programming models demonstrations of subjective and objective approaches, respectively.

A.1 Subjective Approach: Weighted Least Squares

Theorized by Chu et al. (1979) the weighted least square method is a well-known subjective-oriented approached used to obtain the weights of the evaluation criteria. Central to the method is a set of simultaneous linear algebraic equations that reflect the subjective judgments made by the decision-makers in the weight assignment procedure.

According to the weighted least square method, the decision-makers compose a pairwise comparison matrix P in which the relative importance of all evaluation criteria are compared against one another. The pairwise comparison matrix is expressed as follows (Saaty 1977):

$$P = \begin{array}{c} \\ c_1 \\ \vdots \\ c_n \end{array} \begin{array}{c} \begin{array}{ccc} c_1 & \cdots & c_n \end{array} \\ \begin{bmatrix} p_{(1,1)} & \cdots & p_{(1,n)} \\ \vdots & \ddots & \vdots \\ p_{(n,1)} & \cdots & p_{(n,n)} \end{bmatrix} \end{array} \quad \forall i \tag{A.1}$$

in which n = the total number of evaluation criteria; and $p_{(i,j)}$ = the pairwise comparison of the ith and jth criteria. For each $p_{(i,j)} > 0$ the following is holds true (Saaty 1977, 1986):

$$p_{(i,j)} = {}^{1}\!/_{p_{(j,i)}} \quad i, j = 1, \ldots, n \tag{A.2}$$

One should bear in mind that logic dictates the following result (Saaty 1986):

$$p_{(i,i)} = 1 \quad \forall i \tag{A.3}$$

As far as the subjective weight assignment approaches are concerned $p_{(i,j)}$ is interpreted as the relative weight of the ith criterion with respect to the jth one. The following definition applies (Saaty 1977):

$$p_{(i,j)} = {}^{w_i}\!/_{w_j} \tag{A.4}$$

in which w_i and w_j = the importance of the ith and jth evaluation criteria, respectively.

According to Chu et al. (1979), the weights of the evaluation criteria can be obtained by solving the constrained optimization problem described in Eqs. (A.5) and (A.6).

$$\text{Minimize } Z_1 = W^T \times FW = \sum_{i=1}^{n}\sum_{j=1}^{n}[p_{(i,j)} \times w_j - w_i]^2 \tag{A.5}$$

Subject to

$$e^T W = 1 \tag{A.6}$$

in which W = the weight vector, which can be expressed as $(w_1, w_2, \ldots, w_n)^T$; e = a vector composed of ones, which can be expressed as $(1, 1, \ldots, 1)^T$; F = an M-matrix (Graham 1987), defined as $[f_{(i,j)}]_{n\times n}$, where each if its element is defined as follows:

$$f_{(i,j)} = -[p_{(i,j)} + p_{(j,i)}] \quad i, j = 1, \ldots, n \text{ and } i \neq j \tag{A.7}$$

$$f_{(i,i)} = n - 2 + \sum_{k=1}^{n}[p_{(k,j)}]^2 \quad i = 1, \ldots, n \tag{A.8}$$

According to Eqs. (A.7) and (A.8), it can be seen that F is a positive definite matrix if for any i, j, and k, there is at least one $p_{(i,j)} \neq p_{(i,k)} \times p_{(k,j)}$.

An additional constraint for the optimization model expressed through Eqs. (A.5) and (A.6), is that $w_i > 0$. However, it is conjectured that the above problem can be solved to obtain $w_i > 0$ without the nonnegativity constraint (Ma et al. 1999).

Equations (A.5) and (A.6) express a nonlinear programming optimization model. To minimize the objective function of the aforementioned optimization model (Z_1), the Lagrangian function is formed, as follows (Chu et al. 1979):

$$L_1 = W^T \times FW + 2\lambda_1(e^T \times W - 1) \tag{A.9}$$

in which λ_1 = the Lagrangian multiplier for the Z_1 objective function. Differentiating Eq. (A.9) with respect to W and λ_1 the following equations are obtained (Chu et al. 1979; Ma et al. 1999):

$$FW + \lambda_1 e = O \tag{A.10}$$

$$e^T W = 1 \tag{A.11}$$

in which O = a vector composed of zeroes which can be mathematically expressed as $(0, 0, \ldots, 0)^T$. Equations (A.10) and (A.11) form a set of $(n+1)$

nonhomogeneous linear equations with $(n+1)$ unknown variables. By solving Eqs. (A.10) and (A.11), the following results for the optimal weight vector w^* and the Lagrange multiplier (Chu et al. 1979, Ma et al. 1999):

$$w^* = \frac{F^{-1}e}{e^T F^{-1} e} \tag{A.12}$$

$$\lambda_1^* = \frac{-1}{e^T F^{-1} e} \tag{A.13}$$

Details on w^*, which is the vector of weights obtained based on the weighted least squares method, can be found in Wang and Fu (1995).

A.2 Objective Approach: Multiobjective Programming Model

The objective approach, which neglects the decision makers' subjective assessments when it comes to the weight assignment procedure, calculates the weights of the evaluation criteria by solving mathematical programming models. The concepts and mathematical procedure of multiple objective programming model (Choo and Wedley 1985) as a fair example of this branch of weight assignment approaches is briefly discussed below.

The multiple objective programming model dictates the decision-makers must first transform the components of the decision-matrix (D) into dimensionless values through a mathematical procedure better known as normalization. The product of the described procedure, which hereby is referred to as the normalized decision matrix (B), is transformed into the weighted normalized decision matrix (R) (Choo and Wedley 1985):

$$x_{(i,j)} = w_j \times r_{(i,j)} \tag{A.14}$$

in which, $x_{(i,j)}$ = the weighted normalized performance value of the ith alternative with respect to the jth criterion; and $r_{(i,j)}$ = the normalized preference value for the ith alternatives with respect to the jth criterion.

At this junction, the decision-maker is required to define the ideal solution to the MADM problem at hand. Let the artificial alternative a^+ represent the ideal solution, which is expressed as $a^+ = (x_1^+, x_2^+, \ldots, x_j^+, \ldots, x_n^+)$; and whose jth component is defined as follows (Hwang and Yoon 1981; Opricovic 1998):

$$x_j^+ = Max\{x_{(1,j)}, x_{(2,j)}, \cdots, x_{(m,j)}\} \tag{A.15}$$

The jth component is restated as follows (Choo and Wedley 1985; Ma et al. 1999):

$$x_j^+ = Max\{w_j \times r_{(1,j)}, w_j \times r_{(2,j)}, \cdots, w_j \times r_{(m,j)}\} = w_j r_j^+ \tag{A.16}$$

in which r_j^+ = the ideal value of criterion c_j, is expressed as follows (Choo and Wedley 1985; Ma et al. 1999):

$$r_j^+ = Max\{r_{(1,j)}, r_{(2,j)}, \ldots, r_{(m,j)}\} \tag{A.17}$$

The separation between each alternative and the ideal solution is given by the Euclidean distance (Choo and Wedley 1985):

$$g_i = \sum_{j=1}^{n}[r_j^* - r_{(i,j)}]^2 = \sum_{j=1}^{n}[b_j^* - b_{(i,j)}]^2 \times w_j^2 \quad i = 1, \ldots, m \tag{A.18}$$

in which m = the number of feasible alternative under consideration; and g_i = the separation between the ideal solution and the ith alternative. Naturally, the smaller g_i is, the better the corresponding alternative a_i.

The multiple objective optimization model uses the following optimization to obtain the weights w_j (Choo and Wedley 1985):

$$\text{Minimize } G = (g_1, g_2, \ldots, g_m) \tag{A.19}$$

Subject to

$$e^T W = 1 \tag{A.20}$$

$$w_j \geq 0 \quad \forall j \tag{A.21}$$

Assuming a linear equal weighted summation the above model is transformed into a single-objective optimization model, set up as follows (Choo and Wedley 1985):

$$\text{Minimize } Z_2 = \sum_{i=1}^{m} g_i = W^T \times HW \tag{A.22}$$

in which H = the $n \times n$ diagonal matrix, where its diagonal elements, each denoted by $h_{(i,j)}$, are computable as follows (Choo and Wedley 1985):

$$h_{(i,j)} = \sum_{i=1}^{m}[r_j^+ - r_{(i,j)}]^2 \quad \forall j \tag{A.23}$$

H is invertible if for any j, there exists $\sum_{i=1}^{m}[r_j^+ - r_{(i,j)}]^2 > 0$, i.e. if for any i and j, there is at least one $r_j^+ \neq r_{(i,j)}$ (Ma et al. 1999).

By ignoring the constraint represented in Eq. (A.21) the Lagrangian function can be employed to cope with the optimization problem, which has been introduced through Eqs. (A.19)–(A.23) (Ma et al. 1999). The Lagrangian function in this instance is as follows:

$$L_2 = W^T \times HW + 2\lambda_2(e^T W - 1) \tag{A.24}$$

in which λ_2 = the Lagrangian multiplier. Differentiating Eq. (A.24) with respect to W and λ_2 the following equations are obtained (Ma et al. 1999):

$$HW + \lambda_2 e = 0 \tag{A.25}$$

$$e^T W = 1 \tag{A.26}$$

Solving Eqs. (A.25) and (A.26) produces the following answers (Ma et al. 1999):

$$w^* = \frac{H^{-1}e}{e^T H^{-1} e} \tag{A.27}$$

$$\lambda_2^* = \frac{-1}{e^T H^{-1} e} \tag{A.28}$$

in which the elements in vector w^* are (Ma et al. 1999):

$$w^* = \frac{1}{\left\{ \sum_{j=1}^{n} \frac{1}{\sum_{i=1}^{m} [r_j^+ - r_{(i,j)}]^2} \right\} \times \left\{ \sum_{i=1}^{m} [r_j^* - r_{(i,j)}]^2 \right\}} \quad \forall j \tag{A.29}$$

It can be seen that w^* satisfies the constraints expressed by Eq. (A.21).

References

Chang, Y.H. and Yeh, C.H. (2001). Evaluating airline competitiveness using multiattribute decision making. *Omega* 29 (5): 405–415.

Choo, E.U. and Wedley, W.C. (1985). Optimal criterion weights in repetitive multicriteria decision-making. *Journal of the Operational Research Society* 36 (11): 983–992.

Chu, A.T.W., Kalaba, R.E., and Spingarn, K. (1979). A comparison of two methods for determining the weights of belonging to fuzzy sets. *Journal of Optimization Theory and Applications* 27 (4): 531–538.

Custer, R.L., Scarcella, J.A., and Stewart, B.R. (1999). The modified Delphi technique: a rotational modification. *Journal of Career and Technical Education* 15 (2): 50–58.

Dalkey, N. and Helmer, O. (1963). An experimental application of the Delphi method to the use of experts. *Management Science* 9 (3): 458–467.

Fan, Z.P. (1996). Complicated multiple attribute decision making: theory and applications. Ph.D. dissertation. Northeastern University, Shenyang, China.

Graham, A. (1987). *Nonnegative Matrices and Applicable Topics in Linear Algebra*. Chichester, UK: Ellis Horwood.

Hwang, C.L. and Yoon, K. (1981). Methods for multiple attribute decision making. In: *Multiple Attribute Decision Making: Lecture Notes in Economics and Mathematical Systems* (eds. C.L. Hwang and K. Yoon), 58–191. Heidelberg, Germany: Springer Publication Company.

Lotfi, F.H. and Fallahnejad, R. (2010). Imprecise Shannon's entropy and multi attribute decision making. *Entropy* 12 (1): 53–62.

Ma, J., Fan, Z.P., and Huang, L.H. (1999). A subjective and objective integrated approach to determine attribute weights. *European Journal of Operational Research* 112 (2): 397–404.

Mareschal, B. (1988). Weight stability intervals in multicriteria decision aid. *European Journal of Operational Research* 33 (1): 54–64.

Opricovic, S. (1998). Multicriteria optimization of civil engineering systems. Ph.D. dissertation. Faculty of Civil Engineering, Belgrade, Serbia.

Rezaei, J., Wang, J., and Tavasszy, L. (2015). Linking supplier development to supplier segmentation using best-worst method. *Expert Systems with Applications* 42 (23): 9152–9164.

Saaty, T.L. (1977). A scaling method for priorities in hierarchical structures. *Journal of Mathematical Psychology* 15 (3): 234–281.

Saaty, T.L. (1986). Axiomatic foundation of the analytic hierarchy process. *Management Science* 32 (7): 841–855.

Saaty, T.L. (2004). Fundamentals of the analytic network process: dependence and feedback in decision-making with a single network. *Journal of Systems Science and Systems Engineering* 13 (2): 129–157.

Shannon, C.E. (1948). A mathematical theory of communication. *Bell System Technical Journal* 27 (3): 379–423.

Wang, Y.M. and Fu, G.W. (1995). Proof on theory of the weighted least-square priority method of AHP. *Systems Engineering: Theory and Practice* 15 (1): 3–8.

B

A Benchmark Example and a Comparison between Objective- and Subjective-Based MADM Methods

Recall there are two primary schools of multiattribute decision-making (MADM) thought available to decision-makers in their quest for finding the most desirable alternatives with regard to a set of, often conflicting, attributes. First, there are objective-based MADM methods. In essence, these methods provide an objective framework to opt for the solution, that is to say, such approaches are centered on the numeric characteristics of the decision matrix. Alternatively, there are subjective-based MADM methods. Here, the methods mostly revolve around the insight and intuition of the decision-makers to select the most desirable alternative. While both classes have their unique merits and drawbacks, which was discussed in length throughout the book, it is crucial to understand how each class approaches a MADM problem from a practical point-of-view. As such, this appendix aims to exhibit the application of both classes of MADM methods through a practical benchmark problem. Technique for order preferences by similarity to an ideal solution (TOPSIS) and analytic hierarchy process (AHP) methods are herein selected to represent the objective- and subjective-oriented MADM methods, respectively (see Chapters 3 and 6 for more information on each method).

The benchmark problem describes a case where a traveling agency advertises three distinctive locations for the upcoming holiday. In terms of MADM these are the alternatives, which are denoted by A_1, A_2, and A_3. As an enthusiastic traveler, you have decided to contact the agency and book a trip. However, now you are facing a problem: Which location should you book for this holiday? Given your circumstance, you have also come up with three evaluation criteria to help you decide on this matter. First, you want to see how others have enjoyed these places. Thus, you have gone through social media to read how these places have been rated on a 1–5 scale, where 5 represents the ideal case. Next, you want to see how much this trip might cost you. Thus, you have made an inquiry to the agency and got a rough estimation of how expensive the trips are. As for the last criteria, you want to know how comforting each trip is in terms of accommodation, transportation,

A Handbook on Multi-Attribute Decision-Making Methods, First Edition.
Omid Bozorg-Haddad, Babak Zolghadr-Asli, and Hugo A. Loáiciga.

food, etc. The agency's brochure has scored each trip based on a 1–5 scale where, again, 5 represents the ideal case. In light of MADM terminology, these are the evaluation attributes, which are respectively denoted by c_1, c_2, and c_3. Note that, while c_1 and c_3 are positive attributes, c_2 is a negative attribute.

The benchmark problem is summarized in terms of the decision matrix depicted below:

$$D = \begin{array}{c} \\ A_1 \\ A_2 \\ A_3 \end{array} \begin{array}{c} \begin{array}{ccc} c_1 & c_2 & c_3 \end{array} \\ \begin{bmatrix} 4.0 & 5000 & 4.0 \\ 3.5 & 1000 & 5.0 \\ 5.0 & 1200 & 2.5 \end{bmatrix} \end{array} \tag{B.1}$$

While c_1 and c_3 are dimensionless c_2 is measured in US$. Furthermore, the reported values are not of the same scale as one another. To address this issue, one needs to create a normalized decision matrix. Here, we simply divide each value by the sum of its given column. The normalized decision matrix is as follows:

$$D = \begin{bmatrix} 0.320 & 0.694 & 0.348 \\ 0.280 & 0.139 & 0.435 \\ 0.400 & 0.167 & 0.217 \end{bmatrix} \tag{B.2}$$

Next, we need to assign the proper weights to each criterion. As stated in the previews appendix, some methods, including the TOPSIS method, do not explicitly provide a framework for weight assignments procedure. As such, depending on the nature of the problem, we can implement different weighting mechanisms, one of which is Shannon's entropy. For more information on these weight assignments methods, see Appendix A. The weight set, denoted by w, is as follows:

$$w = \{0.034, 0.849, 0.117\} \tag{B.3}$$

These assigned weights are then used to compute the weighted normalized matrix (D_w):

$$D_w = \begin{bmatrix} 0.011 & 0.590 & 0.041 \\ 0.010 & 0.118 & 0.051 \\ 0.014 & 0.142 & 0.025 \end{bmatrix} \tag{B.4}$$

Using the values of the above matrix, one can compose the ideal (a^+) and inferior (a^-) alternatives, which are as follows:

$$a^+ = (0.014, 0.118, 0.051) \tag{B.5}$$

$$a^- = (0.010, 0.590, 0.025) \tag{B.6}$$

Next, one can compute the separation measurements of each feasible alternative from the ideal (D^+) and inferior (D^-) alternatives. These measures are summarized in Table B.1.

Table B.1 The separation measures for the set of alternatives.

	A_1	A_2	A_3
D^+	**0.472**	**0.004**	**0.035**
D^-	**0.015**	**0.472**	**0.448**

Table B.2 The relative closeness to the ideal solutions and the ranking of the alternatives according to the TOPSIS method.

	A_1	A_2	A_3
C^+	**0.031**	**0.991**	**0.928**
Ranking	3	1	2

Lastly, one can compute the relative closeness to the ideal solution (C^+) and rank the alternatives accordingly. The results are summarized in Table B.2.

As demonstrated in Table B.2, A_2 has been selected by the TOPSIS methods as the best alternative. This means that with respect to the structure of the decision matrix this alternative is the closest one could possibly get to the ideal solution while maintaining the furthest distance from the worst possible solution. Note that such evaluation is rooted in an objective point-of-view, given that the whole procedure is solely centered on the reported values of the decision matrix.

Alternatively, one could also resort to subjective-oriented MADM to tackle the problem. Here, we employed the AHP method to select the most suitable alternative. As such, we have to evaluate the alternatives with respect to each attribute using a series of pairwise comparison matrices. Using the Saaty's scale (see Chapter 3 for more information), one compares the relative desirability of each alternative with respect to each attribute based on the decision-makers' intuition and preferences. The pairwise comparison matrices with respect to c_1, c_2, and c_3, which are respectively denoted by P_1, P_2, and P_3, are as follows:

$$P_1 = \begin{matrix} \\ A_1 \\ A_2 \\ A_3 \end{matrix} \begin{matrix} \begin{matrix} A_1 & A_2 & A_3 \end{matrix} \\ \begin{bmatrix} 1 & 2 & -2 \\ 1/2 & 1 & -4 \\ 1/-2 & 1/-4 & 1 \end{bmatrix} \end{matrix} \tag{B.7}$$

$$P_2 = \begin{matrix} \\ A_1 \\ A_2 \\ A_3 \end{matrix} \begin{matrix} \begin{matrix} A_1 & A_2 & A_3 \end{matrix} \\ \begin{bmatrix} 1 & -8 & -7 \\ 1/-8 & 1 & 2 \\ 1/-7 & 1/2 & 1 \end{bmatrix} \end{matrix} \tag{B.8}$$

$$P_3 = \begin{array}{c} \\ A_1 \\ A_2 \\ A_3 \end{array} \begin{array}{c} \begin{array}{ccc} A_1 & A_2 & A_3 \end{array} \\ \begin{bmatrix} 1 & -2 & 5 \\ 1/{-2} & 1 & 7 \\ 1/5 & 1/7 & 1 \end{bmatrix} \end{array} \tag{B.9}$$

Similarly, the decision-makers compare the attributes and measure their relative importance via the pairwise comparison matrix (P_w), which is depicted below:

$$P_w = \begin{array}{c} \\ c_1 \\ c_2 \\ c_3 \end{array} \begin{array}{c} \begin{array}{ccc} c_1 & c_2 & c_3 \end{array} \\ \begin{bmatrix} 1 & -5 & -2 \\ 1/{-5} & 1 & 3 \\ 1/{-2} & 1/3 & 1 \end{bmatrix} \end{array} \tag{B.10}$$

As stated in Chapter 3 and Appendix A, the above-described structure is used as a subjective-oriented weight assignment mechanism for the attributes. Here, the computed weights through this framework are as follows:

$$w = \{0.122, 0.648, 0.230\} \tag{B.11}$$

A comparison between the two sets of assigned weights reveals that the weights in Eq. (B.11) are more evenly distributed than those of Eq. (B.3). This brings us to a critical discussion regarding these two perspectives toward MADM. While subjective-oriented methods enable the results to reflect the intuitions, experiences, and decision-makers' cognitive understanding, it is just as easy to incorporate biased or misinformed judgments to the computation procedure and undermine the whole process. Again, while such methods can evaluate the logical consistency of the decision-makers' judgments (Herman and Koczkodaj 1996; Saaty 1980), it is an entirely different matter to account for biased or misinformed opinions. Such issues could just as easily jeopardize the integrity of the results by not genuinely reflecting the stakeholders' interest in a practical MADM problem. As such, when it comes to subjective-oriented MADM methods, it is often suggested to evaluate each subjective-based assessment cautiously or better yet involve others' opinions in the process through group MADM paradigms.

As for the benchmark problem, the hierarchy structure of the AHP method aggregated the preferences of the decision-makers and ranks the results based on the overall performance of each alternative. The results are summarized in Table B.3.

As was the case with the TOPSIS results, here, A_2 is selected as the most desirable alternative. According to AHP's evaluation, similar to our previous assessment, A_3 and A_1 are ranked second and third, respectively. Thus, while the ranking results from both methods resemble one another, they are not exactly mirroring one another, given that the overall scores assigned to alternatives by these methods differed from each other. TOPSIS calculates that while both A_2 and A_3 can clearly dominate A_1, their performances are somewhat comparable to each other

Table B.3 The aggregated scores and ranking of the alternatives according to the AHP method.

	A_1	A_2	A_3
Aggregated scores	0.151	0.532	0.317
Ranking	3	1	2

even though A_2 is slightly better. As for AHP, while the ranking is identical to those from TOPSIS, the distributions of the scores assigned to these alternatives are slightly different, and there is a more pronounced distinction between the overall performances of A_2 and A_3. Again, note that the results of the AHP's evaluation are heavily derived from the decision-makers' personal intuition, which resonated itself in forms of pairwise comparison matrices. As such, other's preferences may have led to different rankings for the same problem. This notion by no means should undermine the subjective-oriented MADM methods. In fact, from a theoretical point-of-view, a sound, logical, and consistent assessment should help select the best alternative and account for the decision-makers' intuitions on the matter, which is often neglected in the objective-oriented MADM methods. However, the same characteristic could have just as easily become a pitfall, for it provides an opportunity to incorporate misinformed or biased opinions, which needless to say would lead to unreliable results. Thus, one must exercise caution when it comes to implementing subjective-oriented MADM methods.

References

Herman, M.W. and Koczkodaj, W.W. (1996). A Monte Carlo study of pairwise comparison. *Information Processing Letters* 57 (1): 25–29.

Saaty, T.L. (1980). *The Analytic Hierarchy Process*. New York, NY: McGraw-Hill Education.

Index

A Handbook on Multi-Attribute Decision-Making Methods, First Edition.
Omid Bozorg-Haddad, Babak Zolghadr-Asli, and Hugo A. Loáiciga.

Printed and bound by CPI Group (UK) Ltd, Croydon, CR0 4YY